THE BEAST

THE BEAST

Riding the Rails and Dodging Narcos on the Migrant Trail

ÓSCAR MARTÍNEZ

Translated by
Daniela Maria Ugaz
and John Washington

VERSO
London • New York

This English-language edition first published by Verso 2013
Translation © Daniela Maria Ugaz and John Washington 2013
First published as *Los migrantes que no importan*
© Icaria Editorial 2010
Foreword © Francisco Goldman 2013

1 3 5 7 9 10 8 6 4 2

Verso
UK: 6 Meard Street, London W1F 0EG
US: 20 Jay Street, Suite 1010, Brooklyn, NY 11201
www.versobooks.com

Verso is the imprint of New Left Books

ISBN-13: 978-1-78168-132-9

British Library Cataloguing in Publication Data
A catalogue record for this book is available from the British Library

Library of Congress Cataloging-in-Publication Data
Martínez, Óscar (Oscar Enrique)
[Migrantes que no importan. English]
The beast : riding the rails and dodging narcos on the
migrant trail / by Óscar Martínez ; translated by
Daniela Maria Ugaz and John Washington.
    pages cm
"First published as Los migrantes que no importan
[copyrighted] Icaria Editorial 2010."
ISBN 978-1-78168-132-9 (hardback : alk. paper)
1. Illegal aliens—Mexico. 2. Central Americans—
Mexico. 3. Immigrants—Mexico. 4. Mexico—
Emigration and immigration—Social aspects.
5. Central America—Emigration and immigration—
Social aspects. I. Title.
JV7402.M3713 2013
305.9ʹ069120972—dc23
                    2013020580

Typeset in Fournier by MJ & N Gavan, Truro, Cornwall
Printed in the US by Maple Press

Contents

Foreword

By Francisco Goldman

ElFaro.net advertises itself as Latin America's first online digital newspaper. It is based in El Salvador, and was founded in 1998. Many enterprises nowadays, individual and collective, proclaim themselves or would like to be considered "alternative," and as part of a "vanguard" showing the way forward, but ElFaro.net truly is both. It certainly offers an alternative to the kinds of fare provided by El Salvador's familiar newspapers—complicit with the political and moneyed establishment, and thoroughly mediocre at best, as is true of the establishment press and other media throughout Latin America. And ElFaro.net is a vanguard because it is so very excellent in every way that it has become a beacon of the possible, of the ambitious, of the truly revolutionary, to young journalists up and down the continent. To the question of how it can be that the Bloomsbury of Latin American journalists has sprung up in tiny El Salvador and not in Mexico City or Buenos Aires, one answer is, Why not? and another is, Actually, it makes perfect sense, and yet another is, Isn't this just what the digital age promised? No more periphery, the center is everywhere. Except it takes a visionary editorial team, and exceptionally courageous and talented journalist-writers, to fulfill such an idealized and wishful supposition.

ElFaro.net was founded in 1999, six years after the end of El Salvador's civil war, by two young Salvadorans who'd been raised abroad, the sons of political exiles. When they returned home to their war-devastated country, and found it still as violent or even more violent than before, saturated by organized crime and gangs, the infamously sadistic *maras*, terrorizing poor urban neighborhoods and towns, they decided that there really could be such a thing as cutting-edge journalism, and that it should and could make a difference. And what is cutting-edge journalism? It means writing about what nobody else dares to write about, at least not thoroughly or memorably, and getting as close to your subjects as you can, and taking as much time as you need, and then somehow knowing how to write the hell out of what you find—capturing *mareros*'s ways of speaking, their jargon and gestures, as if the writer himself has been a *marero* all his life, deciphering their codes, prising from them their life-stories, their secrets, their most scarifying and gruesome stories, their odd vulnerabilities, learning the layout and nuances of their places, and doing the same with their rivals, their victims, with the police and prosecutors who pursue them, and shaping that material into compelling narratives that engross the reader and deliver much larger and more unsettling meanings than those found in ordinary newspaper dispatches. I hadn't read stories like those published in ElFaro.net anywhere else. Such high-quality and important work doesn't go unnoticed, and the digital newspaper's writers have gathered some of the world's most prestigious journalism awards: cofounder Carlos Dada, the current editor, won the Maria Moors Cabot Prize, and Carlos Martínez won the Ortega y Gasset Award.

Now Carlos's brother, Óscar Martínez, has produced *The Beast* (originally *Los migrantes que no importan*, "the migrants who don't matter"), about the Central American migrants who trek across Mexico to reach the northern border and the United States. With mind-boggling courage and commitment, Óscar Martínez went where no other journalist from Mexico or elsewhere had gone, exploring the migrants' routes, in a series of trips, from bottom to top, that take in not only the infamous train known as "La Bestia"—he rode on that train eight times—but also the desolate byways traveled on foot where the very worst things happen. Despite being a compilation of dispatches published over two years in ElFaro.net, the book has the organic coherence, development, and narrative drive of a novel. It reads like a series of pilgrims' tales about a journey through hell. (Even calling it hell feels like an understatement.)

The Beast is, along with Katherine Boo's *Behind the Beautiful Forevers*, the most impressive nonfiction book I've read in years. I first read it in Spanish a couple of years ago after it was recommended to me by Alma Guillermoprieto, in an edition published in 2010 by Icaria, a small press in Barcelona. In Mexico and Latin America, the book might as well have not existed. How could it be that this book, which should be urgent reading for all Mexicans at all interested in what occurs in their country, was not immediately published in Mexico? Perhaps because it holds up a mirror to a Mexico almost too depraved, grotesque, and heartless to believe. In different ways it holds up just as painful a mirror to the United States, and another to Central America. Finally *The Beast* was rescued and published, in late 2012, by the Oaxaca-based Sur + Ediciones, one of a handful of excellent small presses in Mexico that have reinvigorated the country's literary landscape. Thanks to their initiative the book was discovered by Verso, which has brought out the present edition in English.

Over the last few months, I've had many conversations with people who've read the book, which I urge upon everybody I meet. They always speak, of course, about the importance of what it conveys, and in awed tones about its author's courage. And then they always add, "But how come that *cabrón* writes so well!" Though only in his mid-twenties when he wrote the book, Óscar Martínez writes really, really well, with liveliness, precision, vividly observed detail, with a restraint which it must have been terribly difficult to sustain considering the rage he often felt over what he was witnessing, with astonishing and never superfluous poetry and, most of all, with a genius for conveying human character. Martínez's literary gift is what lifts *The Beast* into a work that delivers much more than journalistic information—though its information is of pressing and illuminating importance—and makes it a masterpiece. Each chapter narrates a unique story. At times the book reminded me of Isaac Babel's *Red Army Tales*.

> "'I'm running,' Auner says, his head ducked down, not meeting my eyes, 'so I don't get killed.'"

So begins the first pilgrim's tale, in a migrant shelter in southern Oaxaca where Martínez meets Auner and his two Salvadoran brothers, embarking on the journey north without any set plan, without knowledge of its dangers, traps, and rules. Yet it's all-important to know what you're doing on this journey, the book will teach us, again and again: it should be required reading for any migrant setting out across Mexico. Along the way only these widely scattered migrants' shelters, most run by the Catholic Church, offer some respite from the hardship and unyielding fear of the journey, though not entirely—because the shelters are also infiltrated by spies working for the Zetas cartel and other criminal groups, or corrupt coyotes who prey on the migrants.

> The first time I asked him, though, he told me he was migrating to try his luck. He said he was only looking for a better life, *una vida mejor*, which is a common saying on the migrant trails. But here in southern Mexico, now that Auner and I are alone, with the train tracks next to us and a cigarette resting between his lips, now that we're apart from his two younger brothers who are playing cards in the migrant shelter's common room, he admits that the better word to describe his journey is not migration, but escape.
> "And will you come back?" I ask him.
> "No," he says, still looking at the ground. "Never."
> "So you're giving up your country?"
> "Yeah."

The brothers' lives have been threatened, but they don't know by whom. At home their mother was killed by gang assassins, perhaps in reprisal for one of the brothers having witnessed and denounced the murder by drunks of a friend who was a gang member, or perhaps it was because their mother witnessed a gang assassination outsider her little store. "Death isn't simple in El Salvador," Martínez writes. "It's like a sea: you're subject to its depths, its creatures, its darkness. Was it the cold that did it, the waves, a shark? A drunk, a gangster, a witch?" Many migrants head north to flee the economic devastation of their countries, the paucity of decent work or pay, in search of "a better life" in the United States: good wages, the chance to send money back to their families, to save enough to build a home or start a small business when they return. But Óscar Martínez also introduces us to many people who are fleeing out of fear. A young gang member running for his life because the rival gang has conquered his gang's turf and had he stayed, his death at their hands would have been assured. A policewoman fleeing because her two successive police husbands had been murdered, and, while she was in mortal danger too, she feared even more being no longer able to endure her dread and despair and turning her own pistol on herself and her baby daughter. Orphaned girls in their early teens, fleeing homes where stepparents, stepbrothers or other informal guardians regularly rape them or violently enslave them.

All are in flight from fear, only to exchange it for the different, unrelenting fear they will discover and learn to endure on the journeys north, with little chance, increasingly little chance, we learn in *The Beast*, of ever actually reaching the United States. Along the way they will be preyed upon by cartels, police, Mexican immigration authorities, *maras* and random rural gangs, robbed, enslaved, forced into narco assassin squads, and raped— an estimated eight out of ten migrant women who attempt to cross Mexico suffer sexual abuse along the way, sometimes at the hands of fellow migrants. Migrants are kidnapped en masse by Zetas, with the complicity of corrupted and terrorized local police and other authorities and of treacherous coyotes, so that their families back home or awaiting them in the US can be extorted; meanwhile the captives are tortured, raped and sometimes massacred. Thousands upon thousands of migrants have been murdered in Mexico, and many others die by falling from "La Bestia"; as many as seventy thousand, some experts estimate, lie buried along the "death corridor" of the migrants' trail. If the travelers do reach the northern border and actually manage to cross into the United States, they most likely will be captured by the US Border Patrol, and be deported or jailed.

Martínez journeys north with the three brothers, Auner, El Chele and Pitbull, on a bus from Ixcuintepec to Oaxaca via a mountain road where there are few Migration Authority checkpoints, because it is so winding and treacherous. How finely and intimately Martínez captures the quiet tension of that ride, the young men's nerves, their quality of strangers-in-a-strange-land:

> El Chele and Auner are sleeping in successive rows behind him. They decided to spread themselves out, in case a cop came looking for undocumented migrants. But they still stick out enough to almost glow: three young men with loose pants and tennis shoes on a bus entirely full of indigenous folks. And they're not just migrating, remember, they're fleeing. You can tell. They're the ones with the light sleep. The ones who peek out the windows when the bus comes to a stop. It doesn't matter if the bus stops for someone to pee, or to pick up passengers, the boys get nervous every time.

In Oaxaca, they part ways; the brothers travel on, first by bus. They keep in touch, texting by cell phone. Martínez names seven other young migrants he's met who, during those months of August and September, are killed on the journey. And then comes a final text: "*On the move. About to board the train.*" After that the communication goes dead, the brothers no longer answer messages. Martínez learns that there has been a mass kidnapping in Reynosa, thirty-five migrants seized from the train.

"*Where are you? How are you?* Nothing. No response." End of chapter.

La Arrocera is what the migrants call the 262-kilometer route through southern Chiapas, from Tapachula to Arriaga, where they climb onto the trains. They avoid the highways and roads because of checkpoints variously manned by the Migration Authority, police and army—"In Chiapas most denunciations filed by migrants are against the police," writes Martínez—and instead hike through mountains, jungles and ranchlands. Migrants consider the route "lawless territory," the most dangerous of the entire trek across Mexico, and it is called La Arrocera only because in a small settlement along the way, there is an abandoned rice warehouse. "En route to El Norte I saw, and began to understand, that the bodies left here are innumerable, and that rape is only one of the countless threats a migrant confronts." Along the paths there are skeletons, the machete-split skulls of migrants. "Bones here aren't a metaphor for what's past, but for what's coming." There are peasant ranchers who pretend to tell the migrants which path to take, instead directing them to where rural gangs—some informal, armed with machetes, others more organized, armed with high-caliber rifles—await to assault them.

Apparently this remote countryside wasn't always populated by murderers, robbers and rapists. What happened was that when the Mexicans living there noticed the migrants crossing their lands, so vulnerable, so frightened of ever denouncing any crime committed against them for fear of being deported, so determined only to reach their destination, their predatory instincts were awakened, and they adapted to what this new situation offered. *The Beast* offers a terrifying lesson in human cruelty, cowardice, greed and depravity. Likewise, the Zetas had never before included mass kidnappings in their criminal repertoire, but when they noticed the migrants traveling through their territories they seized upon what they perceived as a new business opportunity, forcing coyotes to work for them, and police and state authorities into complicity. When one badly beaten migrant managed to escape the house in a small town where he was being held along with dozens of other migrants, and went to the police to make a report, the police returned him to the kidnappers. Martínez and his photographer travel the La Arrocera route:

We walk on, telling ourselves that if we get attacked, we get attacked. There's nothing we can do. The suffering that migrants endure on the trail doesn't heal quickly. Migrants don't just die, they're not just maimed or shot or hacked to death. The scars of their journey don't only mark their bodies, they run deeper than that. Living in such fear leaves something inside them, a trace and a swelling that grabs hold of their thoughts and cycles through their heads over and over. It takes at least a month of travel to reach Mexico's northern border ... Few think about the trauma endured by the thousands of Central American women that have been raped here. Who takes care of them? Who works to heal their wounds?

An expert on the migrants tells Martínez:

The biggest problem isn't in what we can see, it's beyond that. The problem lies in a particular understanding of things, in an entire system of logic. Migrants who are women have to play a certain role in front of their attackers, in front of the coyote and even in front of their own group of migrants, and during the whole journey they're under the pressure of assuming this role: I know it's going to happen to me, but I can't help but hope that it doesn't.

There's an expression among the women migrants: "*cuerpomátic*. The body becomes a credit card, a new platinum-edition 'bodymatic' which buys you a little safety, a little bit of cash and the assurance that your travel buddies won't get killed. Your bodymatic, except for what you get charged, buys a more comfortable ride on the train." A migrant named Saúl tells Martínez atop "La Bestia" about a scene that's permanently branded on his mind, when an eighteen-year-old Honduran girl he was traveling with fell from the train:

"I saw her," he remembers, "just as she was going down, with her eyes open so wide."
And then he was able to hear one last scream, quickly stifled by the impact of her body hitting the ground. In the distance, he saw something roll.
"Like a ball with hair. Her head, I guess."

Throughout Central America and Mexico, as in the neighbor-hoods populated in the United States by migrants who manage to reach it, after years of widespread and untreated, silently endured trauma, there must be entire communities that could be converted into mental health clinics, or even asylums.

The migrants are not just pushovers and victims. Martínez shows how rugged and capable they often are—these working men, stone masons, construction workers, mechanics, peasant farmers—and how bravely they often fight back, protecting their companions and their women from being forced off the train and herded into the forest. "This is the law of The Beast that Saúl knows so well. There are only three options: give up, kill, or die."

On one of his rides atop the train, Martínez witnesses and grip-pingly describes a series of battles between the migrants and their attackers, who pursue them in white pick-up trucks. He notes in conclusion: "After the attack on the train, where there were more than a hundred armed assaults, at least three murders, three inju-ries, and three kidnappings, there was not a single mention of the incident in the press. Neither the police nor the army showed up, and nobody filed a single report."

Out of indifference, moral mediocrity and fear, the Central American migrants' plight has gone mostly unnoticed in Mexico and the United States. Now and then an especially large massacre, like that of seventy-three migrants in Tamaulipas in 2011, brings some media focus, but it passes all too quickly. Catholic Church leaders such as the priest Alejandro Solalinde in Oaxaca have been at the forefront of efforts to force Mexican authorities to provide better protection for migrants. Of the many silences that overlay this story, one of the most profound is that of the United States, where the tragedy of the migrants is what news editors call a "non-story," one to which Washington could not be more indifferent. Throughout the 1970s and 80s the United States fanned the civil wars of Central America, supporting repressive governments, devastating those countries, and helping to create cultures of vio-lence, all in the name of defeating communism—with a promise to nurture just, democratic societies once peace was attained. There was no nurturing, no rebuilding, and even after the wars were over, there was no peace. The United States mostly turned its back, and now it spurns the offspring who flee what it created in Central America.

Óscar Martínez travels the length of the now nearly impregnable northern border, which has become a walled war zone where the US carries out a nightly battle against the Mexican cartels that use ever more ingenious methods to deliver their drugs across it. Here the cartels consider the migrants a nuisance, forcing them to search for ever more remote and dangerous slivers of land where they might be able to pass. Here too, they face kidnappings, assaults, betrayals and rapes. In the book's final chapter, set in Nuevo Laredo, Martínez follows a Honduran migrant named Julio César. It is nearly impossible to cross in Nuevo Laredo, where the strong currents of the Río Bravo regularly drown the desperate migrants who try to swim it. But Julio César studies the river with the meticulous patience of a frontier tracker, walking far outside the city until he discovers a remote spot where the waters are shallower and an island divides and weakens the current. He will wait several months, until April, in the dry season, when the river will be even lower, to attempt his crossing. Julio César incarnates many of the book's lessons: patience, courage, attentiveness, getting as close to the subject of concern as one can, "the difference between knowing and not knowing." Those are the book's closing words. In some ways they encapsulate the methods Óscar Martínez followed in his own crossing over into the hidden and terrifying lives of the Central American migrants.

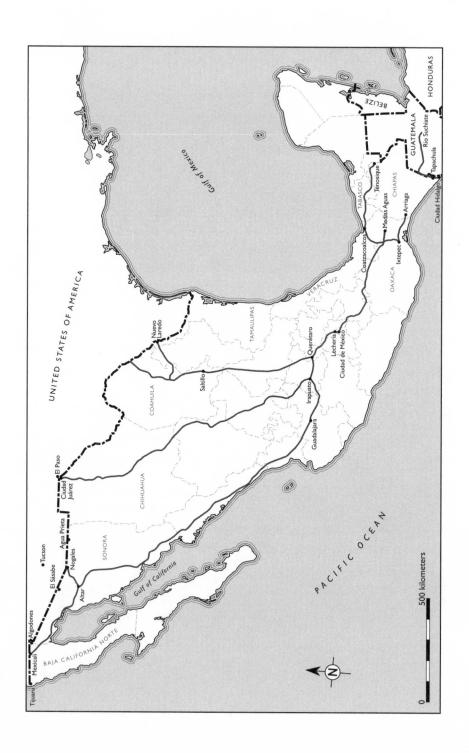

1

On the Road: Oaxaca

There are those who migrate to El Norte because of poverty. There are those who migrate to reunite with family members. And there are those, like the Alfaro brothers, who don't migrate. They flee. Recently, close to the brothers' home in a small Salvadoran city, bodies started hitting the streets. The bodies fell closer and closer to the brothers' home. And then one day the brothers received the threat. The story that follows is the escape of Auner, Pitbull, and El Chele, three migrants who never wanted to come to the United States.

"I'm running," Auner says, his head ducked down, not meeting my eyes, "so I don't get killed."

The first time I asked him, though, he told me he was migrating to try his luck. He said he was only looking for a better life, *una vida mejor*, which is a common saying on the migrant trails. But here in southern Mexico, now that Auner and I are alone, with the train tracks next to us and a cigarette resting between his lips, now that we're apart from his two younger brothers who are playing cards in the migrant shelter's common room, he admits that the better word to describe his journey is not migration, but escape.

"And will you come back?" I ask him.

"No," he says, still looking at the ground. "Never."

"So you're giving up your country?"

"Yeah."

"You'll never return?"

"No ... Only if anything happens to my wife or daughter."

"And then you'll come back?"

"Just to kill them."

"Just to kill who?"

"I don't even know."

Auner knows nothing of the men he runs from. Back home, he left behind a slew of unsolved murders. Now, blindly, he runs and hides. He feels he has no time to reflect. No time to stop and think what connection he and his brothers might have with those bodies on the streets.

Auner left El Salvador, along with his wife and two-year-old daughter, two months ago. Since then he's guided his two brothers with patience and caution. At only twenty years old, he tries hard to keep his fear in check so as not to make a false step. He doesn't want to fall into the hands of migration authorities, doesn't want to get deported and sent back to El Salvador, which would mean starting again from scratch. Because no matter what they're put through or how long it takes, they must escape, he says, they must get north. To El Norte. "Get pushed back a little, okay," Auner says, "it might happen, but we'll only use it to gain momentum."

Without a word, Auner gets up, ending our conversation. We walk down the dusty sidewalk, back toward the migrant shelter. We're in the small city of Ixtepec, in the state of Oaxaca, the first stepping-stone of my journey with them. At the shelter, a place made up of palm-roof huts and half-built laundry rooms, Auner huddles next to El Chele and Pitbull, his younger brothers. El Chele has a boyish face, light skin, and a head of curly hair. Pitbull has the hardened face of an ex-con and the calloused hands of a laborer. Auner is the quiet one.

A humid heat wraps around us, so thick I feel I could push it away. The brothers are talking about the next step in their escape. There's a decision that needs to be made: stay on the train like stowaways, or take the buses through indigenous mountain towns with the hope that they can avoid checkpoints.

A journey through the mountains would take them through the thick green Oaxaca jungle, well off the migrant train trails. But it's a route studded with checkpoints and migration authorities, and usually only taken with the help of a guide, or coyote. Auner first heard of the trail thanks to Alejandro Solalinde, the priest who founded and runs this migrant shelter. Solalinde is a man who understands the value in giving an extra option, even one so dangerous, to those who flee.

In contrast, the voyage by train would have Auner and his brothers clinging like ticks onto its roof struts for at least six hours en route to Medias Aguas, Veracruz, the home turf of Los Zetas. They'd then have to hide in ditches on the outskirts of the town, waiting for the next train, ready at any moment to sprint for their lives.

The infamous gang known as Los Zetas was formed in 1999 by the narco-trafficker Osiel Cárdenas Guillén, founder of the powerful Gulf Cartel, arrested in 2003, and a US prisoner since 2007. Cárdenas originally created Los Zetas to act as his organization's armed wing, composed of thirty-one elite Mexican army deserters—some of whom had trained at the US-led School of the Americas—but the group expanded and evolved, becoming increasingly, violently autonomous. By 2001, the group had already added to its brutal money-making repertoire the mass kidnappings of undocumented migrants for ransom money. By 2007 it had broken away to form an independent cartel. In 2009 the Drug Enforcement Administration (DEA) called the Zetas, simply, "Mexico's most organized and dangerous group of assassins."

The answer to the Alfaro brothers' question might seem obvious to someone not familiar with the rules of the migrant trail. Mexican cartel violence has become increasingly notorious through media portrayal, Mexican and US government denunciations, and the cartels' own use of a gallows-style display of their mutilated murder victims. But the risks of traveling through the mountains, so as to avoid Los Zetas, aren't inconsiderable. Of every ten migrants from Central America, six are apprehended and mugged by Mexican migration authorities—a potential catastrophe for these guys who pocket, as if they were jewels, the $50 their father sends from the United States every four days. They use this treasure to buy their once-a-day ration of tortillas and beans, which they eat quickly, hidden in thickets, before continuing their escape. And getting caught by the Mexican authorities doesn't just mean returning home with their heads down and their pockets empty. Their return could cost them their lives, as could riding atop the train, which continuously throws migrants off its back, dismembering or maiming so many.

Just today I learned that a boy named José lost his head under that train. José was the youngest of three Salvadorans I traveled with two months ago. We skirted highways and ducked from authorities as we ventured through another of the high-traffic points along the migrant trail, La Arrocera. His decapitation, I'm told, was a clean cut. Steel against steel. It happened close to Puebla, some three hundred miles north of where we are now.

Though the dream is easy, the voyage is incredibly dangerous. Sometimes it's simply the exhaustion that kills you. Sometimes it's just one slow moment of slipping into sleep, and your head is gone from your body.

José was shaken off by one of those train shudders that so easily dislodge you when you're worn out. Marlon, who was traveling with José at the time, was the one who broke the news to me. He confessed José was fleeing too. But unlike Auner, José knew exactly what he was fleeing from. He escaped from the gangs that closed down his bakery. They were imposing an unpayable extortion tax: $55 a week or he'd be killed. The entire company went to ground, then fled. Now one of them has already returned to El Salvador in a black bag.

The Alfaro brothers, Auner, Pitbull, and El Chele, will decide what they're going to do tonight. And they know that they need to make the right choice. Otherwise they're going to meet in front of them—their bodies hitting the street—what they meant to leave behind.

THE FIRST BODY

"Hey bitch!" Pitbull heard someone call behind him. He knew the call was for him.

And when he turned he saw the muzzle of a nine-millimeter pistol sticking in his face. That's when he dove. Before he even hit the ground he heard the shots. Two bullets pierced the face and back of Pitbull's friend, Juan Carlos Rojas, a known gang member. A piece of Juan Carlos's brain landed on Pitbull's imitation Polo shirt, which he had bought in a slot machine hall in Chalchuapa, El Salvador, to impress the ladies. It was a sunny February day in 2008.

Pitbull felt, in that moment, nothing but blind rage. It came up from his stomach and shot through his whole body. He lost control. He turned into an animal.

Pitbull looked down for a moment at Juan Carlos, who was covered in gore and plainly dead, and then he took off running, screaming incoherently at the assassin and his accomplice, who were trying to escape. But the one who'd fired the shot looked dazed. He was hunched over and heaving. Pitbull, either not caring or unaware that the man still carried the nine-millimeter, saw him as nothing but prey. The prey, a drunk who was about fifty years old, stopped again, pointed his pistol at Pitbull and said, between gasps, "Stand still, you dumb fuck, so I can aim at you!"

There was nothing to be done. Froth rose in Pitbull's stomach, in his throat. When his prey was only a few steps away he jumped at him, his hands out like claws. The old man's nine-millimeter fell to the ground.

They say around these parts that rage is cured more easily with a clean fist. But Pitbull just started whaling on the man's face.

When two cops finally showed up, they pulled off the still raging Pitbull. Then they helped up the half-conscious old drunk. His accomplice had quietly slunk away. Being in a country like El Salvador, the cops drew all the obvious conclusions: a young man

in the middle of a crime scene—a gangster for sure. The kid was
the first they questioned.

"Which gang are you in?"

"None, you fuck," spat Pitbull, with typical grace.

"You're with the 18's like your friend they killed, aren't you?"

The officer already knew about Juan Carlos, knew that he was
part of the infamous 18's. In the smattering of towns that make
up this single city, Chalchuapa, even with 73,000 people, the cops
know most of the gang members by clan, by name, by nickname,
and even by rank.

"You deaf or fucked up?" Pitbull said. He was calmer now, had
slipped back into his youthful tough-guy jargon. The cop, on the
point of getting violent, took a step toward Pitbull, but the police
sub-inspector showed up, just in time, easing the tension.

"Listen, kid," he said to Pitbull, "they already told me you were
looking for revenge. Tell me now. You want to come to court and
testify so we can close this case?"

"You're in the game too," Pitbull responded, refusing to go
testify.

Pitbull was seventeen years old. Already he was itching for
adventure, for sharpening his edges. And this he did. A few days
later, dressed as a police officer, he went to downtown Chalchuapa
looking for the murderer's accomplice who had gotten away. All
day he searched through alleyways and makeshift street shops. He
told me he even found it pleasurable, another adventure.

"It was ballsy to walk around in a cop's uniform," Pitbull told
me. "Too bad we found the old fuck the easy way."

In the end, Pitbull went to the station to identify both the assassin and his accomplice. Pitbull and the murderers, standing face
to face.

"These are the two shits who killed Juan Carlos," he said to an
officer as he pointed them out.

But the assassins also got a good look at Pitbull that day. And in
the relative calm of the moment, they were even able to remember

that they'd seen him before, that they knew who he was. The Chalchuapa slums are a small world. The assassins recognized that Pitbull was the son of Silvia Yolanda Alvanez Alfaro, the woman who owned the shop next to the *pupusería*[1] and on the other side of the Conal factory. They knew that this kid with a shaved head and a silver earring was Jonathan Adonay Alfaro Alváñez. He was a brickworker, farmworker, carpenter, plumber. A jack-of-all-trades. He was Johnny. He was Pitbull. Of course they knew him.

PITBULL THE TOUGH GUY

"You must have had some idea," I say to Pitbull. We're sitting on the rails of the Ixtepec train line, drinking soda and smoking cigarettes.

After Auner told me why they were on the migrant trail, I asked—feeling as if I were asking a father for a date with his daughter—if I could speak to his two younger brothers. Auner gave me the go-ahead. I started with Pitbull. Silently we slipped out of the commotion of Father Solalinde's migrant shelter and sat down among towering shrubs. I wanted a shielded place so that he'd feel safe, so he'd feel safe enough to remember.

"No, man," Pitbull says. "I have no fucking clue who those bitches are. I was just cruising the game rooms with my friend. He told me he had to grab something at the bar. Then, real calm, he came out. We started walking and then the two old fucks just jumped out and popped him."

"And you don't think it's them threatening to kill you now?"

"I don't have a clue which sons-of-bitches are threatening us."

Nothing. Not even a clue. Pitbull flees, but he doesn't know from whom. If he were a character in a movie, of course, Pitbull would have snooped around, hit up his barrio contacts, tried to put a name to the assassins, maybe put on the police uniform again.

---

1 A street stand selling deep-fried rolls of corn flour with seasoned beef.

But Pitbull lives in the real world. He's just an eighteen-year-old kid steeped in the violence of one of the most dangerous countries on the continent.

What's more, not even the police reports contain many details. When they killed Juan Carlos—January or February, he doesn't exactly remember—nine other men between the ages of eighteen and twenty-five were killed, just in Chalchuapa. And Pitbull doesn't even know if Juan Carlos was his friend's real name.

"That's what he called himself," Pitbull says. "But he was in a gang and he had problems in some of the other barrios. I heard people call him a lot of different names."

William, José, Miguel, Carlos, Ronal, Unidentified, any of these could have been Juan Carlos. All of these young men were murdered in Chalchuapa in the same month. And even if one were to know the facts of the murder, I have a hunch that, like the facts of so many other migrant murder cases, the details would be so scarce they'd simply disappear. Evaporate. It'd be as if nothing had ever happened.

Pitbull turns to look over his shoulder at a couple of migrant women leaving the shelter. "Hey, sweethearts!" he yells. Fleeing, it seems, isn't always a somber procession. At least not for Pitbull. He takes a drag of his cigarette, then sinks back, lying down beside the rails and propping his head on a rock. He looks up at the sky and takes another drag. His posture makes him look like he could be a patient talking to a shrink.

After he saw that body fall, Pitbull got out of Chalchuapa for a while. Two boozy old men were being charged with homicide because he'd identified them to their faces. Leaving was the best thing.

He went to Tapachula, a Mexican town that smells of fritters and lead, on the border with Guatemala, where one of his older brothers, Josué, aka El Chele, had been living for about five months. El Chele was working in a mechanics shop in a factory slum in Tapachula, saving up money to continue his journey to El Norte. He also had some hope that his father would call and tell him that a coyote was ready, the money paid, and all that was left to do was make the trip north.

"Nos vamos al Norte, hijo, verás cómo ahí sí hay chamba, buen jale, buen dinero,"[2] his father had told him in his migrant Spanish, a mix of Central American and Chicano.

The three brothers, Auner, Pitbull, and El Chele, had never been close to one another, but recently their lives have forced them together. Auner was especially distant, working as a farmhand in rural El Salvador, waiting for his wife to bear his first child. None of the brothers called each other. They followed rural codes, a man's *campesino* way, always keeping a tight cap on their emotions.

El Chele was in good with the owners of the mechanics shop, but not quite good enough for them to let Pitbull sleep there as well. The owners did, however, let El Chele bring women to the shop and spend a slow afternoon in the back with them. And so El Chele's time passed in Tapachula, working at the shop and working to lure girls into the back room, but never making steady friends. In his free hours he would take a shower to wash the soot off, slick gobs of gel into his curly hair, put on an imitation designer shirt and fake Converse shoes, and then start his solitary prowl through café corners on the main plaza, through the pseudo-colonial white rotunda and through the *paleterías* or soda fountains where men and women gathered, and, as El Chele hoped, where they fell in love. Sometimes he'd succeed, score a date, flirt with a girl on a bench in the park. They'd eat an ice cream, and then he'd woo her back to the shop where they'd squirm their pants down. Not long after, he'd forget about her and return to his routine.

Part of El Chele's success was due to the fact that he doesn't look like the typical delinquent. Unlike Auner and Pitbull, he's fair-skinned, and the innocent look of his face matches his boyish brown curls. He doesn't have calloused hands, and he keeps his

---

2 "We're heading up north, kid, you'll see. There's work there, good money, lots to do."

nails clean and clipped, so you can't tell that he's already spent most of his young life in laboring. All of it makes him seem like somebody you could trust.

Pitbull, on the other hand, was scraping together his life as best he could. He spent his time in Tapachula, roaming the Zona de Indeco, one of the most dangerous barrios and site of many national and foreign-owned factories. In Indeco—thanks to the giant walls, graffitied with Mara Salvatrucha gang signs, that section off the safer parts of Tapachula—walking the streets is like stepping on a spinal cord, a touchy boundary line between two countries in conflict.[3]

Pitbull worked those months variously as a bricklayer, a mechanic's assistant, and a load-carrier in a market. All of it was under the table and day-to-day. He made a few friends who, as he put it, made him feel like he was living on a tightrope, always on the verge of becoming a nameless dead body lying on the street. It was that same rope on which he teetered in El Salvador when he was weighing whether or not to give in, like most of his hopeless friends, to one of the gangs. As a gang member, he told himself, at least he'd have constant backup, and so be able to make the best of the constant fear.

"It's not that I wanted to join a gang," Pitbull told me, in a sort of self-critical confession. "I know it's a bitch getting into that, but I was just like all those other kids. We were street punks who didn't go to school, just wandering around, trying to live the best we could, looking for a good time."

In Tapachula, having a good time means walking that tightrope. If there's no fear of the fall, it's hardly worth the walk.

And it didn't take long for Pitbull to fall in with a new crowd. Some young thug came up to him and made an offer. "So what, you want to go fuck something up around here?"

"I'm down," Pitbull responded.

---

3   The Mara Salvatruchas gang originated in Los Angeles in the 1980s, but it has since become a transnational organized crime gang, with its largest presence in Central America and southern Mexico.

They started stealing bicycles from kids, grabbing women's purses. They found most of their prey outside of schools, in middle-class neighborhoods, around the markets. One of the wallets that they stole, however, sent Pitbull back to El Salvador. After Pitbull snatched that fated wallet, he jumped on his bike and turned a corner right where a cop happened to be passing by. Since he didn't want to ditch the bike, he pedaled up onto the sidewalk and turned down an alleyway where, for his misfortune, there was another cop. They had him cornered. He was taken down to the station.

"Piece of shit thug," the cop yelled at him. "You come to my country and do nothing but cause trouble. We're going to put you away for three years so you learn not to fuck around anymore."

Pitbull's looks didn't help him any: his hair on end, his head always thrown back, his eyes always squinting like he's about to attack someone. Plus he has that insolent thug walk, that hard, body-teetering limp.

He didn't even try to explain that he wasn't a gang member, that he was only a kid from Central America. The only thing that crossed his mind in that moment was the three years.

"Three years. I'll be twenty-one, almost. A veteran."

And the police wouldn't ask him anything but what gang he was in. Pitbull looked the part, enough to have them convinced.

In the end, the three years was only a threat. Pitbull spent eight months in a juvenile prison in Tapachula, during which time nobody visited him. Not once. Not Auner, not El Chele. Not even Doña Silvia, his mother.

"I was fresh meat," he said.

His first time in the shower, somebody left him naked, stealing his shoes, pants, and shirt. But then, after a few more days, he started figuring things out. The other kids spoke the same language as he did. He overheard words like *perrito*, *chavala*, *boris*, *chotas*, and he started to feel at home. It was gang slang. Mara Salvatrucha slang. Pitbull turned back into the reckless kid he was. Speaking the language opened the door to the dominant gang in the prison.

The Mara Salvatrucha leader was El Travieso (Naughty Boy), an eighteen-year-old Guatemalan who'd been locked up for four years, since he was fourteen, on account of three murders. Three black tears tattooed under his eye laid claim to those bodies. Next in command was El Smokie, with two black tears, and "MS" tattooed on the inside of his bottom lip. Then El Crimen (The Crime), also Guatemalan and also with two black tears. Then finally there were El Hondureño and Jairo, both from Honduras.

"All of them were two-lettered," Pitbull said, referring to the MS of the Mara Salvatruchas. "All of us Central Americans were the big shits of the prison. We sold weed, cigarettes, cocaine, and we kept all the other little shits in order."

What does it take to survive as a young man? According to Pitbull, it takes recklessness. Recklessness like Juan Carlos had, before he was killed back in Chalchuapa. Like El Travieso has. Like El Crimen. Like all his friends from childhood, and like he himself who is now on the run. And what does the recklessness do for him? It gives him "reputation." And what's the best way to gain that reputation? Earn a few tears under your eye, learn to run in the game, learn to make the rules, rather than lose your shirt and pants in a prison shower room.

"The first thing I did when I joined," Pitbull says, "was to get my clothes back." He laughs. "I fucked up those shits who stole them from me too. To make up for the shame. Back in the bathroom, we broke those pigs in good."

After sitting with Pitbull for a while, listening to him reminisce about prison days, we return to the shelter and stand next to a table where some of the other migrants are busy with conquián. As they play the card game it's as if, for this moment, they've forgotten about the streets back in El Salvador, and the bodies that were hitting them.

The card players laugh. They joke around, insulting each other, glad to be surrounded with fellow Salvadorans who understand why they're fleeing. When one of the men puts down the wrong card in this fast-paced game, the other players howl and jeer. Moron! Ass! *¡Pendejo! ¡Burro!* And the one who put down the wrong card laughs right along.

Then Auner takes me aside. He wants to tell me the decision he and his brothers have come to.

"We're going by bus across the mountains," he says. "But, it's like," he hesitates. "It's that … I wanted to see if you could help us out, because … It's just that we don't know anything."

I agree to help them as best I can. I'll go with them to Oaxaca.

We decide to meet tomorrow at the Parque Ixtepec, and then, without any gesture at emotion, we say goodnight.

THE DROP OF A PEN

The morning sun hasn't yet scorched the town. A protest march passes through the cobbled streets, headed by a pickup with a megaphone strapped to its roof, that usually makes its rounds advertising the daily paper. Those with street jobs watch the march, which is about a hundred people strong. The news truck has loaned its services to denounce the alleged rape of a local prostitute by eight policemen. Police crime here doesn't surprise me. Two years ago I wrote a report about a gang of migrant kidnappers made up of municipal and judicial officers in this same town.

"Son of a bitch," I say, "eight of them raped her."

Auner and El Chele look down. "*Qué paloma*," they mutter, an expression meaning something like "What a shame!," and go on absently staring at the magazines of a nearby kiosk. Pitbull looks pensive. He doesn't say anything at first, then he spits out, "But she was a whore, right?"

Who knows what it is that makes three brothers what they are. Auner is paternal. El Chele could be confused with any other adolescent. And Pitbull, he seems like he's been an ex-con all his life. So how did they turn out so differently? Maybe a few more minutes spent one day at the corner store or at a soccer game, maybe a punch doled out by their father in a moment of despair. It could be something that subtle, as random as the drop of a pen.

The three of us hunker down into the beater of a bus, which is filled with indigenous folks on return trips back into the mountains. After a while we figure out why this is the route preferred by migrants who can afford to spend a little extra. The road is a hair-raising series of steep ascents, dives, sharp turns, and broken sections of pavement, winding like an intestine through a no-man's-land of forest and patches of rugged limestone, a path where the Mexican Institute of National Migration still hasn't set up a checkpoint.

Overcoming our fear and our stomachs, we finally arrive at Santiago Ixcuintepec. It's a small indigenous town bathed in mist and drizzle in the thick of the jungle. We come to a church to rest the nine hours we have before the next bus leaves for Oaxaca City. Some young locals glare down at us as if in challenge. Pitbull veers between wanting to shoot them an even more provocative look and keeping his cool, keeping his head down, remembering that he's on the run and that the odds of this road are stacked against him. Luckily, he says nothing.

In just a few minutes three separate locals, wearing kind faces and cheap rubber-soled sandals, offer to take us to their homes which are in small towns farther down the road. But their offers, I know, are two-faced. They tell us we'll sleep well there, stuffed with beans and tortillas—and then each of them asks for $150. Because our bus, they tell us, isn't coming today anyway.

They're scammers, no doubt. Of course our bus is coming, which will cost only $8 a head for the whole ride. This little town, like so many others I've seen on this road, is turning into a nest of thieves. Migrants are the perfect prey because they're invisible, always hiding from authorities.

The brothers, not knowing how to respond, turn to me. The locals' offer clearly doesn't sound too bad to them. Forward is forward.

THE OTHER BODIES

"Hey, old lady, treat us to a couple sodas, would you?" It was Los Chocolates, two dark-skinned brothers from Chalchuapa, members of the 18's. They were shouting at Doña Silvia, the Alfaro brothers' mother. Los Chocolates hung out mornings and afternoons in front of Doña Silvia's corner shop, often asking for free drinks. Their job for the gang was to stand guard, but they spent most of their time on the post getting high.

It was June 19, 2008. A day like any other.

"Them again," Doña Silvia whispered to herself, just before she heard eight gunshots, followed by the screams of her eldest daughter who'd been standing outside the shop with her children.

Doña Silvia came out running and found her daughter and grandchildren hugging onto each other, still screaming. A taxi cut a quick U-turn and sped away down the street. Los Chocolates— Salvador, thirty-six and Marvin, eighteen—were splayed out on the sidewalk. Their faces, chests, and legs all pockmarked with bullet holes.

The taxi, its windows darkly tinted, had parked in front of the store right next to where Los Chocolates were passing their day. Then, as though the driver wanted to ask for directions, both the front and back windows of the taxi slowly rolled down. Out peeked four nine-millimeter muzzles.

Silvia was stunned, her gaze fixed on where the taxi had squealed away.

It was a dizzying scene, the stuff of violence-torn barrios, where members of different gangs openly fight on the streets. Doña Silva's shop isn't in one of those barrios. It's in a neighborhood known for its children's soccer games, for teens chitchatting and mothers working their corner food stands. The peace here is only seldom interrupted by the violence. This violence, though, has lately been encroaching.

Silvia ushered the little ones into the store and closed up shop. When the police finally came to collect the bodies, there were no witnesses, nobody to answer even a single question.

To Silvia it was a sign. She had lived all her life in that city, had raised her kids there, but she felt a tide change that afternoon. The day after the murders she called her sons, Auner and Pitbull, and told them to get out of town, to hang out a while with their grandfather in Tacuba. El Chele was already across the border in Mexico. Silvia let him be. No one told him about the death of two known gang members only steps away from his mother's store.

Auner and Pitbull fled to Tacuba where they worked on the farm, pushing cows out to pasture, sharpening machetes, cutting grass. For Pitbull it was a return to his childhood as a laborer, a *campesino*, a childhood that made him wince. That sort of work, he was convinced, led nowhere. Besides, he couldn't get his mind off hanging out in clubs, flirting with girls, or getting another piercing. Auner didn't like it there either. His new wife's pregnancy had sparked in him the dream of being able to provide for his family on his own. Their grandfather paid the boys nothing but rice, beans, and tortillas. It wasn't enough for them.

And so they decided to leave for Mexico, for Tapachula. Auner spent one last night with his girl. Pitbull got high with his boys in Chalchuapa, his first time smoking outside of prison. And the next day Auner and Pitbull got on the bus and headed north to meet their brother.

They were together again, not by choice but by necessity. They helped each other out, and yet all the while they carried on with that cool affect particular to *campesinos*, leaving little room for comfort or future plans made together.

Then, one night, not too long after he had arrived, Auner was walking home after a day of work, pondering his future, ambling that slow pensive amble that would befit a man ten years older, when he received the call from his uncle.

"Auner," his uncle told him, "they killed your mom."

Doña Silvia Yolanda Alváñez died aged forty-four from two gunshot wounds to the head, one through her forehead and the other through her left temple. The murderers were two men. The getaway vehicle was a bicycle: one man pedaling, the other riding the back pegs. They stopped in front of Doña Silvia's store where she was washing silverware on the sidewalk next to her brother. The two men walked past the brother and surrounded Doña Silvia. Then each of them shot her in the head.

THE ANXIETY OF ESCAPE

"This is a bitch," Pitbull says loudly, with every intention of being heard.

The bus is chugging its way from Ixcuintepec to Oaxaca City, its headlights illuminating moths and mosquitoes and cutting through the pitch dark of the jungle. We've been listening to norteña music since we first boarded, and Pitbull is sick of it. He wants a taste of reggaeton. After a while, though, he calms down and nods off to the trebly beat of the bus.

El Chele and Auner are sleeping in successive rows behind him. They decided to spread themselves out, in case a cop came looking for undocumented migrants. But they still stick out enough to almost glow: three young men with loose pants and tennis shoes on a bus entirely full of indigenous folks. And they're not just migrating, remember, they're fleeing. You can tell. They're the ones with the light sleep. The ones who peek out the windows when the bus comes to a stop. It doesn't matter if the bus stops for someone to pee, or to pick up passengers, the boys get nervous every time.

Dawn comes while we're still in the mountains. We open our eyes and see that the dirt road we'd been traveling is now paved.

El Chele, staring out the window at the distant mountains, has hardly said a word the whole ride. But Pitbull, when awake, is the same unrestrained guy, shuffling around in his seat, trying to crack jokes, insulting passing cars, whistling the random tunes that come into his head. And Auner has been sleeping almost the entire time. When he finally wakes I notice a sad look on his face. With his brow furrowed, he sees me looking at him and shakes his head.

"What's going on with you?" I ask.

"Just thinking the same thing over and over."

"Your family?"

"My family."

"What about them?"

"God. Just hoping the threats against us don't turn against them. Those people are damn crazy. They didn't even say who they were coming for. They only said, *for the family*."

Auner explains to me that by family he means only his two brothers, their older sister who stayed behind, his wife, and his two-year-old daughter. The rest of them, he says—his grandfather, his uncles, all of those who didn't say a word or do a thing about his mother's death—aren't worth a dime to him.

That hot night in Tapachula, when Auner got the call from his uncle, he and his brothers decided to leave immediately to try to make it in time for their mother's burial. None of them want to walk me through that night. They only give me the shortest of phrases: *it was hard, we just had to get back, it was total hell*.

For two days they traveled against the migrant tide, getting farther from the United States, crossing the river that divides Mexico and Guatemala. They arrived too late. They made it only just in time to see the casket lowered into the dirt. El Chele admits he had a child's rage. He was angry, he says, but felt like crying more than lashing out. Pitbull and Auner silently knew they were in agreement—they wanted blood. But whose blood, neither knew.

A shroud of silence fell over the body of Doña Silvia. The uncle who had witnessed the murder claimed ignorance. "No," he said. "I don't know anything. I really don't. I didn't even see them." Their grandfather held his Evangelist bible out in front of him as if it were a shield. "You've got to be quiet," he told the brothers. "Leave everything in the hands of God. It's how He wanted it. Stop asking questions and jump into the hands of God like your mother has."

None of it sat well with the brothers. Months passed. The brothers looked for answers, but none came. Were the killers Pitbull testified against in the Juan Carlos murder finally getting their revenge? Was it the Mara Salvatruchas, trying to eliminate any witnesses to Los Chocolates' murder?

"Or maybe," offered Pitbull, "it was some old witch that hated her for God knows what."

Death isn't simple in El Salvador. It's like a sea: you're subject to its depths, its creatures, its darkness. Was it the cold that did it, the waves, a shark? A drunk, a gangster, a witch? They didn't have a clue.

Months passed: two months of rage and questions, then two of resignation, and another of exhaustion. Eventually the time came for the brothers to reap what they'd sowed. All those questions sprouted not answers but threats. In one week, both their uncle, who was in Chalchuapa, and their grandfather, who was in Tacuba, received the same anonymous note. It was sent to their relatives, but addressed to the brothers.

"Someone wants to kill you," their uncle told them. "Someone told me they're gonna kill you three and then the whole family."

That was it. The tip-off as anonymous as the threat itself.

The brothers felt the purgatory of their country, they felt the force with which their country spit people out or dropped them dead (twelve murders a day in a country with only six million people). They packed their bags and started north, joining the pilgrimage of upchucked Central Americans. They dove into that stream of escapees. Those fleeing poverty, those fleeing death.

Because poverty and death touches them all: the young and the old, the men and the women, the gangsters and the cops.

TWO STORIES OF VIOLENCE

I can't help but think of other stories I've heard on these roads. I can't help but think of the shocking indifference to receiving a death threat as if it were a part of daily life. I remember the nearly identical reactions of a Honduran policeman and a Guatemalan gangster: I had to escape. That's what they both told me, both of them emphasizing the *had*.

The gangster's name was Saúl. He was nineteen years old and had spent fifteen of those years in Los Angeles with his mother. Five years ago he'd gotten involved in the 18's. He was arrested and deported, however, when he was no longer a member—at least that's what he told me—for robbing a twenty-four-hour convenience store.

I met Saúl in Mexico. Both of us were traveling north toward Medias Aguas, hanging onto the tops of cargo trains. The head-lamps cutting a brief path of light through the mountain darkness. Saúl was heading north for his fifth try at crossing over. One attempt after another, five in a row without a break, trying to get back to the United States. We cupped windbreaks around our cigarettes with our hands. He was telling me why he was running, and he kept stressing, again and again, that he *had* to run, that he had no other choice, that for some people in this world there are not two or three different choices. There is only one. Which is, simply, to run.

The effect of riding the rails is always the same. On top of a train there aren't journalists and migrants, there are only people hanging on. There is nothing but speed, wind, and sometimes a hoarse conversation. The roof of the cars is the floor for all, and those who fall, fall the same way. Staying on is all that matters when The Beast, *La Bestia*, a popular name for the train, is on the move.

Saúl was deported from the United States to Guatemala, a country he didn't know. When he was sentenced, still in the United States, he was allowed to make a single phone call. He used it to get an address in Guatemala from an uncle. When he arrived in the country he'd been born in but hardly remembered, he started looking for a man he'd never known, a friend of his uncle. His search sent him to a slum neighborhood, somewhere along a river. This is what he told me. Like he was anybody walking through any neighborhood, he just walked right on in. And what happened to him is what happens to any kid who doesn't know what he's doing in Central America, who thinks any neighborhood is just any neighborhood. A group of thugs turned out of an alleyway and beat him straight to hell.

When the thugs ripped off his shirt and saw the "18" tattooed on his back, they started snarling.

"Aha! A little gangster prick!"

Saúl tried to calm them by offering the name of the man he was looking for. "Alfredo Guerrero, Alfredo Guerrero!" he called.

The gangsters went quiet. Then, like a butcher drags a slaughtered animal, they dragged Saúl's pulped body through the barrio, all the way into a house and left him at the feet of a man. The man had an M tattooed on one of his cheeks, and on the other, an S.

"Why are you looking for me, you little fake-thug piece of shit?" the man said.

"You're Alfredo Guerrero?"

"You got that."

"I'm Saúl," Saúl said, breathless, "I just got deported. And, I swear it, I'm your son."

The man, as Saúl recounted it to me on top of the hurtling train, opened his eyes as wide as possible. And then he exhaled, long and loud. And then a look of anger swept over his face. "I don't have any kids, you punk," his father said.

But in the days following, the man gave Saúl a gift. The only gift Saul would ever receive from his father. He publicly recognized him as his son, and so bestowed to him a single thread of life. "We're not going to kill this punk," Guerrero announced in front of Saúl and a few of his gang members. "We're just going to give him the boot." And then he turned to Saúl. "If I ever see you in this neighborhood again, you better believe me, I'm going to kill you myself."

They left him in his underwear in another Mara Salvatrucha neighborhood. He only got out alive by covering himself (and the 18 tattooed on his back) in mud and pretending to be insane.

I got to know the Honduran police officer a year before I met Saúl. Her name is, or perhaps was (who knows if she ever made it to the United States), Olga Isolina Gómez Bargas. She was around thirty years old. Her story is also about a neighborhood she was barred from. And her story also has to do with two letters: MS.

She decided to leave her country after a bullet almost bore through her head. It was a bullet from the nine-millimeter pistol she carried with her every day. Her own gun.

Olga's first husband was a cop who was killed by the Mara Salvatruchas. He'd made a simple mistake. He entered the El Progreso neighborhood of Tegucigalpa, the Honduran capital, without backup. A volley of thirty bullets left his body like a colander. He was killed two years before I met Olga Isolina crying on top of a train, fleeing, so she told me, from herself.

Olga's second husband, also a cop, was killed only a year and a half after the first. Olga had long been living in a neighborhood where the MS had a strong presence, but she'd learned to disguise herself so they wouldn't know what she did for a living: she worked only in faraway parts of town, and she always changed into street clothes before coming home. She tried to convince her husband to take the same precautions, but he wouldn't hear of it. He'd come home in uniform, his pistol still tucked into his belt.

And then, one day, her husband got shot three times in the neck. Pride and violence, she had learned, are never a good mix. Since her second husband's death, Olga started thinking about her gun as a way to escape that hurricane of violence. "I'm going to kill myself," she would say to herself. "I'm going to kill myself and my daughters and my dog, and then we'll have nothing left to fear."

But she didn't do it. She started the escape to El Norte instead.

Violence, as Saúl well knows, can come from your own blood. Violence, as Olga Isolina says, can thrust you into depression. Violence, as the Alfaro brothers know, can terrorize you, especially when it has no face.

GOODBYE BOYS

Downtown Oaxaca City is shining in its Sunday best when we get out of the taxi at the central bus station. Blonde chubby children hold onto balloons while parents photograph indigenous men and women selling artisan crafts in the central square.

Auner, Pitbull, and El Chele smile at the tourists, but they're distracted, their eyes are darting in every direction, especially behind them. They're searching for a guide in the midst of *paleta* vendors and the pyramids of caramel apples. Following each other in close succession, the travel-worn brothers seem out of place— like a black-and-white picture spliced into a colored film—and they know it.

Though I'm going to accompany them through their next step, we know we'll soon have to say goodbye to each other. Their father has given them the cell number of a Oaxacan friend who he'd worked with in El Norte. He told his sons that his friend would give them a hand. But the brothers don't know what this man looks like, or how much he'll want to help. Will he be their guide? Has their father, hopefully, already paid their transit? Or might he just feed them a meal, let them rest before they continue north on their own?

I lend them my phone to make the call.

The difference between fleeing and migrating is becoming clearer to me. Fleeing takes speed. The boys know how to flee. Migrating, though, takes strategy, which the brothers don't have.

On the migrant roads there are wolves and there are sheep. The three brothers, bumbling naively through the square, look nothing like wolves. They don't even prepare themselves in case the father's friend turns out to be a coyote. They don't think about how they'll try to negotiate to avoid the undeclared taxes and extra charges. If a coyote knows he's working with fresh meat, he's going to try to squeeze them dry.

Auner hands me back the phone. The friend of the father has offered them bed and board and a little advice.

And so the brothers will continue north by themselves, without a guide. And they decide to go by train, instead of paying for another bus. They'll start the ride on the back of The Beast, straight ahead into the region of assailants and assassins, where migration authorities have been expanding their reach and capacity.

The afternoon in the central plaza is calm. Dry leaves fall lightly and blow along the ground. Old men and women rest on benches and nod amiably at the passersby.

On one of the benches, after shooting a look to Pitbull and El Chele, Auner says to me, "I don't want to offend you, but there's something we don't get. Why do you want to help us? Why do you even care?"

At first it seems easy to respond: so I can write your story.

But as we're about to say goodbye, a lump comes into my throat.

The question, I realize, is really a thousand questions. Who wants to hear the story of three more boys condemned to death? Why follow three bumpkin brothers who are running from becoming bodies on the street? What kind of story, in Latin America, is another body on the street? Why even try to help? What's there to say about people spit out of their own country?

But my answer is cut short. A dark man walks up to the bench. It's their father's friend. He makes a quick motion with his hand for the boys to follow him. I give Auner, then Pitbull, then El Chele, a quick, strong hug, and then they turn to go. I lose sight of them as they continue their escape, passing through the crowds of children and Sunday strollers.

WHERE ARE THEY?

For the next few days I keep in contact with the brothers through text messages. They've picked up a phone along the way.

Where are you? How are you?

Good. About to get on a bus to Mexico City.

Days pass. In Chalchuapa and Tacuba, young men and women condemned to violence and death become the new bodies on the street. Roberto, Mario, Jorge, Yésica, Jonathan, José, Edwin. All between fifteen and twenty-seven years old. All of them murdered in El Salvador in August and September.

Where are you? How are you?

On the move. About to board the train.

Then our communication cuts. I keep sending messages, but get no replies. I read about the massive kidnapping in Reynosa. At least thirty-five Central Americans, all riding the rails, all captured by Los Zetas.

Where are you? How are you?

Nothing. No response.

2

Here They Rape,
There They Kill: Chiapas

The most dangerous part of the migrant trail through Mexico, where undocumented Central Americans have no protection and where the horrors seem ceaseless and locals seem deaf to screams, is La Arrocera. Over the course of a year of walking these migrant trails, I've heard the stories of hundreds of attacks, of people beaten to a pulp, of murder, of women screaming while they were raped in those hills, and, just beyond them, Mexico refused to listen.

Paola, a twenty-three-year-old transsexual Guatemalan, says that she expected to be attacked while traveling. "I'd been told this always happens to migrants," she said. Then she told me the story of her rape:

She says that she tried to relax, readying herself to the idea of what was coming. Her shirt had been torn by one of the men standing behind her, all of whom smelled of grass and looked like laborers. They had suddenly come out of the nearby brush with shotguns and machetes. Calm, despite being, as she put it, in doggy position, Paola understood she had only two cards left—her wits and her will.

She listened to the outlaws negotiating behind her. "You can give her a fuck first. I'll go next." "Look here," Paola interrupted, "do what you want, but for your sake I'd put a condom on. I've got some over there in my backpack. It'd be for your own good, you know, I've got AIDS. It's just, well, I didn't expect this sort of problem. I thought you were all macho men, you know, the sort that only rape women." Paola spoke matter-of-factly, although she's identified as a woman now for years and would never answer to her former name.

A short moment of silence passed. Paola imagined them staring at each other, dumbstruck, pop-eyed, but of course she doesn't know. She had her back to them. She was still on her hands and knees, her head raised high and her eyes steady, with all the dignity she could muster.

"Just get the fuck up, you fucking whore," one of them said. "And go to hell."

Paola doesn't actually have AIDS. What she does confess to acquiring, after five years of prostituting herself in Guatemala and Mexico City, is a life-saving resource around perverted men: the combination of wits and will. Mugged and manhandled, without a cent in her pocket, she went on walking the nameless roads toward El Norte. "But at least I was prepared," Paola concludes. "Emotionally, I mean," she adds, referring to being warned about sexual attacks on the migrant trail.

She tells me her story sitting next to a stalled train in Ixtepec, just a few miles north of where she escaped being raped. Tall and dark, she wears heavy makeup, a black, low-cut shirt, and tight cowboy pants. Paola is a true survivor of La Arrocera.

La Arrocera. The place is stained red by the blood of migrants, some say. The place makes you whimper like a dog, others say. But most people just keep silent, only speak to define the place, simply, by name—La Arrocera. One hundred and sixty miles long, La Arrocera is a network of twenty-eight ranches scattered among thick overgrowth that stretches between Tapachula, the first big city one comes to on the migrant trail through Mexico, and the coastal city of Arriaga, which all migrants must reach to catch the train. At the end of this line of ranches lies a large, abandoned rice cellar, which gives the place its name. La Arrocera means, simply, The Rice Cellar.

Paola saw firsthand that something bad happens to nearly

every migrant here. La Arrocera is lawless territory. The forty-five others she traveled with to Ixtepec were all assaulted. Paola, like many migrants, intimately knows the danger of this place. The authorities know it too.

Many of the victims are never found. It's not uncommon that migrants travel alone, without identification and through areas where they have no contacts. The body of one migrant woman, for example, was found on November 20, 2008, strangled in the Relicario neighborhood of the town of Huixtla. Those who met her before her death, in Tapachula, said she was Guatemalan. They met the man she walked with too. They recognized him by the scorpion tattooed on his hand.

She was raped on the dirt-and-straw floor of a cardboard shack. That's all we know. At the time of her rape and murder there wasn't a police force dedicated to these rural areas, and really it's a sorry sight now that there is—seven men from the nearby towns, standing guard with clubs in hand whenever they have some free time.

The picture of the Guatemalan woman who was killed was published in the small daily newspaper, *El Orbe*, displayed on a half-page with two other pictures of tortured bodies. It shows the woman with wide-open eyes, a gaping mouth full of dried grass, dirt and leaves, and a bloodied scalp with fistfuls of hair torn out.

There's no open investigation. What's left of her are the few scraps of stories from people who had met her on the trail. Orlando, who works at Huixtla's cemetery, has a story. He sticks his tongue out as far as he can to show what she looked like when he was finally able to get her shirt out of her throat. The stories are all that's left. Stories and a small purple cross, lost in a graveyard full of anonymous bodies. The epitaph reads: "The young mother and her twins died in Nov. 2008." And her twins, it says.

Who knows why her murderer chose this place. Every day while en route to El Norte I saw, and began to understand, that the bodies left here are innumerable, and that rape is only one of the countless threats a migrant confronts.

THE BELATED WAR

We arrive in hostile times. At the beginning of 2009, the government of the state of Chiapas finally started paying attention to the violence on these trails. The bandits of today were once day laborers and ranch hands, who for years watched lines and lines of Central American migrants sneaking fearfully through, always ready to duck into the scrub. And then one day one of the laborers must have got an idea: the migrants are walking these trails in order to hide from the authorities, so if there were to be an assault, a rape, say, or a robbery, nobody would report it.

Migrants cross the river Suchiate on the southwestern border between Mexico and Guatemala, and from there begin their halting trip on microbuses and *combis* (the local word for public transportation vans). They board buses and then hop off before reaching the migration checkpoints set up along the highway. They duck into the foothills and walk a few miles to bypass the checkpoints, then get back to the road and wait for another combi. They make these mountain bypasses at least five times in the 175 miles until they reach Arriaga, where they can board a cargo train. On the trains they ride cramped and clinging like ticks, all the way to Ixtepec.

For years undocumented migrants have considered robberies and assaults as the inevitable tolls of the road. God's will be done, they repeated. The coyotes even started to hand out condoms to their female clients, while they recommended the men not resist an attack. For the past decade, in this hidden and forgotten part of Mexico, the stories of husbands, sons, and daughters watching women suffer abuses have been commonplace.

At the beginning of 2009, after more than a decade of petitions from human rights organizations, the Chiapan government finally bowed to the pressure. A visit from the chancellors of Guatemala and El Salvador and a letter signed by more than ten organizations, including the Catholic Church, prevailed on the government to take the first steps: creating the Prosecutor's Office for Migrants and convincing Governor Juan Sabines to order police chiefs in Huixtla and Tonalá to start patrolling the most dangerous portions of the migrant trails. In the end, though, they've just barely stirred the pot in the banditry free-for-all. Corruption and wickedness seem to float to the surface in every corner of this part of the country. Those in charge of cleaning up the worst areas are finding that there is simply not enough manpower to get the job done.

The local police commander, Máximo, receives us on a typically humid day. This is the most suffocating month in the region. Keeping your shirt dry is nearly impossible. Commander Máximo is responsible for the area stretching from Tonalá to Arriaga, which is the top half of all of La Arrocera. When we sit down he puts in an order for maps, a stack of documents, and lemonade with extra ice.

"All right, fellas," he says to Toni Arnau (one of *El Faro*'s news photographers) and me, before we're even able to ask our first question. "As you can see, we've attacked the problem at the root, and we've come up with a solution. I can tell you that in my zone there will not be one more assault or rape."

The stack of papers that he slaps on his desktop bears the title: "Operation Friend." On one of the pages is a photograph of eight men, all under thirty-five years old. Above the photo the caption reads: "Alleged perpetrators of the events on the train, December 23, 2008." Supposedly these are bandits who have expanded their field of operation, from attacks on the migrant trails to pillaging the trains heading out of Arriaga. During the assault in which these men were captured, a Guatemalan migrant who tried to stand up to them was murdered. The assailants carried both machetes and automatic weapons.

"And how many are still in detention?" Toni asks.

"I'm pretty sure," Máximo says, "one of them is still locked up."

Máximo takes out another folder to wash out any bad feeling

we may have. He slaps it down and drums his index finger on the plastic surface of the desk.

"This is the guy we just caught in El Basurero. His job at the big migrant crossing point in Durango was to direct anyone he could off the main path, right into the hands of the assailants. But we took care of him."

The photograph is of a man named Samuel Liévano, a skinny fifty-seven-year-old rancher who owns a small plot of land right where the path splits and the trail leads back to the main highway. It's the spot where migrants run past the last federal police checkpoint at the entrance to Arriaga. Liévano, however, guided migrants the other way, toward El Basurero (the Garbage Dump) where the old rail line is and where the bandits lie in wait. El Basurero is an open dump and a notorious site for assaults and rapes. Máximo and his men caught Liévano after the rare event that two Hondurans who were led into an ambush in El Basurero reported the crime at a migrant shelter in Arriaga.

The informants against old man Liévano are two black Honduran men. They get to the shelter, where we're waiting for them, without a drop of sweat on their foreheads. They're fishing divers from the sweltering Atlantic coast, well-accustomed to a scorching day of work. Now, after five days waiting for the prosecution to call them, they're fed up and want to get back home. Elvis Ochoa, an experienced twenty-year-old, says of the trip north, "It's nothing," and flashes a Los Angeles gang sign. He's already lived in the States a few months. Nineteen-year-old Andy Epifanio Castillo, however, is a candid first-timer. He admits he's had his fill, and doesn't want to step any farther on Mexican soil. With slumped shoulders, he laments, "I risked my life for one that's better." If the boys leave tomorrow, Liévano will go back to his ranch, continuing to direct unknowing migrants into a trap, and proving the words of Máximo to be another superficial attempt at resolving a systemic problem.

The bandits who held up Andy and Elvis, even after hearing that Liévano was in trouble, are supposedly still hanging around, one with a nine-millimeter, the other with a 22-gauge shotgun.

Leaving the hostel, we try to figure a way to safely see El Basurero. Máximo offers us a ride, but mentions that things will probably turn out different for us—riding in a truck with four policemen carrying Galil rifles—than it usually does for undocumented migrants.

We're left with one last option. The prosecutor's office that specializes in migration cases has just started a new round of operations. They call on the public municipal offices of various small towns, and assign officers to go undercover as migrants and then fight back against any assailants, with firepower if necessary.

Only three weeks ago, four undercover policemen stumbled upon a robbery in progress in El Basurero. There were two migrants hiding in the underbrush who came out when they saw the police.

"Keep still, you sons-a-bitches," one of the policemen yelled.

One of them moved. The policemen unholstered their pistols and when the hidden bandits saw the guns, they started firing and running. The two migrants were trapped in the middle: Wenceslao Peña, thirty-six, and José Zárate, eighteen, both Mexican. One was shot in the neck, the other caught two bullets in the thigh. When the firefight ended, only two men were standing unharmed. Two of the four policemen were shot with a 22-gauge shotgun. All of the wounded are still in the hospital in Tonalá.

In the public prosecutor's office, three men sit melting in front of a fan. When they notice the half-open door and our heads poking inside, they ask us what we want. After we explain ourselves, one of them, Víctor, steps out to talk with us. He was one of the uninjured officers in the recent gun battle. He has his shirt unbuttoned almost all the way to his waist, his belly taut against the opened fabric and the butt of a nine-millimeter sticking out of his belt.

"What do you really want?" he says in greeting.

"We've come straight from seeing the public prosecutor,

Enrique Rojas. We've been here a week and are trying to get to know the migrant trails, to experience them as the migrant experiences them. We haven't gotten very far."

"I don't get it," he says. "What is it exactly you want to do?"

"Go with you on one of your operations."

Víctor throws a quick glance at one of his colleagues, who stands with his rifle strap across his chest. They exchange knowing, lopsided smiles.

"No," Víctor says, lengthening the vowel. "That's impossible. It's very dangerous, even for us, even though we're armed. There's a gunfight on every corner here. These robbers don't think twice before firing. We always go in armed, and we still need protection from a second group of agents that follows us a couple of miles behind."

We spell out our arguments again, insisting, but with each motion we make, another trickle of sweat drips from our faces and Víctor ticks off another counter-argument.

"It's even worse in La Arrocera," he says. "There the bandits are organized and carry AR-15s. We only go in when we've thoroughly detailed an operation first."

By the time we leave we realize that our only option left is to improvise. It's unusual for someone to want to nose around these parts. By and large, the victims here are only written about once they are dead. Journalists and human rights organizations condemn and take the stories they hear in migrant shelters to court, but the only people who really know what goes on in La Arrocera are the migrants and the bandits themselves.

These mountains, there's no better way to say it, have their own laws.

A year ago, chancellors from Guatemala and El Salvador toured through this region. They staged a whole spectacle: thirty federal police agents with two teams of state police on horseback sweeping ahead, other patrols waiting for them a couple miles up the highway. It was a whole army of uniforms. Honduras is currently preparing its official guided tour under the same conditions. The headlines that come out of these visits are a farce. "IN CHIAPAS THE HUMAN RIGHTS OF MIGRANTS ARE GUARANTEED" appeared in three of the local papers.

Commander Roberto Sánchez, known as Commander Maza, receives us outside of Huixtla. The heat hasn't let up. It's just stopped raining, and the water has sprung back from the ground as an infernal fog.

Sánchez helps us as well as he can, but the conversation is brief and jumps between nicknames, recent deaths, and impunity. Chayote, he says, a famous local bandit who was detained four months ago, was released because his victims kept on their northern march instead of testifying. Chayote, we learn, actually turned himself in, opting to spend a few years in prison rather than get stoned by defensive migrants under one of the bridges in La Arrocera. And then there's El Calambres, a member of one of the older gangs, who was detained in Tonalá, but the plaintiffs in the case—not surprisingly—also wanted to keep heading north. It's normal. In Chiapas most denunciations filed by migrants are against the police. A migrant putting himself in police custody is about the same as a soldier asking for a sip of water at enemy headquarters.

Tomorrow we'll go to the police station responsible for patrolling this sector for the past three months. And we'll remain locked into this paradox, easily traveling around the dangerous Arrocera without even a whiff of the fear that migrants breathe daily.

ON FOOT WITH MIGRANTS

We get to the station at six in the morning. The police like to make their rounds early, before the sun starts to burn. Inside the station, which is set up in an old ranch house, we're greeted with a surprise. Three Salvadorans had come knocking the night before, asking if they could rest there. They'd wanted to catch their breath and be alert before getting to their next hurdle: sneaking past the first checkpoint in Huixtla.

The men are stretching and yawning, having just woken from a four-hour nap.

Eduardo, we learn, is a twenty-eight-year-old baker who's fleeing the Mara Salvatruchas. Marlon is a twenty-year-old distributor who loyally sticks with Eduardo, his boss. José, twenty-six, is described by Eduardo and Marlon as their extra pair of hands. The officers who let them stay the night now plead with them not to leave until the sun is high, because, they explain, not even they dare walk La Arrocera in the dark. I get the feeling they are only being so kind because we are present.

The three Salvadorans join us on our excursion. As we step out of the station we see a one-room cement house with a thatch roof, and a middle-aged man, barefoot and without a shirt, standing on its stoop, holding his daughter's hand. He waves to us and the officers wave back. It's a casual, everyday gesture.

"And them?" I ask the officer next to me. "They're your friends?"

"Spies," he answers dryly. "They work with the bandits. They're the ones who push the migrants off trail and to the spot where the gangs wait to attack them. Every time we do our rounds, they're out here, watching us."

We walk single file down the rocky path that, though still noticeably ravaged by Hurricane Stan which struck in 2005, serves the migrants as a life-saving guide through this jungle that seems like something out of Vietnam. The lush green of the plants blankets us, the ground is an obstacle course, and the puddles we're hopping over are like miniature swamps. To our right, only a few paces behind the tangles of vegetation that tower over the side of our path, there's the stable, called El Hueyate, which migrants often use for a night's stay. And if you look carefully, you can see, behind the scrub brush, like a secret gateway to a parallel universe, narrow tracks marked off by cairns that lead to hidden ranches and other abandoned stables.

"It was right here," one of the officers says, pointing out a cement structure as we're crossing a small bridge. All these officers speak in a matter-of-fact tone.

It was here last year that an officer, one of his colleagues, was killed. A bandit broke his skull with a machete. A newly sharpened machete is, for these outlaws, more weapon than tool. They use it to break up soil, sure, but mostly to attack, or to defend themselves. The officers say the bandits always have a machete, their most loyal companion, in hand, as if it were a natural extension of their arms.

We hear dogs bark, and we look around, but we only catch glimpses of flashing eyes peeking through the cracks of nearby gates and sheds and houses. People want to know who we are and what we're doing.

"They've got us surrounded," the officer says, shaking his head, and then slams us with another of his loosely explained accounts of our surroundings. "What I told you about the bones," he says, "happened here. And over there, that's where we found El Chayote's body."

Vultures continuously circle the area, looking for dead cattle and dead people. Bones here aren't a metaphor for what's past, but for what's coming. The bones the officer was referring to were a perfectly intact skeleton they found here a few months ago. And El Chayote was an infamous Arrocera bandit. His body was found right around here as well. We would have been able to see it from where we're now standing: a big bruise in the middle of his forehead and his face caved in as if he were made of soft clay. El Chayote was found pelted by rocks. While the machete is the most common weapon for small-time bandits, rocks are a migrants' defense.

We're walking among the dead. Life's value seems reduced, continuously dangled like bait on a fishing line. Killing, dying, raping, or getting raped—the dimensions of these horrors are diminished to points of geography. Here on this rock, they rape. There by that bush, they kill.

"They separate the women from the group and take them over there to rape them," an officer points to a cluster of squat banana trees. "And, well, this is also where we head back to camp. This is where our patrol round ends."

We've barely walked a half hour. I can't stop shaking my head. What we've walked is a fraction of what a migrant walks, and we've only reached the beginnings of their journey.

People call this point La Cuña (the Wedge). It's a narrow path that meets up with the highway, just north of El Hueyate, to the right of a mango tree where they rape, to the left of a heap of dirt where coyotes from Huixtla lead migrants straight into the jaws of the bandits they secretly work for.

As the officer goes on describing the brutal facts of the land, the three Salvadorans watch silently, furrowing their brows. It seems they're wondering what they should do next. "We're looking for this one guy," the officer says. "We think he's hiding out here. They call him La Rana (the Frog). He's got a big scar on his face. We know he works around here, but we just can't find him, you know? I know they give him a warning every time we're around here, before we can even smell him. They watch us so closely."

Just as he finishes his last sentence, I shake his hand and, without much explanation, tell him I'm going on with Eduardo, José and Marlon to Arriaga, where we'll catch the next train. The officers shoot me a worried look. I imagine they think of that colleague of theirs who was recently murdered. I imagine that, for them, a dead migrant is commonplace, but a couple of dead journalists is another matter. No one wants those kinds of bodies—the ones that come with names—found in their jurisdiction.

The trails are so rocky and dense with vegetation that within minutes we lose sight of the officers. Now, and just now, our real journey begins. We walk through the thick of the jungle for another three miles until we get to a small road that takes us back to the highway. Eduardo runs ahead to stop a combi on its way to Escuintla, the nearest town.

After our guided tour through La Arrocera it's clear to me that every attempt to eradicate violence in this area has been haphazard and unsuccessful. La Rana is still on the prowl, the rest of the bandits are a little ahead or a little behind, watching, waiting, and the dead bodies are always still fresh in memory.

What helped me understand this area was my conversation with El Calambres (The Cramp). His real name is Higinio Pérez Argüello. He's twenty-six years old and known for being the head bandit and assailant of migrants in La Arrocera. For the past three months he's been in jail in Huixtla, where he let me visit him and listen to his story as long as I followed his only rule: to retell everything in third person, to always say *them*, never *us*.

A CHAT WITH EL CALAMBRES

He was initially charged for rape, arms smuggling, and assault. He was accused of having raped a migrant, but, not surprisingly, the accuser disappeared. The other two charges stuck. And now he's waiting out his prison sentence.

The prison director offers his office for the interview and says that Higinio will probably talk. His reasoning is disturbing, but also not surprising: "He's going to talk because it's not like he's accused of a serious crime. We don't have anyone accused of serious crimes here. They're accused of murder, rape, or robbery. Never of drug trafficking."

And indeed, Higinio, also known as El Calambres, talks.

El Calambres is thin, with sharp features and veiny arms. He wears an oversized shirt which, coupled with his rural mannerisms, gives him the look of a gangster. He's five foot five and has long sharp fingernails, slanted eyes and a thin, lopsided mustache. Six chains hang around his neck, all crucifixes and rosaries. After he's been led into the office, he sits, crosses his arms, locks his gaze on the floor, and starts to talk.

"Yeah, I know the trail through La Arrocera," he says. "I used to live in a ranch around there. They would always be fucking with anyone passing by."

"Who would be fucking with them?"

"The people who lived and worked there. I've seen the gangs that come through. Now there's just one of them around. They came up from Tapachula to do their business. El Chino runs the operation. The other boss is El Harry. They've been around a while now, doing their thing, hunting illegals."

"And why do they only hunt the undocumented?"

"Because they know those people aren't going to stick around and cause trouble. If they mess with someone who's from here, though, they know they're going to have problems, and those problems are going to stick around. The others are just passing through."

I know from word of mouth that El Chino is still working. Everyone knows him by his nickname, and considers him one of the biggest bandits of La Arrocera. El Harry is even more legendary. He's one of the first who capitalized on the impunity in this area, one of the first who started with the robberies and rapes. They caught El Harry once, put him in prison in Tapachula for an assault, but then he paid the 50,000-peso bond and started roaming again.

But before he was ever caught he had the chance to hook up with El Chochero (the Old Man) and El Diablo (the Devil). Those two are now behind bars in El Amate, the largest detention center in Chiapas. The state has almost no control over the prison. From inside, El Chochero and El Diablo continue to run their narco operations, putting taxes on new inmates and keeping guards out of their cells. Back in 1995 they were working with El Harry, riding motorbikes and wreaking havoc on migrants who didn't take the trains and decided to walk the mountains instead. El Chochero proved he had talent, rising in the ranks until he went to prison and was put in charge of one of the prison crews, Crew Green. Now he oversees the prison's underground tax system, and even assigns new inmates their cells. He's become, as they say in prison slang, the new chief general. It took two days of fighting to wrest the position from the last chief general, the drug baron

Herminio Castro Rangel. It's these short-lived, explosive prison wars that decide who runs El Amate.

"Wait," I say to El Calambres. "I don't understand. How much can you make assaulting migrants?"

"Depends on how much the migrants are carrying. Some carry ten pesos, others carry five or even eight thousand pesos. See," he says, "they're not just fucking with them in the hills here. They start fucking with them way down south so that by the time they get here some of them are already broke."

"And how's business? If I were to grab a machete and just try my luck?"

"Nooo, it's all under control. Each group has its turf. Nobody can operate on somebody else's turf. If you just show up, you'll get shot."

"And if you stand up to the gangs, is that a way to get shot?"

"*Ay*! No, no, that's how you get killed, if you try to stand up to them."

"So there's probably a lot of bodies out there that nobody's ever found?"

"A shit-ton."

I explain to El Calambres what Máximo and Sánchez told me. I tell him that they assured me that the problem was resolved. El Calambres, for the first time, lifts his gaze. We share a lingering glance and then he breaks into smile.

"It's like this," he says. "There's not just one guy working these trails. There are gangs. And not just one gang. Which means there's never a pause. If somebody falls, someone takes their place right away. It's a lot of land, and it's remote, and maybe the law does go chasing the bandits. But the bandits who work it, they know the law too, they keep their eyes open, and they know the land even better than they know the law. The law just can't cover it. The place is too big. And if the law does run into the bandits, the bandits will shut it down. They have .22 shotguns, AR-15s, 357s. They even have bulletproof vests."

It's like the public prosecutor said, La Arrocera is something else. Bandits are better equipped there than cops. El Calambres assures us that gangs consider migrants as part of their long-term business plan, though sometimes, "thanks to some connections," they stumble upon other jobs: robbing jewelry stores, cars, businesses. And no gang works alone: they have authorities that are in the game with them.

At my last question, El Calambres shrugs, drops his head, and gazes back at the floor.

"And so, what's with the rapes then?" I ask. "Just for kicks?"

"Yeah, sort of. It's kicks for them. Something extra."

"Sure," I respond. "It's easy to rape someone if you know she's not going to report it."

"Yeah, well," he says. "Yeah."

The bandits leave their houses in the morning just like everybody leaves their houses in the morning, on their way to work. They leave from their neighborhoods, El Relicario, Buenos Aires, El Progreso, Cañaveral, El Espejo. They leave from the ranches and farms, and they station themselves waiting to do their business: rape and robbery. And at the end of the day they haul in their booty and go back home and rest, until the next day of work.

THE RANCHES, THE EXHAUSTION, THE TENSION

As we're pulling in to Escuintla, a small town of squat houses with row after row of street stands, the photographer Toni Arnau gets into a fight with the driver of the combi. Though the driver knows he's talking to three broke migrants and a couple of journalists indiscreetly recording everything, he still overcharges us.

"Just five pesitos for the trouble, damn, all I'm saying is just five more pesos!"

That's what he wants, five more pesos each. It's unfair, surely, but I have to admit, it sounds like a decent tax compared to what I know other unarmed muggers (a very different type of assailant than then ones who hide outside of towns, deep in La Arrocera's overgrowth) demand. Some charge 200 pesos for a ride that costs only ten for a Mexican. Still, we refuse to pay his surcharge and have to get off. We pick up another combi going to Mapastepec but find ourselves with the same problem, and so again, before getting to the next stop, we get off. Now on foot, we spot a man under a bridge who is waiting for another combi and ask him if the train station is very far.

"About three miles that way," he answers, "but don't go on this side of the highway, just two weeks ago some migrant got murdered around there."

We walk on, telling ourselves that if we get attacked, we get attacked. There's nothing we can do. The suffering that migrants endure on the trail doesn't heal quickly. Migrants don't just die, they're not just maimed or shot or hacked to death. The scars of their journey don't only mark their bodies, they run deeper than that. Living in such fear leaves something inside them, a trace and a swelling that grabs hold of their thoughts and cycles through their heads over and over. It takes at least a month of travel to reach Mexico's northern border. A month of hiding in fear, with the uncertainty of not knowing if the next step will be the wrong step, of not knowing if the Migra will turn up, if an attacker will pop out, if a narco-hired rapist will demand his daily fuck.

Few think about the trauma endured by the thousands of Central American women who have been raped here. Who takes care of them? Who works to heal their wounds? Luis Flores, head of the International Organization for Migration, said it well: "The biggest problem isn't in what we can see, it's beyond that. The problem lies in a particular understanding of things, in an entire system of logic. Migrants who are women have to play a certain role in front of their attackers, in front of the coyote and even in front of their own group of migrants, and during the whole journey they're under the pressure of assuming this role: I know it's going to happen to me, but I can't help but hope that it doesn't."

Migrant women play the role of second-class citizens. And they are an easy target. That was made very clear to us a couple days ago when we visited the migration offices of Tapachula and spoke with Yolanda Reyes, a twenty-eight-year-old who has lived here illegally since 1999. She made a life for herself in Tapachula and tried to live normally, but, even after so many years, something wouldn't ease her mind: she was still an undocumented Central American woman. She'd just gotten legal residency the day we met her, after a long process of filing a complaint against her partner, a Chiapan police officer who, in a crazed tantrum, slashed her eleven times (four times in the face) with a machete.

"Whore, you fucking whore, you're going to learn, you're just a fucking Central American and you're not worth a thing!" Those are the words she remembers.

After two hours of walking, our shirts are drenched with sweat, our faces are sunburned, and our legs are sore. We've just reached Madre Vieja, a town indistinguishable from all the others we've crossed: scrubland, mud, silence. The last time a body was found in this area was eight months ago. I can't help but wonder when the next will turn up.

We get onto the highway. The train station is still some 400 plus yards ahead. Another two hours of walking. We'll get there, but we have to go deep into the woods in order to find the path we're looking for. We rest a moment on the slab of a highway median. We cross the highway, looking every which way like scared animals, then pile into another combi. We've successfully sneaked past two checkpoints.

As soon as we get to Mapastepec, we board another combi toward Pijijiapan. We're bone tired. Again we ask the driver to let us off before the next checkpoint. The driver leaves us in El Progreso. It's already midday. When we slink back into the woods, walking among nameless mountains, we feel that hellish heat again. No one talks anymore. Not Eduardo, not Marlon, not José. Knowing that once they reach the station and board the train they'll still have 90 percent of Mexico to cross is enough to make me want to beg them to give up.

We've climbed over seven barbed-wire fences and crossed ten cattle ranches and a river. We're on this road by recommendation of an old man we met during the first three miles of our trek. The man warned us, though, of the danger. He said that we couldn't blame him if we were attacked. He recommended this route in particular, he said, because it had one clear advantage—it stayed close to the highway, which meant potential help, which meant people would be able to hear our screams. It sounded terrifying. There was another path we could have chosen, but it was longer. We figured we only needed water and shade, and the word *shortcut* rang louder than the threat of attack.

We walk another three hours among these cattle ranches, with no idea if we're still on track or if we've been walking in circles. Just before reaching El Progreso, we pass by another route which, now that we're exhausted, seems the better bet—to get off at El Mango, a back road which is more direct and devoid of checkpoints, but where, we were told, getting assaulted is a guarantee.

In the end, in a tiny, abandoned shell of a house, we find the two things we need: an old man who promises to be our guide, and a well. The old man says we're in luck, things are relatively calm now, and yet danger, he knows, is fast approaching. Two weeks ago police caught a man and his son, both of them full-time assailants, just on the other side of the highway in an area called Santa Sonia. And because of that, the assailant's relatives, in the mugging and kidnapping business themselves, had decided to cool it for a little while.

"It won't last long. So let's move it. We gotta move quick."

And so we set off, back onto the highway, managing to board a combi en route to Pijijiapan. Then we get off in time to board another en route to Tonalá. We're told the checkpoint there is highly militarized, but that the officers are only worried about arms and drugs smuggling, and we're promised they won't ask for any documents. Plus, we're tired, we don't care about this new risk that, only a few miles back, I know we wouldn't have taken. What's one more checkpoint? We'll happily take it,

convinced they won't detain us, though we know we're pushing
our luck.

We cross. And sure enough, they're only looking for weapons
and drugs.

After forty minutes on the combi we ask to be let off at a crossroads called Durango. It would have been only a twenty-minute
ride to Arriaga, but our guide advises us not to risk going through
any more checkpoints and so we settle in for another two-hour
trek. Our silence is nervous, angry. We know this place. We've
heard so much about it. We're right around where that infamous
old man, Liévano, would trick migrants off track and lead them
right into the hands of their attackers.

Our surroundings change. There's no longer the thick green
overgrowth, but long, meandering paths of loose rock. The place
looks apocalyptic. Dry. Wild in its dryness.

We pass the famous dump, the place of rape and violence. A
wide and open dump heaving with stuffed plastic bags and mul-
ticolored boxes that swirl around in the wind and get stuck on
the gates of nearby ranches. It looks like a landscape blasted
by bombs.

We trudge on for more than two hours and can feel the blisters
on our feet, after almost thirty miles of skirting checkpoints. The
iron bridge that marks the entrance to Arriaga suddenly appears at
the edge of our horizon—an industrial door to a small, drab city.
We've been on the go since six in the morning, the threat of being
attacked hovering just a breath away from us. The bridge is what
we've been waiting for.

Curtly, we say goodbye.

Marlon, Eduardo, and José are going to a migrant shelter.
We're going back to Huixtla. This time, in all that immensity
that is La Arrocera, there was no attack. Maybe it is calm, maybe
the story here in Chiapas has changed course, maybe the prosecutors, police officers, and lawmakers are successfully reaching
their goal.

NOTHING IS WHAT IT SEEMS

It's been four days since our walk through La Arrocera.

I've been asking how things are in these parts, if migrants have been making it through unharmed or if bandits are still having their way.

Carlos Bartolo, who runs the migrant shelter in Arriaga, tells me that just today four people who'd been robbed showed up. One of these, Ernesto Vargas, a twenty-four-year-old from a small Salvadoran town called Atiquizaya, was robbed by two men, one who carried a machete and another who held a .38 revolver pointed at his chest. They took everything he had: $25 and 200 pesos.

I call Commander Maximino, who says he's checking into it. It seems, he tells me, that a group of bandits have moved a few miles to the north, to the border of Oaxaca, where they've set up a safe house in the mountains. The group has been robbing not just migrants on foot, but those riding the rails as well. I ask him if he's spoken with the Oaxacan authorities, if he's told them what he knows.

"Well," he answers, "they're not that interested. They don't want to touch this stuff. No way we're going to coordinate with them."

Another day passes. I call the priest Alejandro Solalinde, who is in charge of the shelter in Ixtepec, Oaxaca, where the train— The Beast—drops off the migrants who are riding from Arriaga. Solalinde tells me that after eight months without incident, the train that arrived that very morning was attacked. Some bandits armed with pistols and machetes jumped on board at the Oaxaca–Chiapas border and stripped all the travelers.

Again I call the shelter in Arriaga. Three more Salvadorans were robbed in Huixtla, including one woman, a twenty-year-old pregnant Honduran who had been raped in La Arrocera two days ago. She said it was the people she traveled with who raped her. They'd told her they were migrants and convinced her to walk with them. Then all three of them raped her. When her son aborted between her legs, the bandits killed him with blows. Then they beat the woman until she lost consciousness. When she came to, she was completely alone. As well as she could, still bleeding, she managed to walk to the highway for help.

3

La Bestia: Oaxaca and Veracruz

So many questions come to mind on top of the train. Why are we hanging on to the roof if the cars are empty? Why so fast? Who will protect us when we're assaulted? What horror stories do the rest of the stowaways carry? And why do we have to ride this brutal, nocturnal beast?

The roofs of the train cars are where the undocumented Central Americans ride. These are the tracks where the wheels of steel slice through legs, arms, and heads.

The whistle blows long and loud in the darkness. The Beast is coming. One blow. Two blows. The shrill call of the rails. Time to get moving. Tonight there are a hundred or so of them. They wake, shake off their sleep, heft packs onto their shoulders, grab their water bottles, and start onto the path of death.

Some of the silhouettes stand out against the other, more furtive shadows running next to the train. Thirty or so sharp, strong, looming profiles. These are the warriors. From their hands, like extensions of their bodies, flash their makeshift weapons of defense. These are men willing to take a stand against the bandits. They know that together they'll have a chance against the rail-pirates waiting for them in the darkness of the jungle.

The men huddle and plan next to the rails as they wait for the engine to hook up with the twenty-eight boxcars to begin the journey. The group's decision is unanimous: if it's necessary, they'll fight.

The majority of the cars stand on one rail line, but there are also some lined up on adjacent tracks. There's an extended moment of uncertainty: nobody knows which train to board. The hundred or so shadows turn their heads between the two lines, trying to read the train's signals. The shadows move along the one line to get a better look, and then return. It's a lot easier if they can figure it out before the cars take off, otherwise they'll have to board on the run.

Though this will be my eighth trip, I still haven't gotten used to it: the back and forth of hurling, frantic silhouettes, the metal clanking of The Beast enveloping everything, hardly a moment to think. It's a sensation between the excitement of the ride and the fear of the uncertainty. All we know is that we don't want to miss the train, that if we jump on the wrong car we're going to have to wait and wait and wait. And when the time finally comes, we'll only think of ourselves, we'll concentrate on the ladder we've picked out, on climbing it safely, hoping that nobody gets in our way.

The train is a long series of uncertainties. Which cars are going to be leaving? Which one will take you to Medias Aguas and which to Arriaga? How soon will it leave? How will you duck any rail workers? To avoid an assault, is it better to ride the middle or the back cars? What sounds signal you to jump on? When do you get off? What happens when you need to sleep? Where is the best place to tie yourself to the roof? How do you know if an ambush is coming?

Between the two lines, the group of thirty make their decision: the leftmost rails. One after another they scamper up the ladders and settle on the top of boxcars, staking their claim. This sixty-foot radius will be their base during the six-hour journey. They'll cling to any ridge or pole to keep from falling. It's a space they're willing to fight for.

These men have already kicked off one dark-skinned teenage Salvadoran. Earlier in the afternoon, the young gangster, recently deported from the States, was smoking marijuana outside the hostel in Ixtepec and sitting apart from the group. The other men didn't trust him, didn't want to risk having a gangster ride with them. "You're not coming," one of them said simply, clearly an order, the whole group of thirty watching over his shoulder. And then the young gangster, looking back into that group of faces, backed down.

Eduardo and I pick our spot on the top of a car with a group of Salvadorans, Nicaraguans, Guatemalans, and Hondurans.

The few women on board settle themselves on the balconies between the cars. A few lucky migrants even secure the bottom platform, which is safe from the wind and passing branches and wires. The remaining passengers only have metal beams to hang on to. They'll ride on top, dodging wires and branches, shivering in the constant currents of wind.

The group of thirty is composed of bricklayers, plumbers, electricians, farmers, laborers, and carpenters, all recently turned warriors. The four Guatemalan men closest to us are brothers. They've recently been deported from the United States, but are headed back to the country they consider their home. One of them is an ex-soldier who left a job as a bricklayer. We also meet Saúl, who is so skilled at getting on and off the train that, after tying his bag to the roof, he swiftly hops off to snag a cardboard box lying next to the rails. He'll use the box as padding against the sharp fiberglass of the roof.

Finally the engine lurches forward, pulling the twenty-eight cars behind it. The hard clack begins at the head and shudders down each car all the way to the last: tac, tac, tac, tac ... One car after another pulled by the powerful engine, people latching on to whatever they can. Many have been injured in this initial thrust when, ignorant of the rules of The Beast, they've rested a foot between two cars. The molars, they call them. As its cars domino and grind together, The Beast, like a hammer crushing a nut, has smashed many feet.

And yet the danger of the initial thrust is outweighed by one invaluable advantage: you can get on before the train starts moving. There are plenty of other stops—Lechería, Tenosique, Orizaba, San Luis Potosí—where rail workers and guards won't let anyone board near the station, and you have to jump on the train farther down the line, once it's already speeding ahead.

On one of my earlier rides, Wilber, a twenty-year-old Honduran who acts as a guide for the undocumented across Mexico, gave me a beginner's course on how to board a moving train.

"First, you read its speed. You let the handles of the cars hit your hand to see how fast it's going. You have to feel that. If you're just watching, the train will trick you. If you think you're ready, get up next to it, grip onto a handle and run with it for about sixty feet to match its rhythm. When you have its pulse down, you latch on with both hands, then, only using your arms, keeping your legs away from the wheels, lift yourself up. You step on the rung with your inside foot, not your outside foot, so that your body swings away from the train and you don't get sucked under."

When I tried for the first time with Wilber, we were in Las Anonas, a small pueblo between Arriaga and Ixtepec. The train was moving at about ten miles an hour. I made the basic mistake that's maimed so many beginners: I forgot the trick about which foot first and I stepped with my outside foot. I was hanging on by my left hand and the sudden thrust pushed my foot back to the ground. The train dragged me for a few yards until, luckily, a few migrants jumped down to disentangle me.

Wilber thinks that travelers who are mutilated early on in the journey are "lucky." The train is usually going slowly enough, he says, that, after getting maimed, they get the chance to make a new decision.

"I saw one guy," Wilber remembers, speaking as calmly as if he were remembering a soccer match, "who got his leg chopped off by a wheel. The guy just couldn't lift himself up once he was already running. And since the train was going so slowly, he had enough time to see his chopped leg, think about it, and then put his head under the next wheel. You know," Wilber says, "if he was heading north because he couldn't get work down south, what could he possibly find with only one leg?"

Why don't they let them board before the train starts moving? Why, if they know that the migrants are going to get on anyway, do they make them jump on while it's already chugging? It's a question that none of the directors of the seven railroad companies is willing to answer. They simply don't give interviews, and if you manage to get them on the phone, they hang up as soon as they realize you want to talk about migrants.

The ride begins. The Ixtepec rail lights fade into the distance. We cut through dark plains outside of town, which glimmer in the eerie light of the yellow full moon.

These are the migrants riding third class, those without either a coyote or money for a bus. The men repeat this fact over and over. They will be sleeping alongside these rails for the bulk of the trip across Mexico, hoping that as they rest they won't miss the next whistle and have to wait as long as three days for another train. They'll travel in these conditions for over 3,000 miles. This is The Beast, the snake, the machine, the monster. These trains are full of legends and their history is soaked with blood. Some of the more superstitious migrants say that The Beast is the devil's invention. Others say that the train's squeaks and creaks are the cries of those who lost their life under its wheels. Steel against steel.

Once, riding on top of the train in the dark of night, I heard someone say: "The Beast is the Rio Grande's first cousin. They both flow with the same Central American blood."

The stretch from Ixtepec to Medias Aguas, crossing from Oaxaca into Veracruz, is 125 miles long, which lasts, at the very least, six hours. Six hours in which the train curves away from highways and into the desolate wilderness where it sometimes stops in the middle of the mountains to load cement or attach new cars. Sometimes the halt in the mountains can last up to two days. It's a waiting and guessing game. This leg of the ride can last anywhere between two and ten hours.

The best place to chat with a migrant is on top of the hurtling train. You're considered an equal there. You're in their territory and have, by boarding the train, signed a pact of solidarity. You share cigarettes, water, food, and are ready to defend the train from attack if necessary. The pact ends when you get off the train. And then you have another opportunity to sign again, to get back on the train or not.

Talking is the best way to stay awake, to keep yourself from becoming another one of the legends, another victim mutilated in the darkness, bleeding to death by the side of the tracks.

THE BITE OF THE BEAST

That afternoon while waiting for the train we spoke with Jaime, an unassuming thirty-seven-year-old Honduran peasant. Jaime was not the sort of migrant to dream of American cars, new clothes, and bling, or to fantasize about returning to his village wearing an L.A. Lakers jersey. He left his small Caribbean coastal village in January, dreaming of healthy crops, shoots of corn and rice and beans that would one day surround his modest home.

It was his second try heading north. On his first trip he spent two years in the United States, saving up $17,000, enough to build his family a cement house back in Honduras. Then he returned for good. He had what he wanted: a house and some crops to grow. But then, after seven months, what he spent two years saving for was swept away. "A hurricane, one of those storms that hit that part of Honduras all the time. It destroyed everything." All he owned—both house and crops—were gone.

And then, just like the first time, Jaime packed some clothes and a few bucks and said goodbye to his wife.

The only way to get back what he had lost, he knew, was to go back north.

But before reaching the goal there is the journey to face, a journey that can take even more from you than what you're looking to make.

That afternoon in Ixtepec at Father Alejandro Solalinde's migrant shelter, Jaime sat in a plastic chair and talked to us under the shade of a mango tree. His left leg was stretched out, his other leg ended in a stump. White, almost raw-looking flesh marked the stump.

Jaime had been desperate. He wanted to ride the train hard, make the journey fast. He wanted to see the corn bloom around his house again. But The Beast lashes out if you're impatient. And Jaime wasn't only impatient, he was tired. He had hardly slept for days, and had just arrived in Arriaga after an eleven-hour ride. And, with the exhaustion weighing down his eyelids, he hopped a train hauling nothing but boxcars. There wasn't a single good wagon on the train, only boxes. It was a dangerous combination.

Boxcars are exactly that, rectangular boxes of steel, no balconies between them, no top bars that you can grab onto. And between each box, the train bares its teeth—small bars of iron onto which impatient migrants hang as if they were crucified, while the earth blurs below, just a few inches under the migrants' hanging feet. That leg of the journey from Arriaga to Medias Aguas lasts six hours. Six hours on the cross, balancing on a thin bar, your own gripping white-knuckled fingers the only protection from slipping into the mouth of The Beast. The train picks up to seventy miles an hour, sometimes even through a curve. And that's not the same seventy of an automobile. A train is a whole other creature. No rubber tires, no quick stopping, or evasive turns. It's a solid, menacing, half-mile-long, barely controllable worm that squirms, wriggles, lurches, and shrills.

Jaime, crucified on the front of the car, talked with his cousin and two Nicaraguans. He occasionally stretched his arms to try to keep awake. But then he succumbed. "For just one minute I closed my eyes," he remembered. Or rather, they closed themselves. After three days of riding the trains before Arriaga, and then an eleven-hour ride under the beating Chiapan sun to Ixtepec, he was bone-tired. And then he walked from Ixtepec, catching what sleep he could in the ditches along the way. Nobody sleeps well in those mountains. One eye may close, but the other stays half-opened, staring into the night, waiting for danger.

When almost instantly he woke, he felt himself falling, felt the world slowing. He floated, he remembered, more than he fell. It was enough time to realize that he was falling toward the rails. Enough time to pray: "My God. My God, keep me, save me." And then everything became noise. Noise and speed. He was slammed flat to the earth, flattened like a stretch of tape. The Beast broke the air and formed the wind current which slammed Jaime into the ground, his head inches from the steel wheels.

Riiiin! Riiiin! Riiiin! That was all he heard, the deafening *Riiiin! Riiiin! Riiiin!*

And then, while the shrieking wheels split his eardrums, another wind current lifted him off the sleepers like a feather, floated him for a moment, suspended in the air, and then slammed him again against the rails. It was the very last car that ran over his right leg. The tailwind then spat him off the tracks, onto the hillside, like something regurgitated.

"I felt fine," Jaime said. "It didn't hurt."

Most mutilated migrants say the same thing. At first it doesn't hurt. Later, though, the pain nearly tears apart the muscles in your face and a sudden and intense heat shudders into your body so fast you think your head's going to explode.

Jaime didn't know what had happened at first. He felt something was wrong when he tried to stand. He doubled over, fell. Then he looked down. His leg was mutilated. It ended in crushed bone and ground skin and a barely attached, macerated, bluish hunk of foot. He tried to climb up the mountain using two sticks as crutches, but the long loose threads of his skin kept catching in the thorn bushes. With his pocketknife he tried to finish the job, cutting off his train-chewed leg. He couldn't manage. He tore off a strip of his blood-soaked pant leg instead, and used it as a tourniquet.

He succeeded, somehow, in walking an hour, still following the tracks, still heading north.

"I didn't feel pain."

But when he stopped walking he felt nauseated. He finally reached a dirt road that crossed the tracks. He waited there for ten hours. Listening and looking, unable to move. There was nobody. Not a soul. The trains in this part of the country cross mountains and valleys, but almost always skirt the cities. If you fall off, especially in desolate sections like that between Ixtepec and Medias Aguas, nobody is going to find you. You're going to make it by yourself or you're not. It's that simple. If you can't walk you're going to bleed out, and nobody is going to know about it. You probably won't even end up as a statistic if you die there. Not unless your family goes to the consulate.

By afternoon Jaime was surrounded by buzzards. They wanted a nibble of him, a taste of his flesh. Finally a pickup truck drove by. Three men got out. One stayed in the truck. Jaime remembers hearing the one who didn't get out say: "I ain't going. My heart'll stop if I see him. This one's alive."

The men took him to the hospital. There doctors sedated him, and then amputated his leg at the knee. When he woke he was hallucinating. "I saw horns sprouting out of the nurse's head, like she was the devil." The pain kept coming that night. Jaime dreamt he was playing soccer, dribbling the ball with a foot he didn't have. His body jerked in the dream and he woke in intense pain, a heat shooting down his leg, to the bottom of his oozing stump. He screamed so loudly that the nurses came running.

"Rest," is Jaime's advice to migrants who ride the rails.

He was sitting with us under the mango tree, his stump hanging off the plastic chair.

"The train will ruin you. Then you'll never get to the United States," Jaime said. "It's better to arrive late than never."

THE STRAIN OF THE JOURNEY

The train stops at La Cementera, the local branch of a cement manufacturing corporation, Cruz Azul, oddly set in the backdrop of this jungle. The engine clicks and shudders to release some of its boxcars, then changes lanes to pick up other cars to align on the tracks behind it. It's time to be wary, vigilant. Men crouching on top of the boxcars raise their heads to scan the streets and sidewalks surrounding the train.

Assailants hop on the train whenever it stops, to hide among the migrants. Sometimes the conductor, in previously made agreement with the assailants, slows the train down enough so that they can jump right on. On this car, the men suddenly raise all of the sticks and rods they've been carrying for protection. An indigenous Guatemalan raises a branch as if it were a shotgun and peers out into the darkness, as if taking aim. His silhouette, he hopes, will confuse potential attackers. Those who need to get off make sure to do so in a well-lit place, so that if they're assaulted others will see and maybe help.

We sense some sort of a fuss, a stirring. It's moving toward us, but is still distant. Then, behind us, we see movement, a flashlight turning on and off, winking ever closer.

The surest sign that there's a mass assault on a train, a migrant once told me, is when a flashlight moves over the tops of the boxcars. One time, when I was on this same route, I saw, in the distance, the splashing of light over the train. It came nearer and nearer, but then disappeared. I imagine this was when the assailants would duck down in some crevice to count their loot. Then, the small circle of light would blink on again and hover toward us. We saved ourselves thanks to the ingenuity of a Salvadoran who told our photographer to turn on all his lights, including his portable reflector and shine it toward the assailants. He did so. And the small circle of light stopped. It stayed put for a few minutes and then, when the train slowed, we saw the assailants hop off and lose themselves among the trees.

Train assailants, except in the kidnapping of women, which are orchestrated by highly organized gangs, are petty criminals—ranchers who live near the tracks. They're townsmen, hardly armed, with only .38 calibers and machetes. But they're also ruthless, knowing that if a struggle breaks out it will be kill or get killed. Push or get pushed off the train, onto the tracks.

A watch team is quickly put together. A Guatemalan man stands guard at the back of the car, while another is in charge of lookout at the front. Saúl, that nimble nineteen-year-old who until now has seemed so confident on top of The Beast, hides his face under the hood of his sweatshirt. "To look more ghetto," he explains. At the back of the train we still see a flashing of lights, but it's too far away to know what it's about.

Saúl lights a cigarette and loudly repeats, "Fuck it, if it's a robber, let him come. We'll give it to him!" It's Saúl's fifth try at getting back into the United States after being deported a month and a half ago. There, he was part of the 18th Street Gang. He got involved in some petty assault crimes, which is what put him in jail before he got deported.

Five failed attempts. Each time caught by Mexican migration officials. He's spent thousands of miles atop The Beast. He's got one mantra, which he repeats often: "You gotta respect this animal. If you've seen what I've seen, you know you gotta respect." Despite being the young, tough guy he is, he can't go back to his country because the other big Latin American gang, the Mara Salvatruchas, has taken over the neighborhood where he was born. Saúl says he knows exactly where he stands: the steel boxcars are like the backdrop of a nightmare.

"It never stops being horrifying," he says, "never."

The image he can't get out of his head is of an eighteen-year-old Honduran girl he traveled with a few months ago, during his first try at getting across. A nervous uproar washed down the train, because everyone thought a migration bust was going on just a few boxcars ahead, and she fell. She fell.

"I saw her," he remembers, "just as she was going down, with her eyes open so wide."

And then he was able to hear one last scream, quickly stifled by the impact of her body hitting the ground. In the distance, he saw something roll.

"Like a ball with hair. Her head, I guess."

Alejandro Solalinde, the priest who opened the migrant shelter in Ixtepec, is the reason those migration raids have diminished in southern Mexico. Leading protests before the National Institute of Migration, he argued that if raids must continue, at least they shouldn't be conducted at night. The darkness, he explained, is too dangerous: there's the constant roar of the train, the metallic chink-chink and those shrill squeals that sound like faraway screams, and all of the sudden, from every side, come blinding lights and migration officers. The lights and the train and the human screams: Get down! Get down! Get down! And then the train comes to a stop and shadows dive over the tracks where the steel wheels wait to slice through a body. This is unreasonable, Solalinde argued, you have to find a better way. Too many are getting crushed in those stampedes.

A blind crowd running, a blind crowd jumping, a blind crowd pushing.

Since Solalinde's complaints, surprisingly, the night raids have ceased. A little ahead, however, after passing Mexico City and crossing Lechería, we'll no longer be in the priest's territory, and the nightly raids will pick up again.

The flashing lights are nearing us. When they get two cars closer, we'll be able to see what it's all about. Saúl lights another cigarette.

"Let's make a pact," he says, "that we won't let them get us. A .38 has six bullets but those are shot off in a second. If we dodge those, then there's only the law of the train left."

This is the law of The Beast that Saúl knows so well. There are only three options: give up, kill, or die.

"A month ago," Saúl says, "three guys got on the train between Arriaga and Ixtepec. All of them were young. Armed. Two of them had a machete and one a .38. The thing was that this time we just weren't going to take it. The one with the gun walked past this one Honduran man, starting his rounds, taking our money, and it was so dumb, he should've stayed put in the front corner of the car where he could see us all, kept his gun aimed at us and then sent one of the guys with machetes to pick up the money. But he didn't. And so the way it all went down is that the Honduran grabbed his legs, and the rest of us got up and surrounded the other robbers with machetes."

There it was. The law of the train.

"First we beat the shit out of them. Then the Honduran asked another guy to help him out, and so the two of them got hold of the one with the gun. The Honduran got his arms and the other his legs, and they flipped him between two cars. The train cut him in two. They did the same to one of the others. When they were going for the third, one Salvadoran guy said we should leave him be so that he could spread the word that it's best not to mess with our kind. They threw him over the side of the train but there was some sort of ledge there. Anyway, I think he died too."

How many bodies must be out there, in the land surrounding these tracks?

Father Solalinde put it well: this land is a cemetery for the nameless.

The lights are close enough so that those standing guard can guess what it's about: "Hey," one of our sentinels says, "put away any weapons, it's just some of the train crew wanting to charge us."

Three crew members come to our car. The migrants cover their faces however they can, they turn their backs and avert their eyes to the sides of the train.

"Alrighty, boys," one crew member says, "it's my hunch there's a checkpoint up ahead, in Matías Romero, and we can either stop there or dodge it, but let's first see how you're going to treat us."

The train crew hops from boxcar to boxcar, acting like they're doing their duty, as if charging passengers their fare. No one in our car responds or gives them a dime.

"Cheap sons of bitches!" one crew member groans out. "Up ahead you guys're gonna get fucked."

My journalist team and I don't identify ourselves. Most train crews around these parts hate journalists. Eduardo Soteras hides his camera in his jacket but carefully peeks the lens out so that he can capture the extortion that, no doubt, those in the cars up ahead will face as well.

All the guys in this car are experienced train hoppers. They know that if there's a checkpoint it's not up to the driver to stop or not. The train has to stop. It can't evade military personnel or federal police officers.

The train changes lanes. A jerky domino effect. We hold tight, clinging to the roof struts beneath us as the train turns. The journey goes on.

It's so cold it feels like someone is whipping us with glass. The cold slicing through our sweaters, cutting through our skin. Yet some migrants are able to sleep. They tie themselves to the train however they can, looping their belts or a piece of rope around the roof struts. The top of this boxcar, overflowing with people silhouetted by the moon, looks like a refugee camp. Dozing, numb, hugging themselves, hugging each other.

The law of the train reigns again. Things are bad, but they can get much worse. Saúl puts on thin cloth gloves and asks another of his rhetorical questions.

"You think this is cold?"

It's needless to respond. We pass through a freezing wind and everyone starts shaking.

"This is nothing," he goes on. "I've seen people's fingers freeze, seen people slip off the train because the roof got so icy."

Soon Saúl and the others will have to endure that ice. After Medias Aguas they'll go through Tierra Blanca, after which they'll pass Orizaba and its volcano and rattle on through what's called "la Cordillera de Hielo," the Ice Range. They'll endure at least ten hours and up to two days on top of the train, as it labors across snow-capped mountains until reaching Lechería. It gets to be about 20 degrees Fahrenheit on that mountain range. And to make the trip more terrifying, The Beast plunges through thirty-one tunnels that are so dark you can't even see your hands.

"Now that's cold," Saúl says.

A half hour passes, and the glow of nearby streetlights wakes those who were dozing. We've reached the train station of Matías Romero, the halfway point between Ixtepec and Medias Aguas. Again it's time to be vigilant. The train slows to a stop, making it easy for assailants to hop on. Those traveling on the caboose ledges also straighten up with worry. At this point, only the quickest and most cunning could escape a migration bust. There's a tall fence on either side of us, row upon row of boxcars circling us. To escape would mean diving into an obstacle course.

All of the sudden, we hear a violent scream.

"Yeah! Gotcha, asshole!"

It's Mauricio, a forty-two-year-old Guatemalan ex-military man who's on his tenth try at getting back to his life as a cement mason in Houston after he was deported three years ago. He's screaming at the same gangster who, I recall, was smoking pot the entire evening we spent at Solalinde's shelter in Ixtepec. He was already high by the time we scrambled on top of The Beast that night.

The reason for Mauricio's anger is simple: back at the shelter, the gangster stole a pair of pants that he'd left out to dry. Mauricio swore revenge. Throughout the night, he eyed the gangster who sat a few boxcars back.

The gangster had just walked up to our car and, not yet seeing Mauricio, tried to convince a Salvadoran man that he, his wife, and twelve-year-old daughter should go back to the caboose to sit with him and his friends. He said he'd offer him and his family protection if there were a migration bust. Why would this gangster want to take this family under his wing? How many friends is he with?

Everyone responds to Mauricio's scream as if it were a war cry. A shower of rocks pelts the gangster, who runs away terrified while the other migrants convince the Salvadoran man that he would've regretted accepting that offer.

Then, moments before the train is about to take off and start the next chapter of our journey, the warriors deliberate. They decide on confrontation. Mauricio, Saúl, a Guatemalan carrying a two-yard-long iron rod, and three Hondurans will go to the caboose and give the gangster and his friends two options: get off or get thrown off.

The expedition readies itself. Rocks, whittled sticks, junkyard poles, and cheers: "We're going to smash his nose!" But with that, The Beast jerks and blows its whistle, reminding everyone that on this road, any control over what happens or doesn't happen belongs to The Beast alone. The train speeds up. Again the domino effect: tac, tac, tac. Everyone is forced to cling to their spot. The journey goes on.

The next stop will be Medias Aguas. It's a two-hour trip through multiple checkpoints along La Cementera and Matías Romero. Dawn is breaking.

The first sun beams from behind nearby hills and melts away any last shreds of darkness. The cold, though, is still unbearable, the struts we're sitting on slippery and frozen. Our faces are numb and rigid. Our fingers are so tired they can barely grip the cold metal. Around us is hill upon hill of dried shrub. Here and there a leafless tree looms. The hills are flooded by fog, an impenetrable gray thickness that stretches to the farthest corners of our view. After eight hours of the intense cold, we're beyond tired and our clothes are soaked by the permeating fog.

By the time we get to Medias Aguas it's late morning. We reach the grand station, the station of stations where the Atlantic route and the Central route, the one we're on now, merge. They won't separate again until Lechería, three long stops ahead.

The train wails its whistle, waking everyone from their stupor. People try to shake off their exhaustion and quickly get their bags to scramble off the sides of the train before it comes to a complete stop. Most mass kidnappings happen in these moments, when the victim-laden trains come into mid-sized cities, like this one, which are dominated by organized gangs. We have to jump ship as soon as possible.

There's no migrant shelter here like in Ixtepec, and there won't be another at the next three stations either. Everyone looks for a patch of grass to rest on or the shade of a tree to protect them from the sun. The dirt road running parallel to the train tracks fills with Central American beggars asking for any little thing to eat. Then, with a little something or absolutely nothing in their bellies, they'll doze with eyes half-closed until The Beast calls to them again, and the journey to the United States resumes.

4

The Invisible Slaves: Chiapas

The strangest thing is that I got used to it. My fear turned to helpless-ness, then to rage, and then, finally, to acceptance. The sordid lives of the women who live together in southern Mexico's brothels were just as horrifying as the lives they lived before they came to the brothels. With these women, everyday words take on new meanings. The word sex *means rape. The word* family *refers to a fellow victim. And a body is little more than a ticket from one hell to another hell. It's called "The Trade": thousands of female Central American migrants, far from their American Dreams, trapped in prostitution rings in Southern Mexico.*

Three women are laughing furiously at the back table. In a gallery of metal, asbestos, and wire fencing, at the last white plastic table, the women, thinking back on the previous night, are roaring with laughter. The reason for their excitement isn't quite clear. Standing some steps away from them, the only sentence I can make out is: "The old drunk was tripping over himself." And then the guffaws ring out again. I couldn't have imagined then that these same women, while explaining how they got here, would later be crying over their recent pasts.

It turns out they're laughing about a client: some dipso who was trying to dance the night before, trying to pinch whatever body part he could get a hold of, jerking and jiggling in the middle of the bar until, finally, he fell flat on the face.

The women, chuckling along at the table, are waiting for the night to begin. They'll soon start taking turns climbing onto stage to strip naked in front of a crowd of drunk and howling men.

This cantina (locally known as a *botanero*) is enormous: some fifty yards long and twenty wide, with thirty-five scattered white tables and a plain cement floor and counter. From the back of the bar come the buckets of beers and the *botanas*: small plates of beef, soups, and chicken wings.

The twenty-five women who work here are just arriving, coming in from the dirt road outside. These women are known as *ficheras*, waitresses who work for *fichas*, or little plastic tokens they collect, one for each beer, chat-up session, or dance a customer pays them for. At the end of the night, usually as dawn is breaking, the waitresses cash in the chips they've earned. Each beer bought for the girls costs the customer 65 pesos worth in *fichas*, or about six dollars.

The bar, which I'll call Calipso, is one of the ten or so strip clubs that light up the night in this part of the city. This border region, on the Mexican side of the Mexico–Guatemala border, is known as the "zone of tolerance." What is tolerated is prostitution. There are whole strings of similar bars, with the same process and the same sort of clientele in the small towns and cities that run along this border. Tapachula, Tecún Umán, Cacahuatán, Huixtla, Tuxtla Chico, Ciudad Hidalgo … all small towns smelling of alcohol and tobacco, sweat and imitation perfume, and cheap sex. And in all of these bars, just like in Calipso, you'd be hard pressed to find a single Mexican woman. The bars are brimming with Hondurans, Salvadorans, Guatemalans, and Nicaraguans. Here, "the market," as the women are referred to, is exclusively Central American.

The owners run the bars tightly, even hermetically. Most of them have dorms attached where the women are cloistered after the nights dancing and working clients for chips. They do have to pay rent. The prostitutes in this region often refer to working one of the bars with the self-reflexive term, *me ocupé*, meaning, literally, I occupied myself, I employed myself. They speak as if they were two, as if one of their selves managed the other, as if the body that had sex with the men was a puppet that they themselves only temporarily occupied or employed.

I came to Calipso by way of a series of contacts. One NGO worker, who preferred to be left unnamed, directed me to Luis Flores, a representative of the International Organization of Migration (IOM), who sent me to Rosemberg López, the director of A Friendly Hand, an organization that works for the prevention of HIV, who sent me to the owner of Calipso, who he knew because the owner allowed him to come and give HIV awareness talks to the women who work there. López had to press hard to be given access to Calipso's dancers, access which he wasn't allowed in any other bar along the border. Most of the bars didn't let him through the door. Some of the owners have even threatened to lynch journalists who've tried to film and interview their female workers. But the Calipso proprietor not only let López in, she told her employees to be open with him, assuring them that he wasn't an undercover cop.

In recent years, public concern has begun to close down some of the bars that prostitute Central American women and girls against their will. Since 2007, when a new law was passed in Mexico against human trafficking, various civil organizations have increased pressure against the bars, making "trafficking," especially trafficking women, a much more publicized issue.[1]

Modern people trafficking, it turns out, is not the image many expect—a scar-faced man tending a cage of women. It's a complex system of everyday lies and coercion that happens just behind our backs. For this very reason, for its open secretiveness,

---

1 The Law to Prevent and Punish People Trafficking was passed under Felipe Calderón's administration, and promises perpetrators prison sentences of up to twenty-seven years and fines of up to 3,375 days' worth of the minimum wage. Norma Gutierrez, "Mexico: Government Promulgates Law Against Human Trafficking," *Global Legal Monitor* Library of Congress, December 2, 2007. Accessed online December 11, 2011, loc.gov.

it's important to look closely into the shadows, to speak with the victims of trafficking, with the women themselves.

The three women still laughing in the back of Calipso have offered their testimonies.

ALONE IN THE WORLD

Erika (I've changed all of the names) wails with laughter. Though she has a thin thread of a voice and occasionally falls into silence, when she laughs, she shrieks, opening her mouth wide and even clapping her hands. She has white skin and reddish, curly hair pulled back by a headband. She's Honduran, from Tegucigalpa, and thirty years old. A dancer, she has round, thick legs, a thick torso, and a curvaceous body. She is short, cheerful, playful, and a good teaser.

"All right Daddy, what is it you want? What can we help you with?" Erika sits at my table. She orders a beer. It's one thirty in the afternoon. She'll keep drinking—beer after beer, all bought for her by clients—until well after midnight.

When Erika was fourteen years old she left her country and twin babies behind. "I had to go to El Norte … looking for what we're all looking for, a better life." *Una vida mejor.* She traveled with five other girls around her age. "Things happened to them. What can I say? Bad things. We'd all heard that women on the trail get raped." El Norte, meaning the United States, may not always be the final destination. Erika preferred to stay in the first state she came to north of the border—Chiapas, Mexico. She settled in Huixtla, known for its prostitutes, those shadows that anyone can see but few openly talk about. She arrived on a Monday or Tuesday, she's not sure exactly when, and then went to the Hotel Quijote to ask for work.

"But how is it," I ask her, "that a pregnant fourteen-year-old has the guts to leave home all by herself?"

A loud guffaw bellows from a table in the back. Erika turns to look. It's early yet, and there are only two tables of customers, but men are already dancing with a couple of the prostitutes. A waitress swoops over to the tables with overflowing plates of chicken wings and shredded meat.

"Let's get out of here," she says, "I hate it when my coworkers see me cry."

Tears are a defect in this world of stone.

We step out onto a dirt road that leads to another dive bar. This city is like a dead-end alley. Up ahead there's another brothel followed by a guesthouse, a euphemism for the row of motel-style rooms where prostitutes take their clients.

"I never met my family," Erika tells me. "See, I'm from Honduras but I never had papers. I never had a birth certificate either. I'm like an animal."

When she was still a girl she was told that her mother worked in the fields, "whoring like me." Her mother had given her and her twin sister away as a baby to a woman by the name of María Dolores, who Erika remembers very well. "That old whore had seven kids, and we, my little twin and me, weren't treated like her kids, we were like her slaves." She always calls him her "little" twin, though had he not died at the age of six, he'd be thirty years old.

What was her life like? Like a slave's, she says. At five years old, her job was to walk the streets, selling fish and firewood. If she came back with something still in her hands because she hadn't sold everything, María Dolores would whip her with an electrical cable until she had open sores on her back. Then María Dolores would cover those cuts with salt and oblige her "little twin" to lick it off. It was on one of those days, one of those sore-licking days, that her brother died on the floor where they both slept. They said it was parasites, Erika says. She's convinced that those parasites came from the sores on her back.

She cries and clenches her teeth. A truck pulls up and parks beside us. Three more clients open the door into Calipso.

"The day my brother died, I got sick. They took me to the hospital but never came back to pick me up. After that, I lived like a drunk on the streets, sleeping between dumpsters."

She lived like that for two years. Selling this, carrying that, begging wherever, sleeping on corners. Eight years later she bumped into María Dolores, who talked her into coming back.

"I was little," Erika says. "I didn't really get it. So I went with her." The physical abuse wasn't as bad, but, in general, life was worse. Omar, one of the woman's sons, was fifteen years old and repeatedly raped her.

"That's why I wonder if I'll ever understand what it is to have normal sex. I got so used to him tying up my legs and arms and having sex with me like that."

Sitting on the curb of a dirt road, weeping just outside of Calipso, Erika paints a typical portrait of the Central American migrants whose suffering lights up the nights of these border towns. Many of the women have no previous schooling. They flee from a past of severe family dysfunction, physical and sexual abuse, and they often come to these brothels as girls, little girls, incapable of distinguishing between what is and what should be. They're fresh powder, ready to be packed into the barrel of a gun.

"If you're not from the social reality of our countries, you're not going to understand," explained Luis Flores who, as head of the IOMin Tapachula, leads community education projects in the area and case-manages Central American human trafficking victims. Here, he explains, migrant women are turned into a product. "They come having already been raped and abused. They come from dysfunctional families in which it was often their father or uncle who raped them. What many of them won't tell you is that they knew they'd be raped on this journey, that they feel it's a sort of tax that must be paid. According to the Guatemalan government, it's estimated that eight of every ten Central American migrant women suffer some form of sexual abuse in Mexico. It's six of every ten, according to a study done by Mexico's Chamber of Deputies. They travel with that lodged in their minds, knowing that they'll be abused once, twice, three times … Sexual abuse has lost its terror. That's the vantage point from which to understand human trafficking. At a certain level, they know they're victims, but they don't feel that way. Their logic runs like this: yes, this is happening to me, but I took the chance, I knew it would happen."

There is, as Flores says, an expression for the transformation of the migrant's body: *cuerpomátic*. The body becomes a credit card, a new platinum-edition "bodymatic" which buys you a little safety, a little bit of cash and the assurance that your travel buddies won't get killed. Your bodymatic, except for what you get charged, buys a more comfortable ride on the train.

Erika, the girl who was repeatedly raped from age eight to thirteen, gave birth to twins and then, as if her suffering were inevitable, her story goes on.

"I didn't understand what pregnancy was. I only felt I was getting fat. That woman accused me of being a whore. I told her it was her son that did it, but she told me I was like my mother, a prostitute, and that just like her I'd ditch my future kids like dogs. She dragged me out of the house naked and walked me five blocks to a nearby park and left me there. And so I had to start completely from scratch."

It meant begging again, picking through trash, sleeping on street corners. She gave birth there, on the streets, and then she decided to, as migrants say, "try her luck." She left her kids with one of María Dolores's neighbors, and started her trek north to the United States with another five young women. Here's where, after hearing that the journey would be full of death and humiliation, and after witnessing many of those she'd been traveling with get hurt, she decided to stay. She doesn't remember if it was a Monday or a Tuesday when she came to Hotel Quijote.

Flores describes a typical transition: "Most start out as waitresses. Then they become call girls and finally end up as prostitutes. Usually they get to that point because they've been lied to." An illustrative case study by Rodolfo Casillas delineates the range in ages that traffickers target: "Between ten and thirty-five years old, hardly ever older. And the trafficking problem is exacerbated with underage migrants, specifically those between eleven and sixteen years of age."[2]

At the Hotel Quijote, Erika was propositioned.

"It goes like this," she explains. "Some asshole comes in and says, 'Let's get out of here. You and me. I can easily get you a job at another bar where you'll get paid more.' And then, if you're not careful, it can get to be a big problem. And all the time a ton of guys tell you that. 'I'll get you a place to live, I'll get you all the papers and documents you need, I'll get you a job.'"

She doesn't share any more details. Like most trafficking victims, she tells her story in the third and second person, and it's hard to tell what pieces of her story are directly autobiographical. It's as though the horrors of their lives were shared by all, as though what happened to one them has inevitably happened to all of them.

Erika assures me she didn't let herself get tricked. "I was no fool." She says it was by her own volition that she left her post at Quijote and sought out a dive. She says that even as a girl she knew to go straight to the managers and lay out her ground rules: "I said to them I'm not here to work only as a dancer, but I don't want to be locked up like the others either. I'm not an idiot. I'll work here every night, finish, and get paid right away.' See, it's because I grew up on the street that I at least knew how to look out for myself."

I ask about the other girls.

"They were locked up. Never let out. They ate only once a day. Whatever man took them there said to them, 'It's not so bad, you're gonna be able to work, but you also have to pay.' Whoever brings you there asks for his cut from the owner of the dive, and that, of course, is taken out of your pay. They sell you. But that never happened to me. Only to the others, because they're stupid."

This rationalization is commonly used as justification—those

---

2   Rodolfo Casillas, *Trafficking Migrant Women and Minors at the Mexican Southern Border: An Exploration into an Unknown Reality* (Mexico City: FLACSO, 2005).

who let themselves be exploited have only themselves to blame. But, as Flores explains, such passive victims are young girls with no education, who don't know how to condemn or report anything that happens to them, who are easy to intimidate. *If you try to escape, I'll call Migration and they'll get hold of you real fast!* "It's a problem of submissiveness," Flores explains. Of 250 sexually abused migrants surveyed by the IOM, only fifty accepted medical and counseling help. Many didn't see the point, because they expected it would all happen again; there was still a lot of road left to walk.

Though solidarity among Central American migrants isn't unheard of, the world of migration tends to isolate people. The journey is hard; tender moments are rare. Those recruiting fresh bodies to work in the brothels are the same Central American women who, against their will, were tricked into prostitution and now, years later, are offered extra pay to trick other newly arrived girls by making them the same false promises they once heard: you'll become a waitress, you'll be well paid.

Flores has a term for this: spiral logic. "I, a Honduran, a Salvadoran, a Guatemalan, got here when I was fifteen years old and I had to go through it, but now I have my own job which is doing the same thing to other girls who have to get through this before they can do what I'm doing."

Erika remembers her first days of prostitution with disgust. She'd close a deal with a man at a dive, and they'd go to a motel for a half hour. The room would fill with the smell of beer and sweat and she'd let herself be used. Sometimes it was like these men felt that they owned her for that half hour, that she was like a house that they'd rented and that they could do inside her whatever they pleased. She remembers that many times the sessions ended with what she'd gotten to know so well as a girl: insults and violence.

She takes out a small, circular mirror from her purse and looks into her eyes. She puts away the mirror, lights a cigarette, takes a drag, and then looks ahead, her eyes narrowing as though she's concentrating on returning from her past. She has sixteen years of this under her belt. Her vulnerability quickly fades. The laughing, teasing woman comes back, and she says goodbye to me with a playful slap on my arm. She walks into Calipso swinging her white, wide hips.

Flores explains that Salvadoran and Honduran women are particularly sought after for this business because, unlike the Mexicans of this indigenous area of Soconusco, Chiapas, or the small, dark-skinned women of Guatemala, their bodies tend to be fleshier and they tend to have lighter skin.

It's three in the afternoon and Calipso is filling up. Another batch of men have come in. The jukebox pop music clashes with the mustachioed, big-bellied clientele. Keny, a Salvadoran with small, button-like black eyes, is in the middle of delivering a round of orders to a table when a manager stops her. They talk a moment and then Keny walks toward my table.

Calipso is, relatively speaking, not a bad place to work. Here pimps don't decide who the women sleep with. If they feel like closing a deal, they do it on their own. If they only want to serve food and drinks, they can. At other clubs, or on street corners, most Central American sex workers have two pairs of eyes locked on them at all times, watching every move.

Flores remembers one time, while trying to do interviews, he approached a woman working a corner at the central plaza of Tapachula. He explained that he was putting together interviews for his organization and asked if they could talk. The girl glanced nervously over her shoulder. "I can't, my boss'll hit me," she excused herself, while imitating, with her gestures, a typical negotiation with a customer. Smile, no, no, thank you, goodbye.

Keny asks for water. She'll switch to beer later. Today is Friday, and she needs to last through the long night to make it all worth it. The difference between a Friday and a Saturday is that white-collar office workers come in on Fridays, because they have both weekend days off. On Saturdays it's the laborers who like to end their work week with a Central American girl.

TWICE BANISHED

Keny speaks in a whisper. It's a soothing sound that issues from somewhere deep in her throat, but sometimes the whisper turns hoarse, her voice tiring, pausing as she closes her small black eyes to add emphasis. "I'm here," she says, speaking slowly, "because I don't have anyone on the other side." She lets her eyelids fall shut, straightening her long black hair.

Her life has been marked by that huge magnet that pulls Central Americans north. When she was just a baby her grandmother left for El Norte. When she was fourteen, her father went north as well. Then her mother followed. When she was fifteen her older sister was pulled by the magnet, and Keny was left living with an aunt and uncle.

"They didn't even feed me," Keny recalls. "They took the money my father sent and they beat me instead of raised me." Her grandmother, after getting US papers, returned and saw that Keny was living like a martyr. She arranged for her to move in with some of her grandmother's friends. But the change didn't help. Keny stayed with the new family until, when she was sixteen, the mother of that family died of a heart attack and the newly widowed husband started beating and molesting her. For help, Keny called her older sister, who had moved to Guatemala City on her way north. Then she too decided to try to follow the family north.

She moved in with her sister but only for a few months. The sisters didn't get along. They got in a fight and Keny almost lost a breast when her sister stabbed her with a knife. "She left me mutilated," Keny explained. "And so I went to the streets. That's when I started to work in a cantina."

She bounced between a number of different bars and cantinas, eventually moving to Puerto Barrios to try dancing at a joint called the Hong Kong. When she first arrived she was wearing a child's

T-shirt with cartoon dinosaurs on it. The other waitresses, after having their laugh, decided to show her the ropes. They taught her how to dance, how to put on makeup, how to woo men, how to smoke pot and crack, how to snort coke, and how to drink, and drink a lot. "When I left that place," she said, "I was showing all of my cleavage." She had left the dinosaur shirt behind.

One of the older girls from the Hong Kong kept taking trips over the border and into Mexico, coming back with a lot more money than anyone was earning in Puerto Barrios. "They just pay more in Huixtla," the girl would explain to the newbies, like Keny, who was still only seventeen.

Keny took the hint. She moved to Cacahuatán, Mexico, and started working at the infamous El Ranchón. For a while El Ranchón was closed after some clients got into drug trouble, but after a change of name, to Ave Fénix, things seem to be back in swing.

Keny's been working these joints for seven years now, from Huixtla to Tapachula to Cacahuatán, from bar to bar.

I ask her if she also works as a prostitute, or just for the chips.

"I worked a little bit at first," she says. "I didn't like it, though, because you had to be with someone that you didn't feel anything for. You never know who you're going to run into. Some of them like to hit. A john's gotten aggressive with me a few times, but when you try to cool them down they start hitting. So now I just stick with dancing, chips, plus drinking."

The price of a prostitute in these parts varies. A youngster has more value than a veteran. And a youngster means a minor. A veteran means having passed thirty. Older than that hardly even counts.

On one evening, after returning from an interview in Tapachula, I asked my taxi driver about finding some young prostitutes, twenty years old or so. The driver responded: "Later on, buddy. My cousin and I have a little business with the girls. We drive them to hotels or houses, wherever you like. They're all real young. Not twenty, more like fourteen or fifteen. Two hours for 1,500 pesos [less than $150]."

Like I said, the prices vary. The older they are and the more indigenous they look, the cheaper they come, 400 or so pesos for half an hour. Younger though, with whiter complexions, you could pay up to 2,000 pesos. Flores says, "They call the more indigenous or more Guatemalan migrants *coppers*. The more Honduran or younger ones they call *escorts* or *teiboleras*.[3]"

The pop song playing in the bar ends. A slow-swinging norteña number by Valentín Elizalde—"El Gallo de Oro," The Golden Rooster—picks up. I ask Keny if it was true what the other waitress from Hong Kong had told her, that she would earn more in Mexico than in Guatemala.

"Yes, definitely," she responds. "Sometimes I waitress by day and dance by night and earn as much as 2,000 pesos."

"And your family," I ask, "do they know where you are?"

"I only speak with my father. He doesn't know. My sister might suspect something. They probably think I'm a waitress, not imagining what I've come to, that I also dance. I want to go back to El Salvador now. I don't want my son, who is nine months old, to grow up and see me like this. There nobody knows who I am. Here everybody knows. Over there I'll be just another single mother. I can't let my family know about this. They wouldn't understand."

I see a stream of tears fall from Keny's small black eyes. She wipes them neatly with a napkin, trying not to ruin her makeup.

I go to visit the women's shelter on the Mexican border, looking to interview women who have been raped or abducted while on their way to El Norte. The administrators who run the shelter agree to speak, but ask me not to identify the place. "As you know," they say, "the cartels are involved in all this." They explain that there are two principal reasons why women decide to stay in these border towns.

One is simply that they make more money than they could

---

3   A phonic rendering into Spanish from *table*, for table dancers.

make in Central America, and after a month of being forced to dance or have sex, before they fall all the way into this life of darkness, vice, and vulnerability, they start to accept their situation, realizing how much money they're sending back to their families.

The second reason, the directors explain, is shame. The past. To have to explain where they've been. What they've done. The fear of being discovered. Flores describes a common trap: "They recruit an indigenous girl from her land, tell her that she'll be a waitress, and then sell her as a prostitute. They tear up her papers and assure her that if she escapes, or if she doesn't obey, they'll contact her family and show them a picture of her sitting on a man's lap at the bar. They tell her that her whole village will know that she's not a waitress, but a prostitute. Now ask that girl if she's willing to go home. Of course not."

"Have you also come across girls who've been kidnapped and forced into prostitution?"

"They've mostly been coming voluntarily. I've heard stories of girls that have been sold, but once they see where they'll be working, they decide to stay put. They tell me they like the money."

But here we're confronted again by the tricks of trafficking. The subtle wording that makes trafficking not sound exactly like trafficking; the suggestion that it's the girls' decision if they want to stay. Blackmail camouflaged as proposals. In the end, it seems it's nobody's fault. Things are as they are. How they've always been. The girls themselves are used to suffering: they "choose" to suffer, they "choose" to be treated like market goods.

The threats and consequences of human trafficking in Mexico are grossly underappreciated. In the entire country there are only three Special Offices for Crimes against Women and the Trafficking of Persons (FEVIMTRA is the acronym in Spanish). And yet according to a 2009 United Nations report on drugs and crime, Mexican authorities' negligence and lack of acknowledgment of human trafficking are coupled with both increasing and more widespread incidents. The National Institute of Statistics and Geography affirms that there are an estimated 20,000 boys and girls enslaved or being exploited by sex traffickers throughout Mexico. Though Mexico signed international agreements on the matter in 2003, it wasn't until September of 2007 that the trafficking of persons was finally considered an official crime and the authorities were asked to combat it. The law, however, didn't create or equip an agency to properly define trafficking, or explain to authorities how it should be fought. And there are only three offices, in a country with thirty-one states, to address the issue. One of them is in Tapachula.

David Tamayo is the official anti-trafficking prosecutor in Tapachula. Though he responds to my questions, he also does a lot of complaining and dodging, not quite giving me a straight answer.

"How frequently do you receive Central American trafficking cases?" I ask.

"Very few come to us. These types of crimes are almost never reported. Migration and other agencies don't communicate with us. Or they deport the victims before they can file anything. It's troubling. All of it goes on under the table. You don't see it. We've only had four official complaints."

"And how many convictions?"

"The four cases are all still pending."

"Can I talk with a prosecutor who's handling a case?"

"No, they're all confidential."

"And do you pursue the crimes even when the victims don't?"

"It's too politicized. Our job is simply to inform the public of the law and their rights. The police are supposed to actually enforce the law. Sometimes they talk to us, sometimes they don't. Communication is a huge problem. The cartels have infiltrated the police forces as well."

"The criminal networks are pretty well organized, then?"

"Organization is one of the cartels' strongest characteristics.

They're involved in everything: kidnapping, drug trafficking, human trafficking. We don't even know which cartel is responsible for what. It's impossible to identify them."

This last comment, however, I recognize as a flat lie. A few days before speaking with Tamayo, I had visited Ciudad Hidalgo, the small city on the shores of the Suchiate River that divides Guatemala and Mexico, to talk to someone from the mayor's office. I told him that I was working on a story about female prostitutes. The official took me to a bar called Las Nenitas (The Babes), ensconced between two dirt alleyways. At about two in the afternoon, there were only two women behind the bar. Tesa, a beautiful Honduran woman, tall and dark, took our orders. She was wearing platform boots, tight pants, and a low-cut shirt. Before arriving, the official had told me that all the women who worked in Las Nenitas were prostitutes. I told Tesa, without mentioning the word trafficking, that I was interested in talking with her. She said she'd be glad to talk, but on another day, and gave me a number to call. She never answered my calls.

When we left the bar that day, the official told me that the owner of Las Nenitas was a well-known Zeta. I asked him how people knew. He told me that it was a small city, and the owner usually left the bar carrying an AR-15 rifle and followed by three armed bodyguards. He explained that in Ciudad Hidalgo the Zetas control all trafficking, sending men to recruit women in Central America and sometimes even kidnapping migrant women riding the buses. They sell the women to truck drivers for a night and then throw them away like unwanted scraps.

"Please," the official said to me as we parted, "don't use my name."

So, regarding Prosecutor Tamayo's statement about the impossibility of identifying cartels, it must be said that there is a big difference between wanting to know and being able to know. Between trying and being too scared to try.

~

It's four in the afternoon. Keny gets up from the table and puts on an apron, getting ready to waitress. She'll work a double today. Later she'll remove her apron, sandals, and pants, and put on black platforms and a yellow dress with buttons down the side that she'll rip off after climbing onto stage.

Connie, another *fichera*, crosses paths with Keny and says, "What's up, old lady?"

Connie doesn't waitress. She only works the nights, dancing and flirting for chips. She came in because the owner asked her to, to talk to me about her past.

I WON'T STAY

Her look says it all. Connie doesn't trust me.

"What do you want to know?" she asks again. "And where exactly is this going to get published?" She makes sure to keep her guard up. I've been warned she's a fighter.

"I came here," she says, "with all five of my senses. No one brought me against my will."

She's eighteen years old. When she arrived here aged fifteen, she already had everything figured out. Or so she says. She's quieter than Keny and Erika, but the details she offers are enough to give me a better sense of that tremendous ghost of a problem, the brothels that proliferate in these border towns.

She says that an acquaintance, a fellow Guatemalan who worked as a waiter, promised her a way out. He told her that the first thing she had to do was run away from her barrio. Something she already wanted to do. Her brother had been killed only a month earlier. Three shots. He worked collecting fares on a public bus in Guatemala City. He was sixteen years old and a gang wanted to recruit him. The Mara Salvatruchas—the most dangerous gang in the world, according to the FBI—offered him the job of killing bus drivers that had wronged them. They promised safety in exchange for his participation and death in exchange for his refusal. If he refused he'd receive three bullets: chest, abdomen, head. He refused.

"That same month," Connie remembers, "the Mara killed fifteen kids in my barrio, all of them between fourteen and sixteen years old. No one could live in peace."

While boys and girls were dying or turning up mutilated throughout the barrio, the rest of Connie's life went on as usual: her father drank every night and harassed her as he had since she'd turned eight, and her mother, as Connie put it, kept busy "getting pregnant again and again." Connie is the eldest of eight brothers and sisters.

Salvadoran and Honduran consuls explained to me that many Central American women who decide to migrate are running away from this type of precarious situation, in which they live in perpetual fear of a gang or find living at home to be as bad or worse than living on the street. They come from circumstances that encourage the normalization of prostitution, rape, and human trafficking. It's a reality in which kids die by the dozen, fathers are aggressors, and neighborhoods are war zones.

That's why Connie, who's worked in brothels since she was a girl, answers my question by dividing her surroundings into what she finds normal and what she doesn't.

I ask, what is her worst memory since she arrived?

"At one point," she says, "I went to go work in Huixtla. I was working at some dive, but migration detained me in Huehuetán. They put me in prison. I was so nervous I got sick. I got depressed. I'd never been in a place like that, with so many people crammed together. I was the only woman in the cell. There were so many men. And I got harassed all the time. The guy in charge of the migration unit told me that if I slept with him, he'd let me go."

According to a report put out by the Mexican National Commission of Human Rights, it's not uncommon that a migration official abuses a woman in custody. Who is going to report a human trafficking violation to an agent who has offered you freedom in exchange for sex? And the abuse doesn't end there. As a trafficking prosecutor explained to me, the National Institute of Migration often plays a leading role in preventing human trafficking victim testimonies from getting a court hearing.

The Guatemalan consul refused to talk about the topic. But I got Nelson Cuéllar, of the Salvadoran consulate, to sit with me and explain why certain things don't work here. He says that in his three years as an official in Tapachula, he's only seen two cases of human trafficking tried in court. In both cases the court ruled in favor of the defendant. For the most part, it seems that prosecuting human trafficking is more a matter of luck than of official and concerted cooperation.

"We're not told when there's going to be a migration raid at a brothel,[4]" Cuéllar told me. "They just send them back to their countries without letting anyone know. Migration should let us know before deportations take place, so that we can interview them and see if they've suffered any abuses. But they send them back as though they've just caught any regular migrant walking down the street. And what's more, it's not just that they don't tell us, but they go to great lengths to cover up the whole raid."

On one of those hot, southern nights we visited a popular "tolerance center" in Tapachula, called Las Huacas. Just before, I'd naively spoken with the municipal secretary of public security, Álvaro Monzón Ramírez, asking him if we could use the police station in front of the row of brothels as a sort of home base throughout the night. I talked to no one else. When I arrived at Las Huacas, only one bar in the street was open. The others had closed for the night, quite unusual for a Thursday. When I asked someone in the middle of locking up a bar what was going on, he told me, "Some municipal cops came by and warned us that there'd be a bust today with officers, migration agents, and reporters."

The next night I came back to Las Huacas without telling anyone. This time, at about one in the morning, all the Central

---

4   The term he used was *Centro de Tolerancia*, the common euphemism for brothels in Central America: literally, Tolerance Center.

American prostitutes stampeded to a black door at the back where they poured out of the bar and into an alleyway. One of them yelled that a migration agent had called the owner of the bar next door to let her know that a raid was coming.

Connie orders a second beer. She looks restless. Though it's still early evening, new clients are starting to fill up the bar. Through her dancing and prostitution, she's been able to bring all her family to Mexico. All of them: her two toddlers, her mother, her father, her seven brothers, and even a niece.

Though they've just barely crossed the Suchiate, some of the Central American women who bring life to these brothels are their family's sole breadwinners. That's why, Connie explains, "so many Guatemalan boys and girls accept the offer to come here and earn good money."

That's how they come, as boys and girls. Just recently, on February 13, federal police and members of FEVIMTRA busted into a house in Tapachula. Inside they found eleven Guatemalan children locked up, all of them in one reeking room where they slept on a tarp on the floor. The authorities accused the owner of the house, a forty-one-year-old Mexican, of forcing them, like an army of slaves, to work in the streets for as long as fourteen hours a day, selling balloons, cigarettes, and candies. They also accused him of refusing them water and food and of hitting them if they didn't sell enough.

It's time for me to leave Connie. The busiest hours are around the corner, and soon she'll have to jump into the scene and start flirting with her clients. She's still young, and on a good night she makes up to 6,000 pesos. On the other hand, Keny, who's twenty-four and blends into the mass of other prostitutes, makes a third of that on a good night.

Before leaving, Connie turns to look at me and answers a question I never asked, but that she must have been wanting or expecting to hear.

"I don't really get busy here anymore. I did it at first, but not anymore, I don't like it. And I don't plan to stay here. In a few weeks, I'm going to leave. My boyfriend says he's going to get me out of here once he has enough to provide for me and my family. I don't want my kids to see me like this."

Unfortunately, none of that will happen. I know how Connie works the bar. I know that just a few nights ago she locked herself into a room with a man and that she'll do it again tonight. And unfortunately, when she said what she said, Connie didn't know that in only a few days her boyfriend would leave town.

The night in Calipso takes off. There are two scenes here. The first, inside the bar, where men yell, dance with *ficheras*, and sit with them perched on their laps. The second, just outside where a neon light splashes over the window view of the dance floor, ten men have lined up, waiting to join the spectacle. As the night wears on, the dance floor empties and the edges of the bar swell with clients, those who want more from the night, waiting to lock themselves in rooms with a *fichera*.

In Calipso, Erika, Keny, and Connie have taken their positions and are making money however they have to, which is what they've been doing since they first crossed the border, when, their lives already falling to pieces, they were barely teenagers.

After midnight, Keny, the Salvadoran, gyrates naked on a bar top and, in spite of the twenty-three beers she's downed, tries to control her movements. For Erika, the Honduran, the thirty beers she's drunk have loosened her up and she bends over a table, pushing her bare butt into the face of a mustachioed man knocking off his hat. He's bought her five beers and it's time to pay him back. Connie, the Guatemalan, dances in a miniskirt and six-inch heels with a pot-bellied man she'll later have sex with.

Tomorrow, with other names, with other men, the scene will start over in Calipso and dozens of other clubs along the border. The Central American women will shake and dance again as they do every night, as they have done since they were only girls.

5

Kidnappings Don't Matter:
Veracruz, Tabasco, Oaxaca

It's this tremendous problem that brings us back to the beginning. The reports we did in these three states changed the coming year for us. We realized that no longer were assaults and rapes concealed, confined to isolated corners of the country. We realized that the problem was going beyond migrants mutilated by the train. We realized that machetes had given way to assault rifles, that remote mountaintops had given way to safe houses, that your everyday delinquent had joined Los Zetas, that robbery had turned into assaults and abductions. The scale had changed, but the authorities were the same, and the migrants kept coming without anyone but robbers and kidnappers even glancing in their direction.

It was raining in Tenosique, the small border city in Tabasco, when El Puma and his four gunmen walked up and down the rails demanding money from all the stowaway migrants. It was the last Friday of October. The torrential rain had stalled the trains and some 300 undocumented migrants piled into the muddy shoulders of the tracks.

El Puma is a thirty-five-year-old Honduran with a nine-millimeter in his belt and a *cuerno de chivo* (goat horn), the Mexican nickname for an AK-47, hanging off his shoulder. His crew, all Honduran and each with a machete and a *cuerno de chivo*, surrounded him. El Puma's turf stretches over the entirety of jungle-shrouded Tenosique, nestled between Petén, in Guatemala, and the Chiapan jungle, the Lacandona. People who know him say, baldly, "He works for Los Zetas."

You have to pay him to get onto the train. Those who don't pay don't go. Those who resist get to meet him, his crew, his machetes, and his *cuerno de chivo*.

Most of the migrants paid. Those who didn't have the money went around to beg for it. Then El Puma radioed the driver of the next train to hit the brakes in Tenosique so he could catch up with him and give him his cut. The migrants piled on top of the wagons or on their lower balconies. Four *polleros*[1] rode atop the middle train car, tightly surrounded by a score of clients. Most of the migrants were Honduran, along with a few Guatemalans and Salvadorans. You could count the Nicaraguans on one hand. Everyone besides the group riding the middle car traveled on their own, without a *pollero*.

It kept raining. The train crept forward, leaving Tenosique behind and digging into the thick of the jungle that was only seldom interrupted by cattle ranches. There was still no sign of a town or highway.

After arriving to Pénjamo, one of the many ranches in this part of the country, the trip got a lot harder. José, a twenty-nine-year-old Salvadoran, was the first to notice the eight men taking advantage of how slowly the train was creeping. They clambered on. "No worries," they said to José's group, "we're headed to El Norte." But José's forebodings were confirmed when he saw that after they'd rested a few minutes, four of them took out nine-millimeter pistols, four more unwrapped machetes, and they all put on ski masks.

"See ya," they said and left the Salvadorans in peace, jumping onto the next car. When the masked men got to the car that Arturo, a forty-two-year-old Nicaraguan cook, was riding, their group had already kidnapped two women. One of them stood out to Arturo

---

1 People smugglers, like coyotes. The name means poulterer; their clients are the *pollos* or *pollitos*, chickens or chicks.

because of her white skin. He said he can still remember her face. He thought she was cute. The other woman he couldn't see well.

The first to be murdered was a Honduran man who traveled with Arturo. He sat perched on one of the train's hanging balconies. From the roof one of the masked men reached down and pressed a gun to his head. He handed over one hundred pesos, but the gunman didn't believe that that was all he had, and he hopped down to Arturo's balcony to inspect. More money was found in his sock. The failed trick cost the man his life. "You're done, you son of a bitch," the assailant said, and shot him through the neck.

The next car was the *polleros'*. There was a prolonged silence, followed by gunshots. Some fifteen minutes of sporadic gunshots. The *polleros* were fighting back. They had forked out the money, but refused to hand over a woman. One masked man fell off the slowing train. And even though he looked dead when he rolled off the uneven rails, his pals quickly jumped off to help. No one knows what happened to the woman Arturo thought so pretty. In the end the *polleros* won the battle, forcing the thugs off the train.

Revenge came, however, in the city of Palenque, about thirty miles north of Pénjamo. Five of the assailants came back for the *polleros'* migrant woman. They killed another Honduran, again in Arturo's car, hacking through his stomach with a machete and throwing him off the train. But they had to shield themselves from the *polleros'* fire. This battle as well the *polleros* won.

The assailants, though, hadn't given up yet. By nightfall they'd caught up. They moved quickly, speeding ahead of the train that, a half hour after the second shooting, stopped in an area known as La Aceitera. The dark of night was interrupted by the glow of town lights. The train picked up its new cargo. The sound of steel against steel piercing into the windy night. All the migrants stood, looking every which way. Something was about to happen, we could feel it. Then gunshots. The *polleros* were forced to give up their car and finally left the woman in the hands of the masked men. They dragged her down and into the nearby forest. But their new loot left the assailants falsely self-assured, and they turned their backs on the train. The *polleros* wanted revenge. They hopped off the train, shot another assailant dead, got the woman back and got onto the train before it took off. Then, minutes later, once the crime scene was out of sight, the *polleros* and their twenty *pollos* abandoned the train to look for another way north. It was obvious those assailants would come back for more.

And they did. In Chontalpan, about twenty miles north of La Aceitera, three white vans surrounded the rails: one in front of the train, another keeping up beside us, the third behind. Without any *polleros* to put up a fight, the rest of the migrants ditched the train.

"It was Los Zetas," Arturo says.

"It was Los Zetas," José says.

It was Los Zetas.

The train emptied. Hundreds of people ran into the pastures to hide, pursued by some fifteen armed men. During the stampede at least one migrant went down, shot dead. Many were hurt. Three women were held at gunpoint in one of the vans.

Mission accomplished, the vans left. The train started chugging. The remaining migrants climbed back on, resuming their journey toward Coatzacoalcos and Tierra Blanca, both cities in the state of Veracruz, Zetas home territory. A place of mass kidnappings. The worst was still to come.

LOS ZETAS' OTHER BUSINESS

The history of the beleaguered train that left from Tenosique could be a manual for anyone who wants to understand the current plight of migrants in Mexico. The manual tells the story of why this region has become the worst leg of an already extremely dangerous journey.

The defenders of migrants who live in these parts pray that somebody does something to improve the situation. They gesticulate, ask us to turn off our recorders and put away the cameras, and then they describe what everybody here knows: that every day Los Zeta and their allies kidnap tens of undocumented Central

Americans, in the broad light of day, and that the migrants are kept in safe houses which everybody, including the authorities, knows about.

The business logic of the kidnappers is sound: it's more profitable to kidnap forty people, each of whom will pay between $300 and $1,500 in ransom money, than it is to extort a local business owner who might alert the press or the police. The national authorities, including a unit of the National Commission of Human Rights (NCHR) that is investigating migration, admit the gravity of the problem.

These are the kidnappings that don't matter. These are the victims who don't report the crimes they suffer. The Mexican government registered 650 kidnappings in the year 2008, for example. But this number reflected only reported cases. Time spent on the actual migrant routes proves that such numbers are a gross understatement. It would not be an exaggeration to say that in any stop along the migrant trail, in just a single month, there are as many kidnappings as the official national figure for the year. In the first six months of 2009, the NCHR visited Veracruz to record testimonies of kidnapped migrants and logged as many as 10,000 cases, claiming that if they had had more personnel the figure would be twice or three times as high.

There is, simply put, nobody to assure the safety of migrants in Mexico. Sometimes a week or more will pass before a migrant on the trail will have the chance or the money to call a family member. Migrants try to travel the paths with the fewest authorities and, for fear of deportation, almost never report a crime. A migrant passing through Mexico is like a wounded cat slinking through a dog kennel: he wants to get out as quickly and quietly as he can.

After the attack on the train, where there were more than a hundred armed assaults, at least three murders, three injuries, and three kidnappings, there was not a single mention of the incident in the press. Neither the police nor the army showed up, and nobody filed a single report.

~

Tenosique is the launching point. Then migrants run the gaunt-
let of Coatzacoalcos, Medias Aguas, Tierra Blanca, Orizaba,
and Lechería. Then the last tolls, the border cities themselves,
Reynosa and Nuevo Laredo. These are the stops along the kidnapping route. All of them, except Lechería, which is outside of
Mexico City, are on the Atlantic coast, and all of them, according to the crime map of the Antinarcotics Division of Mexico, are
dominated by Los Zetas.

From the capital city to the migrant hostels in the south, there
is no doubt that people know what's going on. Mauricio Farah
of the NCHR explains: "The migrant situation is complex and
alarming. The number of kidnappings is booming. And they're
happening, even to large groups of migrants, in broad daylight.
The kidnappers show up with guns and simply take people away.
The Mexican government is supposed to be responsible for the
safety and the lives of those who are in its territory. It's incredible
that this is continuing to happen."

NCHR has often reminded the state of what is happening, but
the authorities continue to deny or simply not respond to official
complaints. The word "kidnapping" has lost its weight in Mexico.
The tangle of normalized, constant violence is complex and con-
fusing, and now even the *polleros* have to submit to its rules.

THE *POLLERO* TAX

Though hundreds of thousands of Central Americans pour into
Mexico each year—Mexico's National Institute of Migration estimates 250,000 annually—those who walk this road know each
other: Los Zetas know the *polleros*, the *polleros* know the assailants, the assailants know who works at migrant shelters, and those
who work at the migrant shelter know the municipal authorities.

Ismael—a fictional name—is a local and has worked at the
nearby migrant shelter for two years now. Previously he had a gig
that forced him to get to know the inner workings of organized
crime.

He looks for a table apart from the others and points with his chin, "Let's talk over there. It's just that so many of the informants for these kidnapping groups pose as migrants, and often they're Central Americans themselves. They listen in on migrants' conversations and then find a good moment to ask them if they have family on the other side, if they have anyone to pay for the *pollero* on the border. If the migrants answer no, they tell their boss to look out for so-and-so who won't have anyone looking after them. Easy prey."

We sit.

"What else can I tell you?" he asks.

"I've got eight testimonies of kidnappings that happened in eight different places. Each of the victims said that the kidnappers identified themselves as Zetas. You think it was really them?"

"Not necessarily. It goes like this: no one can say they're a Zeta without permission. A lot of them, though, are just local delinquents who work for Los Zetas, who make sure that the *polleros* pay their dues," he tells me, his face not breaking from its steady glare.

I've known him for a few months now, and the only parts of his face I've ever seen move are his lips. The constant roar of the shelter doesn't turn his head. A group of migrants are showering, others are washing their clothes, some are playing soccer while the nearby trains squeal, their cars shifting from side to side. Ismael looks on with his steady gaze as though absorbing everything. At times, without pausing from what he's saying, he moves his eyes, following an undocumented migrant move across the shelter. He comes off as stoic, and yet he's willing to talk, to describe the inner workings of orchestrated kidnappings. He's been surrounded by abductors, as well as their victims, for two years now nonstop. He's even dodged the bullets of a few assailants who tried to kill him after he chased their car, trying to save a kidnapped Nicaraguan woman.

"What dues?" I ask.

"This all comes from way up, all the way from the northern

border in Tamaulipas. There's someone by the name of El Abuelo up there. He's the guy who controls all the *polleros* passing through his turf. I know he's in business with Los Zetas. He pays some sort of tax so that his *polleros* can work here, down south. And Los Zetas have people to make sure that whoever isn't paying isn't getting through."

"And the kidnappings?"

A migrant comes over to us, and picks up his backpack, which sits on our table. Ismael looks at him out of the corner of his eye. He waits to respond until the man leaves.

"It started as something against the *polleros* who didn't pay. They'd take away their *pollitos*, their little chicks, and since they already had them in their hands they figured they'd go ahead and get a ransom from their families in the US through a fast deposit from Western Union. And then it got to be a habit. They started picking up any migrant who walked alone."

"When did all this start?"

"We started recording victims' testimonies in the middle of 2007."

At the end of the conversation Ismael tells me that *polleros* often pass by the shelter. "They can give you more details," he says.

The sun begins setting, everything dimming to orange by the time a *pollero* shows up. Ismael points him out to me. He keeps them in check and knows their every movement, but says that he can't introduce him to me. A relationship between migrant shelter workers and *polleros* would look very suspicious. Instead he gets someone else to introduce us.

"So, you're a journalist?" the *pollero* asks.

"Yeah, and I know you were kidnapped by Los Zetas six months ago in Tierra Blanca. I just want you to tell me a bit about it. You don't have to give me your name."

With a sideways nod he signals me over to a mango tree. The tree is some twenty yards from the rails, across a wire fence in a large empty wasteland lot. We jump the fence and sit beneath the tree.

"Nowadays I only lead people through the Tapachula route [on the Pacific coast], because Los Zetas are on the other side and they already got me once."

"That's what I want to talk about."

"Yeah, well, one has to have a sort of boss up in El Norte so that they can let Los Zetas know that you're okay, that no one should touch you, but that time my cell wasn't charged so I couldn't make the call to my boss, which is when they ganged up on me and hauled me into their car. I was guiding six people. They asked me who I worked for. I told them, but they didn't believe me. Then they tortured me, burning my back with cigarettes."

When he's sure no one's watching, he lifts his dirtied white shirt as if to say, here's the evidence. I see six round scars.

"What happened after they tortured you?"

"They asked for money. I had to cough up because if I didn't they'd take away my migrants. I knew those people, we were close. They were two Guatemalans and four Salvadorans from Santa Ana. If I didn't pay, I knew they'd kidnap and torture them. Anyone who says they don't have anyone in the States to send money gets burned. I know people who've had fingers and ears cut off. And plenty of them just get killed."

"And how do you know it was them?"

"People say it's not them. They say they're gangs of nobodies, just delinquents who work for them. The real Zetas control these guys from the northern border."

The *pollero* says he found out how this all works in January. If it's true, then he and the US Bureau of International Narcotics and Law Enforcement Affairs found out at about the same time. The bureau's report, published that same month, stated that Los Zetas charge *polleros* for the use of their turf.

"And your boss, what would he have done had you been able to call him?"

"He would've paid to get everyone released."

"And these bosses are in contact with Los Zetas, with the infamous El Abuelo?"

"I've heard people talk about him. He's in control of the Nuevo Laredo and Reynosa turfs. He's one of the ones that pay the tax. But there are other big guys like that—El Borrado, Don Tono, Fidel. You risk a lot as a *pollero*. Because if the boss doesn't let everyone know that you're going, then everything gets thrown your way and you're fucked. They kidnap you, maybe even kill you. There's been a lot of murders. One guy got killed in Coatzacoalcos, and another in Rigo and another in some place called Las Anonas. The ones in charge of oversight go by train, many are Central American. The one who gave me away was Honduran. He got on the train at Medias Aguas."

"How does it work? How much does the boss have to pay?"

"He pays 10,000 dollars a month and he has to let everyone know that you work for him and how many 'chicks' you have with you. Then no one can touch you. This all started last year, first in Coatzacoalcos, and then they took over Tierra Blanca in the beginning of January because they know that that's where the two routes merge."

He's referring to the two main railways, the one that borders the Atlantic coast and the one that goes upcountry, closer to the Pacific.

The *pollero* is nervous. He smiles, purses his lips, smiles again. He doesn't stop moving his hands and feet. A lot of *polleros* are addicted to cocaine, amphetamines, or caffeine pills that they use to stay awake through the night.

"What about the police?"

"They're all connected! That time they got me there were police watching and they didn't do a thing. After that I'll never work for anyone. That's why I don't guide people anymore. Because if they see me again, I know I'm dead."

COATZACOALCOS

Having arrived on the same train that brought Arturo and José from Tenosique, about twenty-five undocumented migrants are inside the church hostel. Most of them are resting on cots. Some of them are washing clothes. A few are sitting with their gaze fixed on nothing. They look worn out. At ten in the morning there were fifteen people picked up by Migration who are now on their way to being deported.

We're in an industrial zone, one of those places that seem half factory and half town, not quite what you would call a city. There's one main drag, a partly dirt road, that's flanked on both sides by industrial warehouses. There are almost 300,000 people living here, mostly in narrow rows of wood-and-tarp shacks that run alongside the train tracks.

The word *Coatzacoalcos* comes from the Nahuatl, an indigenous language of Mexico, and means The Snake Den.

After an entire night riding the train, the newly arrived migrants do what they do at every stopping point: they ask and they listen. And what they hear today, news from a Honduran man, convinces them all to register their names at the hostel. "This morning," the Honduran tells the crowd, "fifteen people were held up at gunpoint in front of a house just down the way."

It's typical. Eduardo Ortiz, from NCHR, explains: "At least ten people a day give themselves up to Migration authorities here."

After a night of shootings, kidnappings, murder, white trucks and car chases, the migrants realize that they've arrived at what may be the worst leg of the journey. And yet from Coatzacoalcos they still have to get through Tierra Blanca, Orizaba, and Lechería.

A group huddles in the bunkroom to talk about the kidnappings. Some of them have tales to tell and others are just listening, imagining what may be in store. The Honduran is talking to Pedro, who's also Honduran and is resting in his bunk. The first man talks of a friend who was kidnapped. Pedro looks visibly distressed, and then goes on to tell his own story.

He says that it all started here in Coatzacoalcos, in a house along the tracks. The ambush was well-orchestrated, he explains. He says he'll have to keep on heading north; he doesn't have any other option. He insists that anybody who has family in the United States should never admit it. To anybody. Ever.

"There was this woman named Mother," Pedro says. "She was the coyote. She charged 2,500 dollars to get you across the border. Everything seemed good, all the way to Reynosa. But that's where they kidnapped me. They threatened me with a pistol and smacked me around. I'm pretty sure they were Zetas. They took the 800 dollars I had on me and got 2,500 from my wife. Then, after a month and eighteen days, they finally let me go. And the police," Pedro concludes, "were working with them." He lies back on his cot and settles into silence.

There are some places where the fear is so thick you breathe it. For a migrant, Coatzacoalcos is one of those places. The stories tumble over each other:

"They kidnapped me on my last try."

"I escaped from a kidnapping yesterday."

"Three months ago I saw two women being grabbed."

Just this morning, among a group of ten migrants waiting in the shelter, seven of them had stories of either being kidnapped or knowing someone who had been kidnapped.

I tell Ortiz, of NCHR, that right in front of us there are loads of kidnapping victims; that people are getting kidnapped blocks from his office, right where the train rails snake through town. But he's not surprised. Kidnappings are his daily bread.

"The scope of the criminal gangs," he explains, "has increased by about 200 percent. We have many reports saying that their modus operandi is the same here as in Tierra Blanca. Each kidnapper covers about fifteen ransoms. Which makes me think that the money wiring companies must know [based on the number of wires a single person receives] who they're dealing with. We have trustworthy reports that municipal police have detained migrants and handed them over to the kidnappers."

"I have three testimonies," I tell him, "where someone who was kidnapped claims that another from his group who managed to escape came back after having been beaten, saying that he went to the local police to report the crime. And the police, instead of investigating, sent him straight back to the kidnappers."

"Yes," Ortiz responds, "it's not that we don't know about these cases. We know that the migrants get delivered. We haven't heard about exactly this type of situation, but we know that the police are involved, that there is co-participation. We've had meetings with the Municipal President of Tierra Blanca, along with the of Salvadorean and Honduran Consulates in Veracruz, and an INM [National Institute of Migration] delegation. Usually the officials claim that what's going on is not going on, and get uncomfortable when we start talking about kidnappings. Actually, only a month after they denied the abundance of kidnappings, the army stepped in and rescued twenty-eight victims. In the last few months everything has been happening in the light of day, with or without the presence of authorities. There are migrants who have told us: 'The army patrols were passing by. They turned and saw that we were being held on the ground at gunpoint. And they kept on going.'

"It's no joke. There are cases of one hundred people being held in a single house. All the neighbors know what's going on, but nobody says anything. Nothing happens and nothing is going to keep happening to those who are passing through, because nobody claims to hear anything."

Erving Ortiz (no relation to Eduardo), the Salvadoran consul, denounced this past August of 2008 that there are "about forty undocumented migrants kidnapped every week" in the state of Veracruz. He made the claim after the army rescued the twenty-eight victims in Coatzacoalcos. And this time the most influential newspapers in the country, *Reforma* and *El Universal*, picked up the story.

I try for the tenth time to contact Alfredo Osorio, the municipal president of Tierra Blanca, but he doesn't answer my call. His secretary, Rafael Pérez, after promising me a few minutes on the phone, doesn't pick up either. In the mayor's office another secretary answers, and tells me that both Pérez and Osorio will be away all week. I call the press secretary at INM and they feed me more of the same, that they're looking for the right person to answer my questions. I reach another of Osorio's secretaries who tells me that the best person to talk with at INM (though I never learn this person's name) is out of the office and will be for another few days. When pressed they say that they don't know when he'll be returning.

Meanwhile, just down the street from these same offices, the kidnappings continue. It's so well-known, I figure, that there's no way that if I finally did get an official on the phone they'd be able to answer me without a resounding yes. And with that yes they would be admitting that migrants are being systematically kidnapped just outside of their offices. Which is why, I figure, they don't pick up their phones.

On April 4, 2008, the head of INM, Cecilia Romero, along with the secretary of the interior, Juan Camilo Mouriño,[2] received a forty-page document titled "Kidnappings and Organized Crime." The document contained a detailed account of what was occurring nationwide, along with three personal testimonies of victims. It was sent out by Leticia Gutiérrez, director of the Pastoral Dimension of Human Mobility, a Catholic organization that runs thirty-five migrant shelters across the country, including in the cities of Tierra Blanca, Coatzacoalcos, and Reynosa. But neither Romero nor Mouriño ever responded.

The upspoken question becomes evident. How is it possible that the kidnappings are still happening when the local governments, the countries of origin, the media, the Mexican government, and the US government all know exactly what's going on?

The NCHR continues to document cases and, about once a year,

---

2   Mouriño died in November 2008 in a plane crash, widely suspected to be the work of the Sinaloa Cartel.

publishes recommendations and files official complaints calling for action. And the data are specific: these government agents, of this agency, on this date, in front of these witnesses, committed this violation of human rights. But it's almost impossible to file complaints of omission—that, for example, a government patrol passed the scene of an in-process kidnapping without lifting a finger. And the smattering of migrants who, out of legitimate fear, are willing to stick around to file a complaint cannot help prove what the government did *not* do.

What Consul Ortiz says is clear: everybody knows, nobody acts, and the kidnappings continue.

TIERRA BLANCA

In Veracruz floods are slowing the trains. Only a few migrants are on route to Tierra Blanca. The sky is clear now, and the air very hot.

I see two men about a hundred yards from me. They look young. One, about twenty years old, is lying in a hammock outside a store. The other looks about fifteen and is sitting on a trunk beside his friend. Edu Ponces and I walk down the tracks. The landscape is empty. The lot we're on is enormous, and there isn't a single train. When there's only a gap of fifty yards between us I turn to walk toward the two men. The youngest—very dark, extremely short—stretches his legs out. When I'm thirty yards away I try to meet their gaze. They both open their eyes wide and freeze. I open my mouth to say something. Then they jump and start running.

"Hey," I say, "I'm a journalist!"

They stop.

"What happened? Did I scare you?"

"It's just, things are really hot here."

Five minutes later a youth of about eighteen, ragged and smelling of wood glue, comes up to us. He'd been sitting at a nearby corner alongside two drunks, watching us. The drunks, while smoking a joint, stretch out on the ground to gaze at the sky.

"Hey, you're a *pollero*," one of the supine men says to me as he relights his joint.

"No," I say. "No, I'm not."

"Yeah, you are, I've seen you around."

"I said I'm not."

"Oh yeah, you're a *pollero*, and I'm going to call the Zetas boss so he can come pick you up."

I feel a fit of anger come over me. I grab hard onto the man's arm and pull him away with me down the tracks, gaining some distance from the rest of the group. All I wanted was to talk to the two migrants in peace. The guy yells at me to let him go. He says he was only kidding. Edu asks me to let him go too, and I do, but then the guy says again that he'll call the local Zetas chief. Edu and I turn to leave, walking in the direction opposite the rails. It's better not to find out if he'd actually have made that call.

We stop at a stand near the rails to buy a juice. It's obvious we're not from here. The vendor wants to know what we're doing. We explain. He seems kind. He was born in Tierra Blanca and had previously migrated to the United States. Without preamble, as if I were asking about the weather, I ask if there are Zetas in Tierra Blanca. "You know," he says, "there are things I can't talk about. You guys are passing through, but I live here and I don't want anyone asking, 'Who said that about us?' If they hear something about someone, they can control even where he walks. They can bring him down." Without meaning to, he said much more than we'd expected. And we feel it's time for us to leave the tracks.

Just one person in Tierra Blanca gives us permission to use his name, along with his testimony of the abductions. It's Miguel Ángel, the deacon in charge of the parish and the small house that serves as a migrant shelter. He echoes what others have said in Coatzacoalcos, but with more detail, and exhibiting greater fear. It happens, he says, it always happens. It happens in broad daylight to dozens of migrants. It's so common that there isn't even much to say. The question answers itself.

After talking to Miguel Ángel, we finally find someone who's been recommended to us a number of times: Osiel (not his real name). The rule Osiel gives us is clear: everything is off the record. That's how everyone, or at least everyone who lives here, talks on Zetas turf.

We meet in a garbage dump full of old dishes and keepsakes from first communions and funerals. At this point it's hard to get any new information, even if it's all off the record. "I can tell you this at least," Osiel says: "everyone knows the boss of all bosses. People call him Chito, and he lives there on the hill. He's the one behind the kidnappings, but no one would give him away."

A warning we had gotten back in Coatzacoalcos comes to mind: "If you go there asking about the kidnappings, Los Zetas will know in eight minutes. If you talk to any of the town's authorities, they'll know in three."

"WE WON'T PASS THROUGH HERE ANYMORE"

In 2006 it was common to hear stories of terrified migrants complaining about the train raids in southern Mexico. During these migration checks (about two a week on each route, almost always at night), when migration authorities, federal police, or the military flashed on their headlights, the train would screech to a halt and everybody would start running. It was a free-for-all. The train raids typically took place in sites where on either side of the tracks there were steep embankments, making escape dangerous or impossible.

In both 2006 and 2007 there was an uptick in the incident reports of crimes committed not by bandits but by the authorities themselves: military, police, and even migration officers. Between May 2006 and April 2007, the investigator Rodolfo Casillas of the Facultad Latinoamericana de Ciencias Sociales (FLACSO, an international institute with a branch in Mexico City) surveyed 1,700 undocumented Central Americans in Mexico. Among those interviewed, Casillas registered 2,506 human rights violations. The NCHR in Mexico also documented three cases in which common prisons were used to detain Central Americans charged with nothing more than a migration violation.

One female migrant who was thus imprisoned, as documented in Casillas's report, was sexually abused by two other inmates in her cell. A Salvadoran migrant held in a Mexican prison nearly died of pneumonia after spending an entire night handcuffed to a cell bar. Two other cases detail migrants being tortured by government officials. There was a case of a minor who was beaten and urinated on in a migration detention center after he had tried to escape. There was also the documented case of an entire group of migrants forced by military officers to walk barefoot for miles, while two migrant Guatemalan men were forced to carry all of their shoes. Every time one of the men dropped a shoe, they were hit by the guards.

Since those years, 2006–7, the number of complaints by migrants against government officials has decreased, and yet at the same time the number of complaints about members of organized crime groups has risen. The voices of migrant shelter workers and human rights activists were heard, resulting in a decrease in migration checks on dangerous sections of tracks where amputations were common. However, this single success—decreased train raids—has been overshadowed by the stalemate in the government's fight against organized crime.

Even the Mexican attorney general has publically recognized that kidnappings have passed from a "sporadic" to a "systemic" problem. Of course he is only referring to the kidnapping of Mexican citizens, who very rarely report these crimes not only for fear of the kidnappers, but also for fear "of the local authorities who are connected with and protect the groups that they should be combating."

If not even a Mexican citizen, who votes and pays taxes, is

willing to report a crime, what is the likelihood that an undocumented migrant will?

In 2008 the number of assaults maintained a steady pace. Assault became an expected toll for those traveling without papers across Mexico to the United States. And it was in this year that kidnappings—victims and reported incidents popping up all over the country—started to get more attention.

On September 30 in Ixtepec, Oaxaca, quite far from what is considered the most perilous leg of the journey, I meet Gustavo and Arturo. They are sixteen and eighteen years old respectively, both from El Cimarrón, Puerto Barrios, a Caribbean port town in Guatemala. When I meet the boys they are already on their way home.

Earlier, while riding the train north around four in the morning outside of Orizaba Los Zetas kidnapped the boys. "Okay motherfuckers," someone yelled at them, "if you run we'll shoot!" Seven armed men took them away. They were locked up for three days, beaten, and repeatedly threatened in a closed room. Their ransom was set at $500.

"They beat us," explains Arturo, "and said that if we didn't give them our family's phone number they'd cut out one of our kidneys." His kidnappers, he told me, held up a horse branding iron heated with a blowtorch and threatened to brand him with a Z. Arturo recognized a chubby guy who had befriended him back in Arriaga, and to whom he'd mentioned that he had family members in the United States. The kidnappers told the boys that the day before they were seized, they had released thirty other migrants.

"Overhearing their conversation, it seemed that they were a new group joining forces with the Zetas," Arturo said. The kidnapping business had been going well. New agents were in demand.

One night, the boys saw a few of the kidnappers return to the safe house bloodied and bruised. One of them explained: "There were about a hundred migrants, armed with rocks, machetes, and sticks, who beat the shit out of us. But that's not going to happen again. As soon as our own guns come in we'll give that shit right back to them."

When Arturo and Gustavo's ransom was paid, the kidnappers demanded more money. Gustavo pleaded with them: "But we already paid! Let us go and we swear we'll never pass through here again. We're going home."

And the kidnappers relented. But they didn't even bother to release them at night: they simply marched them at pistol point to the central train station. It was four in the afternoon. Gustavo and Arturo recall that as they were being marched through the streets, the windows and doors of the houses along their way slammed shut one after the other.

6

We Are Los Zetas: Tabasco

After a year of hearing their name everywhere, we decided to find them. But where? Where do you find Los Zetas? We decided on Tenosique, the small town in Tabasco that marks the beginning of the route they control. What we found surprised us. We found them in a group of girls selling sodas, in a police officer, in a journalist, in some petty delinquents riding the rails. We found them everywhere, in a town riddled with fear.

After seeing this place in action for a week, I tell him, I guess that his life must be very complicated. Hell, I have no idea how he's even still alive.

The undercover agent smiles proudly as he looks me in the eyes. He remains silent a moment. He turns to glance toward the door, though he knows we're alone in this small, aquarium-like café. We could be seen through the huge windows lining every wall, if it weren't for the large mango tree blocking us from view.

"I'm alive thanks to smarts," he finally responds. "I don't go places in a brand-new car. I don't walk around with a pistol showing, and I don't show my face at any events unless it's necessary."

By "event" he can only mean the murder of an officer, the scene of a shoot-out between military personnel and drug traffickers, or an armed bust at some hamlet hidden among those crime-reaped fields where the bosses, Los Zetas, carrying out their famous "kidnapper express," have a group of Central Americans locked up.

"But sometimes it must be impossible to do that," I insist. "You must live on your tiptoes! You never know who's who. It's impossible to be sure if the man selling tacos is only selling tacos or if he's selling them to be able to keep watch."

The agent knows. He lives under these rules. His eyes are constantly scanning, noticing whether that car passed twice or if that man is watching us out of the corners of his eyes. That's why he only accepted to meet me after I'd given him the word from someone he's very close to. It was a long slog, getting a hold of that state administrator who knew another administrator in Tabasco who happens to be one of the few people this agent trusts. And even then, he didn't start talking until he'd carefully scrutinized my credentials. He looked at my picture and then at me, then back at my picture, then back at me. Anonymity is the only way he can keep on. His game is to be no one, to look like anyone else from among the flocks living in terror; to lower his gaze, never taking it off the hot sidewalks of the towns surrounding Villahermosa, the capital of Tabasco. He agreed to see me on condition that I wouldn't report where he works or who he works for.

He smiles again, finding it funny, watching my face flicker with the recognition that he works in the heart of enemy territory. All the time. With dozens of eyes looking for him.

"That's why it's necessary to move slowly," he says, "very slowly, and to be careful, when the time comes, in asking any questions." He finishes his coffee in one gulp and changes topic. "In the end, did you guys go to the ranch I told you about? Were you able to get the pictures you wanted?"

"Yeah, we went. And he took all the ones he could. The scene gave us goosebumps."

THE CEMETERY RANCH

The rain makes La Victoria ranch seem like a film set. It looks staged, the perfect backdrop for a kidnapping—as if a bad guy

Crossing point at Suchiate River, which separates Guatemala from Chiapas.

The crossing of the river marks the beginning of the journey across Mexico for undocumented Central American migrants.

On many stretches of the trail through Mexico, migrants are forced to travel on foot, avoiding roads in favor of areas of dense vegetation. La Arrocera—the Rice Cellar—is one of the most notorious of these stretches, a network of twenty-eight ranches scattered across one hundred and sixty miles of thick vegetation in southern Mexico, where migrants endure robberies, assaults, and rapes.

Toni Arrau

A woman from the group Las Patronas. For almost twenty years, the women of La Patrona, Veracruz have been bringing food and water to the migrants as they pass by on the trains.

Stowaways. The journey from Ixtepec to Medias Aguas takes six to eight hours. Falls, assaults, and kidnappings are common on this stretch.

Toni Arnau

A man murdered in one of the dangerous neighborhoods of Huixtla, Chiapas. Violence against migrants also affects many others areas and has prompted the formation of community patrols.

Toni Arnau

At El Bambi, a brothel where a number of Central American migrants work.

Toni Arnau

A Guatemalan mother and daughter, inside a car traveling north. On this trip, they were intercepted by Mexican agents, but were able to continue their journey after delivering a payment of 1,000 pesos (about eighty dollars).

Edu Ponces

Waiting at the Casa del Migrante in Nuevo Laredo. A loose network of nonprofit and Mexican government organizations tries to help migrants.

Two groups of migrants in the Sonoran desert, guided by their coyotes.

At the border wall in Tijuana.

Toni Arnau

Detained at the border.

with an eye patch, an overcoat, and a large pistol were about to step through the door.

When we arrive, three policemen are showing the place to two agents from the Public Prosecutor's Office, who post a CLOSED sign on the front gate. The main residence is just beyond the gate, a few feet away from the rail lines. The house, whose green paint is faded and chipped by time, looks typically Dixie-American, with a wraparound porch where in another context owners might be whiling away the afternoon.

This is the basic, gloomy shell of the house. Above the front door hangs a cow skull with wide horns. Inside the front hallway lie hundreds of crushed beer cans, and to the rear of the house are scattered sardine, tuna, and bean cans. Through a front window you can see that the floor in the front room is covered in stains and scattered sawdust. The whole house smells wet and fetid, like there is some indiscernible leak somewhere. A back room is littered with discarded clothes, more crushed cans, scraps of wood. But this is all perceived from the outside. The public prosecutors won't let us set foot inside the house. Toni Arnau, the photographer I'm traveling with, after stubborn insistence, is permitted to take a few photos by peeking in through the front door.

Last Thursday, fifty-two undocumented Central American migrants were released after being kidnapped and kept crammed in the house for days. They were held by the commander of an *estaca* (Zeta terminology for squadron) who is said to run this small town of Gregorio Méndez.

Two of the migrants who were traveling on top of the train passing through Gregorio closely escaped the fate of the fifty-two others when the conductor, Marcos Estrada Tejero, suspiciously decided to stop the train close to the ranch and fifteen armed men approached. Two days later, the two men ran into an army commander on patrol and told him what had happened. Soon twelve soldiers along with twelve state policemen from Tabasco and thirty state policemen from Chiapas suited up in search of the kidnapped migrants. The train conductor, who was located while driving another train outside of Veracruz, was arrested and accused of working with the same branch of Los Zetas later caught near La Victoria. One of Los Zetas' chiefs, a Honduran named Frank Hándal Polanco, was arrested as well, but was seen leaving the police station in a taxi only an hour after his apprehension. There were eight others arrested in the joint military-state police operation, while at least seven, still armed with AR-15 assault rifles, escaped into the nearby mountains. On the ranch itself the officers found and confiscated nine-millimeter pistols and M-16 rifles.

"The worst part is how they were treated," one of the soldiers tells me. "They were in a state of shock. And all of them had bruises on their lower backs. A strip of purple." I didn't yet understand why.

By the time authorities found the ranch, the migrants knew that they'd met the famous storybook wolves: Los Zetas. They already knew by heart the chilling threat the kidnappers used to introduce themselves: "We are Los Zetas! Don't move or we'll kill you!"

In these small towns, there's no need of an ID, or any other kind of credential, to prove Zeta membership. If someone says they're a Zeta, they're a Zeta. If they say they're a Zeta and they're not a Zeta, it won't be too long before they're dead.

At La Victoria ranch, the kidnappers put on a show. They arranged the victims into five groups, lined them up to face the wall and forced them to their knees. Then they started paddling them in the small of their backs. It's a method of military torture used in Mexico, and it's one of the identifying marks of Los Zetas. The verb to paddle, *tablear*, is well known in the overlapping world of both Los Zetas and undocumented migrants passing through Mexico.

Any attempt to break Los Zetas' rules is punished by death. Two of the kidnapped migrants learned this when, making the best of an unusually inattentive guard, they escaped from the ranch. The men ran for the mountains: an area their captors knew like the back of their hands, but that they didn't know at all. One of the Zetas soldiers went to hunt them down. He shortly returned with one of the migrants, who was marched in front of the other captives and forced to his knees.

"See what happens if you fuck with us!"

Melesit Jiménez, from Honduras, was shot dead in the back of the neck.

Only a few minutes after the body of Jiménez fell, two more shots rang out from the hills. The second fugitive was hit once in the neck and once in the stomach.

In the next few days, while the group now numbering fifty learned to submit to their captors, Los Zetas entertained themselves by raping the two women in the group, both from Honduras, and occasionally paddling the men in the back. They were waiting for the ransom money: between $1,500 and $5,000 apiece, wired from each of the victims' families.

This massive kidnapping occurred only a few days after the National Commission for Human Rights (NCHR) presented a paper on the current state of migrant abductions. A mass of reporters jostled for photos and sound bites of the event. The NCHR stated that, even with their limited resources, they were able to document 10,000 firsthand reports of kidnapping, including documentation of the police conspiring with Los Zetas. The conference made national headlines. But the next day everything returned to normal: silence.

In this world of pilgrims without papers, kidnappings have become just as common as migrant assaults in La Arrocera, or the torture and mutilation of train hoppers throughout Mexico. It's so common that in Tabasco we don't need to go looking for it. After months of watching Los Zetas infiltrate the country, making it clear that they are an independent cartel (after splitting from the Gulf Cartel), after months of hearing their name and smelling the fear in the small towns of southern Mexico all the way to the northern border, we're starting to understand who they are, how they work, and, above all, how they have such wide-ranging control.

Their secret is simply fear. They shake the bones of policemen and taxi drivers, lawyers and migrants. All you need to do to get someone to dance the dance of fear is to utter the famous, simple motto: we are Los Zetas.

In Tabasco, which marks the beginning of Zetas' turf in Mexico, you can almost taste the fear. It hits you in your sixth sense: that feeling of walking round a dark corner and knowing you're about to get mugged. It was the fear we saw on a taxi driver's face when we asked him to take us to La Victoria ranch and he responded: "No, I can't go there, they won't let us through. No. I'm not going." He shut his cab door and split. We could feel it in the looks of the men sitting in the parked black truck on the corner, where we waited for the bus that would take us to the ranch. And in the almost trembling words of the driver when he realized where we wanted to go: "But you guys … You wouldn't be … I just don't want any trouble."

Before leaving the ranch, we even saw the fear in the three policemen. While they were hanging the seized property sign, one of them, holding tightly onto his AR-15 and glancing up toward the mountains, said: "We can't show you the tombs because they're still hanging around, keeping watch."

By "they" he meant Los Zetas. Los Zetas always keeping watch.

The same nervous policeman later told me, "Of course they're hanging around in the mountains. They have more arms buried somewhere around here."

And indeed it was close by the ranch, in the tangle of mountain shrubs, that two Honduran men who were presumed to have been part of the hostage group, and who had already been apprehended and put in chains, led police to Jiménez's body. Worms were crawling through the wound on his neck when they uncovered him. Close to his body, an Uzi and two of its cartridges were dug up as well.

Police had to take the two Honduran men out of the Tapachula detention center. Apparently a brawl broke out in their holding cell. And when authorities tried to break it up, they saw what looked like a lynching in progress. The fifty undocumented migrants were beating the two Hondurans. They were, it turned out, both Zetas.

"They're Zetas!" people screamed. "They were armed and paddling us at the ranch. They're part of the gang!"

So the police took the two men back to the ranch in Tabasco, where they were forced to help uncover the other body. The other escapee that these men themselves had killed and buried.

Los Zetas are like a metastasizing cancer. Migrants are recruited. Soldiers are recruited. Policemen, mayors, businessmen—they're all liable to become part of the web.

SURVEY FOR THE ENEMY

"So then," I ask the agent, "everything they found out about La Victoria ranch was due to dumb luck? I mean, it wasn't uncovered because of good military work, but just because two lucky migrants escaped and bumped into a squad and told them about the fifty-two other migrants held captive?"

The undercover agent smiles at my question. It's a smile that flashes with complicity. A smile that says that both my question and its answer are obvious.

"Why do you think I move like I do?" he asks. "Slowly, step by step? Because Los Zetas find out about most operations even before the military. They have ears all over the place. And when there's a bust like that, it's for one of two reasons: either things went down fast, without any planning, with some impressive whistle-blowing, which in this case was done by two migrants, or because an extensive undercover operation went down silently, slowly, without anyone even knowing about it."

It was, in fact, dumb luck, an unraveling of will and time. If the two who escaped had been too scared to confront the soldiers, worrying that they'd be detained and questioned, if instead of talking they had run into the hills, if minutes before bumping into the squad they had stopped to rest, hidden under the shade of a tree, at the edge of a trail, then the squad would have passed them and no one would ever have heard about the ranch called La Victoria, hidden in the outskirts of Gregorio Méndez.

"I already told you, they have ears everywhere," the agent goes on. Like a good informant, he knows how to surprise. "So tell me," he says coyly, "were there any police at the ranch?"

"Three."

"Well, okay, one of them is under investigation because allegedly he works for Los Zetas."

For over a half hour we'd talked to and questioned someone who is possibly a Zeta. This is what enables them to do whatever they want. This is how they know of almost every undercover operation planned against them. This is how they almost always know the who, the when, and the where. This is why it's hard to act or react on their turf. This is why our photographer, Toni Arnau, was only able to take out his camera for a minute. And this is why this agent moves so cautiously, because Los Zetas see everything.

It's becoming uncomfortable moving through their domain, and walking the streets of Tenosique. One afternoon, a city official showed us around. As we made our way down the main road that divides the city of 55,000 in two, our driver started pointing out the businesses we were passing.

"See that place? The owner's son was kidnapped a month ago. The owner of that place," he points, "was kidnapped and killed four months ago. Our ex-mayor, Carlos Paz, was kidnapped over on that street in May, and I've heard that Los Zetas have the wife of the owner of that pharmacy locked up right now."

This is a showcase of kidnappings. A tour through a town taken over by narcos, where there are plenty of landmarks, but instead of pointing out a café where someone famous once ate, we gawk at the business where the last kidnapping happened, or the block with the most recent murder.

When Los Zetas take over, they take over everything. They've monopolized crime—kidnappings, extortions, murder, drug trafficking, retail, pirated movies, migrant guides. These crimes are all part of the same enterprise, and whoever wants a job, any kind of job, has to somehow work for Los Zetas.

"They control everything," the agent explains, "every institution. Notice how so many of the kidnappings in Tenosique happen near the rails, right in front of the migrant trail. City and state officials know that one of them will die if they do so much as lift a finger. Better to keep quiet and take what Los Zetas pays them."

"It must have taken them a long time to create such a network," I say absentmindedly, as though thinking out loud.

"No. Don't be so sure," he says. "They came one day and hit hard. They swept up all the small criminal organizations that already existed. We actually just started hearing about them in July 2006, when authorities caught Mateo Díaz, known as El Comandante Mateo, or Z-10.[1]"

Before that it was the Gulf Cartel that roared loudest in Tabasco, but back then few knew about them, or their heavily armed unit which later peeled off to form Los Zetas. Mateo was arrested back in his hometown, a small city in Tabasco called Cundiacán, because he made a big scene one drunken night at a bar called La Palotada. They arrested him along with one of his sidekicks, a Guatemalan by the name of Darwin Bermúdez Zamora. The city police didn't know who they had, but might have guessed he was important when just minutes after his detention, an armed commando unit of fifteen attacked the police station with bazookas, grenades, and AR-15s. Two policemen were killed in the fray, another seven were injured, and the station was destroyed. Only afterward did they find out exactly who they had locked up next to the other petty troublemakers.

It was Z-10, El Commandante Mateo, who in 1998 deserted the feared Army Special Forces (GAFES) to help form Los Zetas. One of the most wanted criminals in the country, he lorded it over the plazas of Tabasco, Chiapas, and Veracruz, three important

---

1   In Spanish, the word "zeta" is the name of the letter Z.

states in the smuggling of Colombian cocaine and Guatemalan military arms. He now hovers near the top of the U.S. most wanted list.

El Comandante Mateo had brought order to Tabasco. He and his henchmen explained the rules to the small local gangs like this: join or leave the state. They took over the gangs of some thirty boys and men, between the ages of twelve and thirty-five, who made a profession out of charging every migrant a hundred pesos to hop on the train to Tenosique. From now on you work for us, they announced. From now on, you won't have any problems with the migration authorities. From now on, any games worth just a few pesos are over. We're going to take over this route, charge any coyotes who pass through here, punish those who don't pay, and kidnap those who don't travel with someone hired by us. That was their offer.

"The gangs already existed," the agent says, "and now they're in charge of a bunch of the businesses that make a profit for local Zetas members. We've even found out that they've taken over the business of pirated CDs. And they do it all their way. When they first arrived they got a hold of businessmen and dealers and burned them. First they show how they work, then they negotiate."

"But are these gangs Zetas or not? I've heard them called *zetitas* [little zetas]."

The agent laughs. "I like that name—zetitas. That's more or less what they are. They're not Zetas in the sense that they don't help structure the greater gang, they don't manage drug loads, and they don't have any responsibility within the cartel. But in practice they're Zetas. They have permission to identify as Zetas, and they have the protection of the big men. So in practice they're the same: a migration officer denounces one of the zetitas on the rails, and he's meddling with a business that's protected by the big Zetas, and these guys are going to get their revenge. But the ones that walk the rails only have the job of picking up migrants. These are the guys who used to be the big fish, the leaders of the small gangs that used to exist. Their job now is to talk migrants into coming home with them. They tell them that they'll help get them to the US border, but instead they take them to cartel gunmen, like the ones at La Victoria ranch."

LOS ZETITAS

Standing under the burning Tabasco sun, we decided to go to Macuspana, a small rural municipality along the train route about 150 miles north of Tenosique. Those who ride The Beast from Tenosique pass through Macuspana. And there, just like in El Águila, El Barí, El 20, Villa, El Faisán, Gregorio Méndez, and Emiliano Zapata, there are bands of zetitas.

Instead of a shelter in Macuspana, there's just a bare-bones church where migrants get a nap with a roof over their heads and a bowl of food before continuing their journey. A thin man with a sharply featured face, who turned out to be the parochial administrator, came out of the church to greet us. He calmly pulled a bench up to a table and there we began what turned out to be a very short conversation.

When we explained that we're looking for information about gangs and kidnappings, the man quieted, his eyes started darting. "I don't know anything about it," he said. "I just serve food to migrants. I don't know a thing." And that was all he had to say.

We went to sit down on the patio with a group of eight Hondurans and one Guatemalan. The conversation proceeded as usual. First thing they wanted to know was who was asking. The trick, we've learned, is to talk about the trail, let them know that you know something about it, know its secrets, its dangers, that you know about the train and where it stops. This trick is getting past the initial response—"No problems, man. All fine so far, thanks to God"—which is always false, and to persist until the migrant starts talking about what he or she has actually been through.

Following these steps I learned that three of the men out on that patio had nearly been kidnapped in El Barí. The Guatemalan man from El Petén, who was leading the group on his second try north, reacted quickly when a truck pulled up in front of them. The passenger had a pistol at the ready and said into his cell phone "I got a small group here." The three migrants bolted.

One of the people in the group, a chubby Honduran man with a black rosary around his neck, dropped a few telling comments. I mentioned that it was common that cartel members lie to infiltrate migrant groups, and he quickly responded, "So they can get your phone number, which is what matters most."

"And they politely ask for your number," I added, "like a coyote taking you north."

The Honduran agreed: "Yes, but it's all lies. Later on you figure out that you're kidnapped and on your way to Coatzacoalcos."

You could see that the man was street-toughened. You could hear it in his words, catch it in his gestures. He went on to talk about his last trip north, when some cartel members recognized that he was a bit reckless and invited him to crash at the house of El Barí's gang leader, El Cocho. They were trying to woo him into the group of zetitas. "They knew I didn't have anyone to pay my ransom, so instead of kidnapping me they gave me a place to stay."

I'm not sure whether to believe this. It could be he was actually working for them as he spoke to me, scouting the trains for potential victims. What I do know, however, is that a lot of his stories were later confirmed by the agent.

The Honduran man told me that El Cocho, about thirty years old, is Honduran as well. That he works with eight other Hondurans and never lets his nine-millimeter out of his sight, "not even to sleep." El Cocho's band is still active, but for the moment they've taken to the mountains "because of a recent raid." He explained that some of the cartel members told him all this before he arrived in Macuspana.

Two months ago there was a military raid in which twenty-four kidnapped migrants were discovered. When the soldiers showed up, however, only the municipal police were there; the zetitas had already split.

"They're all in it together," the chubby Honduran said. "When I was crashing with them, a couple of police dropped by to eat. I saw El Cocho give them an envelope full of money."

He went on to describe the group running Hotel California.

In years of covering immigration as a reporter, this is one of the most outrageous examples of impunity I've come across. The Hotel California in Tenosique is known by every authority in town as being Zetas turf. And everybody knows they store arms and drugs and house kidnapped migrants in the hotel. And the hotel itself is just down the street from the Migration offices, which are next to the train tracks where numerous mass kidnappings have occurred.

"There," the Honduran said, referring to Hotel California, "about ten or so guys work for the Train Man."

The Train Man is an ex-coyote, around forty years old, who back in 2007 was apprehended by Los Zetas for not paying their tax. He pleaded that he hadn't known the rules, and was willing to make up for his mistake. He spent the next year on a corner in Coatzacoalcos selling tamales and bags of cocaine. After paying off his debt, just when the the police detained the Zetas chief, El Gordo, the Train Man was promoted to zetita chief. And now, when he shaves his head, you can see on the top of his skull the loyal tattoo of a Z.

"Yeah, the cops paid me to show them where El Cocho lives, where the Train Man lives. A few others as well. That was the day I showed the cops all around." This was the last comment the Honduran made to me before we left Macuspana.

THOSE WHO ARE BOUGHT AND THOSE WHO ARE SCARED

"Everyone knows about Hotel California, but no one wants to get involved. They've bought up half the world, not just city and state officials. You know the two women who stand on the edge of town every day, selling sodas. Do you think that's what they're really up to?"

The agent pauses, gives me another of his mysterious smiles, and then looks me in the eyes before answering his own question.

"Nooo. They're in charge of seeing if any military convoys come in, if a suspicious car comes in, if more cars than usual come in. Of course, all you see is two young women selling sodas."

They hire small-town women, Central American migrants, policemen, politicians, and businessmen. A town has been taken over once half of it is on the payroll and the other half is scared. Anyone who speaks up is threatened, like Fray Jesús, a young, brave priest at the Tenosique church who publicly denounced Los Zetas during his sermons and in front of the media. Fray Jesús got three warnings: two written (one stuck onto his windshield wiper, the other onto the front gate of his parish church) and one by word of mouth: "Tell the little priest that if he keeps getting into things that don't concern him, he won't end up so hot." Fray Jesús has since learned to speak out against Los Zetas without crossing the invisible boundaries they've set for him with their threats.

Everyone is confined to one of two roles in this town, a fact at the forefront of each individual mind in every encounter between residents: is this person among the threatening or the fearful? The woman who works the pharmacy counter and lowers her head when she sees a stranger pass by is someone who fears. The men driving the yellow car who pass us three times in less than five minutes are those who threaten.

"We're talking about people with money. Los Zetas are pushing between 50,000 and 200,000 pesos a month to every gang of zetitas in this area. The gangs have enough money for themselves and to bribe authorities. And keep in mind that this is a small slice of their business. They get money from drug trafficking and arms trafficking. Migrants are their third business."

He ponders for a moment. Silence hovers over our table. The sun sinks, the light around us dims.

"Yep, it's their third business, but they don't have any small businesses, only money-making gigs that require turning on their entire machinery of corruption. It's a conservative estimate that 40 percent of all state police units have been bought by Los Zetas."

THE JOURNO AND THE COP

The two meetings began with the usual reverberation of the fear that steeps this region of the country.

After talking to a few of his colleagues, we found the reporter without much trouble. We called him one afternoon and, as he already knew what we wanted to talk about, simply set up a time to meet in person. We took a bus from Villahermosa to a small outlying town, and walked into a modest restaurant. A half hour later a hot and sweaty man came in with a stack of papers under his arm. It was the reporter we were looking for, the man who for ten years had been covering the drugs, the shootouts, and the corrupt military and police beat in this region, where the high number of military convoys driving down the dusty streets makes it look like we're in Iraq.

The reporter typed notes into his laptop while talking and cocking his head every which way, always attentive to who was around him. He eyed a scruffy old man at the next table. With juice sellers working as lookouts and corrupt officials in every direction, anybody could turn out to be listening and anybody could turn out to be a Zeta.

We chatted for a bit, but it was obvious that we should move to another spot, somewhere where we wouldn't need to whisper every time we said the word Zeta. We eventually found ourselves in an electronics repair shop, where the nervous reporter opened up. He even turned on his computer to show us some of his photos.

The pictures were of old ranches, captured Zetas, corrupt policemen caught in the act, as well as corpses, lots of corpses.

But what we wanted to know, the reason we had come to him, was why nobody was talking about what everybody knows, what even outsiders like us know in just a few weeks of poking around. That is, why does nobody name the corrupt officials, if everybody knows who they are? Why do they only open up when there's a crackdown and a few of them get arrested and paraded before the media? Why does nobody talk about how deeply involved many officials are, or how widespread and everyday the corruption is?

"Because I live here. And my family lives here. And, like you say, if they have half the village bought off then they definitely know your name, where you live, how old your kids are and where they go to school. And if you decide to risk it and publish something, you're going to face the same thing I faced. A black truck filled with armed men pulling up outside your house. A knock on the door. 'We've come to ask how you want it to turn out,' they say. 'You want it to turn out good? Then stop writing that shit you've been writing. Or you want it to turn out bad? Because if you continue we're going to murder you and then murder your whole family.'"

The reporter had a point. A point for reporters on the ground, but not necessarily for the media companies safely holed up back in their offices in the capital. For those who live in the middle of the violence in these towns, for those who travel without bodyguards and earn a pittance for their work, for those who work from their homes where their kids live and play, silence is understandable.

Because when the thugs pronounce their famous motto, when you hear, "We are Los Zetas," you either fold or they are going to fold you. The reporter understood the dynamic all too well. Kidnapping victims understand it, too. But Mario Rodríguez Alonso, the transit chief of the town Emiliano Zapata, understood it too late. Rodríguez chose not to fold when he arrested a man for drunk driving and the man started yelling that he was a Zeta. The next morning (in July 2008) a group of armed men showed up at the police station and took Rodríguez away. The following morning they dropped his corpse back at the same police station. His head was covered in a black plastic bag, his arms were handcuffed behind his back, and his body showed signs of being tortured and was riddled with bullet holes.

~

A few days after talking with the reporter, we tracked down a cop and asked him what he thought of the public's fear. Getting hold of a cop willing to talk, it turned out, was more difficult than finding a willing reporter. We contacted him originally through some relatives who had a friend in the government, and we never actually spoke with the man until we met him. Instructions were relayed to us through our contact: two o'clock, the small corner restaurant along the river.

He arrived on time. This policeman, on his off days, worked as a security guard for the restaurant. He suggested a walk, so we headed down an alleyway and stopped in the shade of a tree on the riverbank.

"We've heard it said that sometimes," I started, "they call the police station and play narco-corridos at full volume."[2]

"Yeah, those shits call us sometimes. They've even been calling some of the commanders' houses recently too, to threaten them, to let them know that if we act against them, they know where they live and won't hesitate to kill their families."

"And this happens a lot?"

"Look, there's always something. Only five days ago we found another body in Tenosique, in Colonia Municipal. He was a cattle herder. Three months ago they killed a police commander who thought it was all a game, and started messing with some of Los Zetas, nosing around Hotel California."

He was talking about Tirson Castellanos, the Tenosique police commander whose second job was as a used car salesman. One day a truck full of assassins followed him on his way home. He gave them the slip at first and tried to hide, shutting himself in the bathroom at a mechanic's shop. But they found him. He was shot fourteen times.

"And yourself, what do you do to stay alive?" I asked.

"I wash my hands of it all. Focus on other problems, on

---

2 Narco-corridos are popular norteña or country-style songs celebrating the big drug barons and their deeds.

pickpockets and drunks. They've gotten to me, though. I was on patrol once and they pulled me over. 'We are Los Zetas,' they said. Then they showed their weapons and said that I was going to work for them now. I told them I wouldn't do it. When they started to get rough I told them that I wouldn't get in their way either. 'All the better for you, then, you son of a bitch,' they said."

"Once," he went on, "I even saw three trucks full of men in AFI uniforms pass through one of our checkpoints.[3] We asked if they were on a mission and they told us, 'We aren't the government. We're Los Zetas.' The police commander at the checkpoint was smart enough to wave them through, saying that he didn't want anything to do with them and hadn't even seen them. I'd never seen so many weapons in one place as I saw that day in those three trucks."

"I imagine there are guys in your station that work for them," I said.

"Yeah, I know there's some. But I try not to get involved, not to dig around too much. Not to trust anybody."

"So there's no solidarity at the station."

"Forget it. Almost everybody's bought. If you stop a Zeta, other Zetas will turn you in, spread your name around, put your family at risk. Everybody's looking out for themselves. In El Ceibo the other day the police reported capturing two guns when what they actually got were five guns and an AK-47."

He was referring to an operation a few days earlier when in the small Mexico–Guatemala border town of El Ceibo, known as an arms smuggling hotspot, police arrested a young man driving a car with five nine-millimeter pistols and an AK-47. A photographer and I were close by when it happened, waiting to see if the Guatemalan army would follow through with their planned operation against arms dealing in the area. However, as it was publicly announced beforehand, the operation was a failure. And the same

---

3 AFI stands for Agencia Federal de Investigación, akin to the FBI, currently subsumed into the federal police.

day, after the Mexican police caught the kid with the weapons in his car, they reported that they found only two pistols. The AK and the other three guns, who knows where they ended up.

Los Zetas have infiltrated everywhere. Not even the army is clean. On July 1, 2009, Mexican Intelligence detained sixteen soldiers on bases in Villahermosa and Tenosique, accusing them of working with Los Zetas. They were charged with warning Zetas about military raids and even plotting to assassinate Gilberto Toledano, the police commander who was in charge of the operation at La Victoria ranch.

NO LIGHT AT THE END OF THE TUNNEL

The sun hangs low, but the heat is still suffocating in this café, when the conversation with the undercover agent comes to an end.

"All of this is complicated," he says as though in summary. "It's complicated because the first thing we have to do is fight off their deep infiltration. We have to build a front, and the entire state apparatus has to be in on it, fighting against them. Then we'd have a real battle."

"So what's being done now, what do you call that?"

"A quaint little game, one that doesn't get results."

Then, as a form of goodbye, we exchange futile, broken thoughts. "It's hard … Yes, complicated … A tough job … Little by little, with care."

Hopelessness takes hold of me. I think it must be the same feeling that overcame the journalist, the policeman, the priest, and now this agent. As we walk the streets of these southern Mexican towns and make way for people with lowered gazes we will be witnessing the fear. And we will witness the fear in the people making vigilant rounds in their cars. And we will witness it in the streets where soon there will be another murder, and where soon many more migrants will be kidnapped.

"It's complicated," the agent repeats. Then we shake hands and say goodbye.

7

Living among Coyotes:
To the Rio Grande and Back

They live to push the limits, working under constant risk, repeating over and again this lethal journey. They are coyotes, polleros, *the pirates of the migrant trails. They live in a world they don't control, taking orders from narcos, those who run the migrant trails in this country. Many of the* polleros *don't like the new rules, and so they've started infighting, devouring each other. This is what a man named El Chilango taught me about coyotes in Mexico.*

He looks like a frightened animal. He whistles, calls out: "Hey! You!" But when I turn to look at him he lowers his hat, almost covering his eyes, dropping his head. And then he darts back into the bushes, glancing at me over his shoulder. A crazy person, I think.

I ignore him, but he calls out again. We're a few steps outside of the migrant shelter in Ixtepec, Oaxaca. He retreats into the bushes and then peeks out when I don't respond.

"Pst! Hey!" he calls, jerking his head, inviting me into the bushes with him. I shoot him an annoyed glance, then turn back to the card game I'm playing with a group of Hondurans. At first he seems to give up. He buries his hands in the pockets of his thread-bare pants and shoulders deeper into the bushes with a face like thunder. As the card game continues, I see him occasionally poke his head back out and shrug at me.

Definitely crazy, I think. I keep an eye on him as the afternoon passes, watching him grumble to himself. He has a spotty gray beard and an abnormally large jaw that juts out from his face. His shiny head, which he occasionally uncovers from under his hat to scratch, has only a few stray hairs on it. He's dirty and has a crazy, undecipherable look in his eyes.

David, the head of security at the shelter, walks past carrying firewood for the kitchen. He tells me that the man in the bushes wants to talk to me. I tell him that I'll go over in a minute, and David, a military/police veteran with a good eye, says, "I bet he's a *pollero*."

That brings me to my feet. I leave the card table and move toward the man in the bushes, who steps out to meet me.

"Not here," he whispers. "I'm going to sit over there. Wait a minute and then come join me."

I watch him walk away. I understand his plea for privacy and try to look indifferent for a minute. I pour myself a coffee from the large pot that's usually bubbling over the fire, and light a cigarette. Then I give away nearly half my pack. The migrants always notice when I have cigarettes. And then, after a few minutes, once I think nobody's paying attention, I walk over to the crazy man and sit down next to him. We're protected from view of the shelter by a tree and from view of the railroad tracks by bushes. After a moment of silence, the man looks at me squarely and starts to talk.

"You can call me El Chilango, but I'm not going to tell you my real name. I'm a *pollero*, a coyote. A Mexican. I'm going to talk because I've already seen you on these trails. I've seen you around and know that you know a little about how it is. And I'm fed up with what's going on here. These assholes are taking my job. So, yeah, if you want to hear me out, grab me a coffee and give me a cigarette and I'll tell you."

I look at his eyes, which are black and small and surrounded by a circle of wrinkles. The iris of his right eye lazes up and out, his left stares straight ahead. The skin on his face is dry, slightly burnt, and covered in dust. Even up close he has a crazed look.

I don't ask a single question. El Chilango, smoking and talking without pause, lays out his life for me. He is forty-one years old, though he could probably pass for seventy. He was born in Mexico City and for the last twenty years he's been working as a coyote. He started when he got fired from a trucking company he hauled for after he stole a load of bananas. He approached some migrants in southern Mexico and offered to drive them to the capital in his trailer. In those days there weren't the migration checkpoints that there are now. He got to know a few other coyotes, and soon learned the routes on foot as well as by train. He learned like all coyotes learn, apprenticing to someone more experienced. He doesn't tell me who his teacher was, but mentions that they ended their relationship with machetes. I notice the two, long, raised scars on his right forearm.

Since then, he explains, he's been working alone. He never had another teacher and he never took on a student. He had contacts in Guatemala, Honduras, and El Salvador that would send him clients, and he'd pick them up himself in Tapachula, on the north bank of the Suchiate River, and take them to Nuevo Laredo, on the south bank of the Rio Grande.

"I never used to ask anything from anybody," he tells me. "But that's all changed now. I had to accept that a year ago. I had to start paying out and working for Don Fito, one of the big-time coyotes. But I'm sick of these assholes now. The coyotes who actually walk with the migrants, who take care of them, we can't work in peace anymore. We're all employed by the big fishes that live up north. And they're all mixed up with Los Zetas who make sure to take their cut."

THE COYOTE WHO'S NOT A COYOTE

Ten years ago, the image of the coyote as custodian started crumbling. The friendly neighbor who, for a small, reasonable sum, would take his *compadre*, his friend, to El Norte, is now a sullen man, covered in scars, and often a danger to his own clients.

Sometimes he's even a Zeta ally, who migrants go with because there's no other choice. Sometimes he's a kidnapper, and most of the time he's a swindler. This new breed of coyotes lives on the road. And the road, malicious and deceitful as it is, has turned against them as much as they've turned against the road.

The good coyote no longer has that option—to be a good coyote. He has to pay his dues to Los Zetas, or hand over human loot instead. The good coyote has to give up his reputation, relinquish the essence of his trade, abandon the routes and cantinas that once served as hangout and pickup spots. He's had to start calling himself a *guía*, a guide, instead of a coyote, and his fees have been slashed. And yet these old pros carry on. The inevitable vice of the road awakens something in them. Life off the road is just too calm, lacking the speed, fear, and constant adrenaline that keeps one awake. That keeps one alive.

I met Wilber, one of these *guías*, in 2007 when he was only twenty-two years old. He had already been detained seven times, had been a coyote for nine years, had taken part in thirty assaults—at least—in La Arrocera, and had witnessed eight murders. Observant and smart, Wilber is from El Progreso, a barrio in Tegucigalpa, Honduras. He never submitted to the new wave of his trade, and never contacted or let himself be contacted by any Zeta. He stayed on the migrant's side. He was and is afraid of Los Zetas, and yet he doesn't pay them. And that's why Wilber now mostly lives off of what he makes from a small market garden and the two horses that pull his banana cart. That and guiding relatives or friends to the north.

Wilber has the wiry, tanned body of a *campesino*. Nothing about him makes him stand out, and no one would imagine that when he's not selling bananas he's running the narco-controlled migrant routes of Mexico. I've seen him five times since I first met him while he was crossing a cousin, the head of a private insurance company Wilber occasionally worked for. I've traveled with him twice now, and I've learned to trust him.

There's a difference between Wilber and other coyotes these

days. Wilber still eats with his migrants, stills sleeps with his migrants, and he doesn't abandon them so he can go on a spree. He doesn't get together with strangers on the rails, and he doesn't show off. He travels like a migrant, and he defends himself not with machetes or AK's, but with sticks and stones.

And his migrants, his flock, as they wait for the train in an open plot of land, they treat him like a friend, like any member of the group. He humbly takes the lead whenever The Beast blows by and tells them which car to get on and when, and he always hops on last.

He would guide his migrants all the way to the Rio Bravo, and when they arrived he would tell them which coyote to approach for crossing into the United States. He'd send them to someone connected with El Abuelo, one of a handful of bosses guiding Central Americans over the border. El Abuelo deals directly with Los Zetas. Wilber is a good guide, but the northern border has its own rules and, if he wants to stay out of trouble, he has no other choice but to follow them. So the best he can do is tell his migrants to seek out specific coyotes. Besides, El Abuelo is famous for sticking with his end of a job.

Last time we got together we had a lot of time to talk. It was a night in October 2008. The train we waited for in Arriaga hadn't come for two days. The lot was full of migrants who, sick of waiting, were sleeping on the rails. The shelter in Arriaga is about three quarters of a mile away from the tracks, and many didn't want to waste time in walking all that way. The two of us lay with our heads resting on the steel track, about ten yards away from the four cousins Wilber was crossing.

Our cigarette smoke, dense in the glow of the nearby lights, lingered in the air. We sat up on the rails and, though the air around us was still, Wilber smoked his cigarette between his thumb and index finger, toward the inside of his hand, as if he were smoking on a moving train trying to keep the wind from eating at his drags.

"I thought you were going to retire, old man," I said.

"Oh?"

"Last time we were in Ixtepec you told me everything had gone to shit and that you didn't want Los Zetas to find you. You said it was going to be your last trip."

"Sure. The thing is, these kiddoes want to go north, and since we're cousins and all, I know they're not going to burn me."

"Burn you?"

"Sure, you know, the problems that come when Los Zetas get a hold of you, them or the police that work for them. If they see a group bigger than five, they're going to want to know which one the coyote is and they won't stop fucking with you until someone talks. They take aside the ones that look dumbest and tell them that if they point out the coyote, then nothing bad will happen to them. But I keep my *pollos* in check, well trained. They know that the deal is to say we're all cousins, which is why I brought my papers with me this time, and they did too, so they'll see we all have the same last name."

"So you're counting on having a run-in with them."

"No, but last time we got off at Tierra Blanca, they got thirty of the ones that were with me on the train. I had a brother-in-law in tow and we just booked it. We hid in a factory somewhere near the rails. They saw us, but they didn't bother to go after us."

"But Wilber, if you're fine with dropping them off at Nuevo Laredo, tipping them to one of El Abuelo's people who works for Los Zetas anyway, why don't you just work for Los Zetas yourself?"

"Because it's all fucked. It's not as simple as working *with* them, and crossing people whenever you want. They control you. They want your home phone number back in Honduras, and they call you once in a while to cross groups they've reserved for you. If you take too long in crossing, or if they don't see you on the road for a month, they fuck you over. They'll think you're working for someone else, or that you've found another crossing point. They want you to watch their routes for them, they want you to get them people."

"People to kidnap?"

"Yeah. And even the other coyotes, they're always fucking with each other. Sometimes someone who isn't getting any work sees you crossing big groups of people and always coming back for more, and they start thinking that your slice is getting bigger than theirs, then they try to burn you, making up stories about seeing you with another boss or that you crossed more migrants than the ones you reported. No, it's fucked. It's better this way."

"Sure, better to be a guide."

"Much better."

"Until they catch you."

"No, they won't catch me. This is going to be my last trip."

I laughed. Wilber laughed too. Then he called his cousins over and we told each other jokes to keep ourselves from falling asleep.

Morning broke and there wasn't any sign of a coming train. Wilber looked serious. He hadn't slept all night, and he still had eleven hours of riding on the train under the pitiless sun. He walked toward the bridge, away from the milling of all the migrants who hadn't gone to the shelter for a cup of coffee or a bowl of food. I followed him. When he'd gone far enough, down to where the rails are covered by weeds, he crouched, set one hand on a pile of construction debris and another on the ground, and put his ear to the rails. He stayed that way for a minute. Then he got up, serious. He asked me for a cigarette.

"It'll be here in less than a half hour," he said, taking his first deep drag.

Quickly, he made his way back to gather his cousins who were buying food at a nearby market.

The train came a half hour later. I wasn't able to find Wilber amidst all the commotion. Some of the migrants on my car were fighting with two drunks who wanted to board. The drunks stank of liquor and each carried a handle of moonshine. Everything got settled when a black Caribbean Honduran, tall and muscular, offered to split their heads with an enormous log. The two drunks, grumbling, decided to give up.

The cars were properly arranged and the train about to leave when I heard a shout from below. It was Wilber who, with his brow furrowed, was waving at me to get off. I didn't move. He waved again, this time with both arms.

"What's going on?"

"Now's no time to play around. There are three Zeta spies on those cars."

"How do you know?"

He didn't answer, only stared at me, his eyes wide and insistent.

"So what, then?"

"So nothing. Time to wait for another train."

I ran to warn a group of Hondurans who I'd gotten to know the day before. They looked at each other, but didn't move. The train started to pull forward. I saw a Guatemalan who was traveling with her husband and I made the gesture Wilber had made to me. But the Guatemalans just waved goodbye.

"Shit," I said.

"They're going to get fucked," Wilber said calmly, taking a bite of a scrambled egg taco, "because about five of those bandits had guns."

"Bandits? You said they were Zetas."

"Well, yeah, Los Zetas are why I got off. The bandits are fine. I gave them fifty pesos and that was that, they were going to leave me be. The problem is that the spies saw me hand the money to the bandits. So now they know I'm the coyote."

THREATENED BY RACE

El Chilango's enormous jaw starts to tremble. For a moment I think he's going to cry. He's put himself in a terrible situation, and he knows it. He's scared. And with good reason.

After an hour of conversation he's laid out his defense for me. It turns out he broke the rules. He took three Hondurans from

Tenosique to Reynosa, on the US border, without telling his boss, Don Fito. He picked up the migrants at the bus station, thinking he could jump a step ahead of his boss and Los Zetas. He says he did it because, after he made a few mistakes, Don Fito hadn't given him work in more than two months. He doesn't explain what the previous mistakes were, saying that they're not important, that he's been a good worker for years.

His plan was going fine at first. He got the migrants to Coatzacoalcos without a hitch, but then La Doña appeared on the tracks. She's a sixtysomething who looks like she might be in her eighties. She sells food to migrants along the side of the tracks, mostly enormous tortillas called *tlayudas*, which are topped with meat and cheese. But the tortilla stand is only a front. La Doña is actually the kidnapping boss in Coatzacoalcos. She runs the business with her three fat and violent sons. I know about her sons. They once pulled the photographer Edu Ponces and me off the train and threatened us. La Doña also monitors the low-level coyotes, making sure they pay their bosses, Los Zetas, so they can send full buses of kidnapped victims to Reynosa.

La Doña likes to approach migrants like a mother at first, sometimes even offering them a free *tlayuda*. She tells them that her sons are coyotes and will give them a good price, but then she pulls out a pistol and forces them into a truck.

El Chilango says that the day before yesterday La Doña came out of her stand just as he was getting off the tracks. "Hey, you son of a bitch!" she called to him. "Who the fuck do you think you are?"

El Chilango says he's sure they had their eyes on him the whole time on the train. La Doña screamed at him to follow her so they could ask Don Fito what he wanted to do to his rebel coyote.

But catching La Doña in an inattentive moment, El Chilango grabbed his group of migrants and dove into a taxi. They sped to the bus station where they caught a bus to Oaxaca, and then caught another to Ixtepec. And here we are, under a tree outside the shelter. His migrants are resting inside, hoping not to get caught in the crossfire between El Chilango and Don Fito's people.

"What the hell were you thinking?" I ask him.

"I don't know, man, I don't know. It's that these migrants still needed to pay me for the trip. And I knew that if we didn't get out of there Don Fito was either going to beat the shit out of me or kill me," he says, his voice trembling up and down with each word.

"Stupid idiots," he says. "I worked well for them, but the boss just wasn't giving me any *pollos*. I have two women with kids I need to send them money. The stupid idiots!"

"And so what now?" I ask.

"Now," he says, still trembling, "I'm going to get on this train, avoid Coatzacoalcos, and see if I can get to the US. And I'm going with my *pollos*. And if I get there, I'm gonna stay. I know how it works here, that all the other coyotes working for Don Fito and El Abuelo already have a kill order on me. Plus all the spies that ride the trains. Stupid idiots."

I tell him that his plan is flat-out dumb and isn't going to work. They're going to find him, and it'll be his fault if his *pollos* get killed as well.

"Can't you talk to anybody from the army for me? Tell them I know where all the Zetas kidnappers are, that if they give me witness protection I'll give them all up. I'll give up the coyotes that work for them too, plus the spies, the whole lot of them."

He shows me the list of contacts on his two cell phones. In one of them there are three numbers for "Doña Coatzacoalcos." In the other there are numbers for "Don Fito" and for "El Borrego" (the Sheep), the famous Zeta chief of Tierra Blanca. I agree to consult the head of the shelter, Alejandro Solalinde. His idea isn't crazy, I tell the *pollero*, but Solalinde rather than me would know who to approach in the army. I ask him to let me talk with the Hondurans, his *pollos*, saying that afterward I'd call Solalinde and tell him what's going on. El Chilango accepts. We exchange numbers and he takes off.

~

Once in a while, to turn yourself in as a witness offers a way out of the game, but I have a bad feeling that El Chilango is going to get killed, that there's no way out for him.

I decide to spend the night looking for possibilities.

El Chilango, I learn, had first come to the hostel the day before. He was supposedly loitering around outside of its gates. He walked up to Solalinde once, but never said anything, and never actually set foot inside the shelter.

I won't say who I spoke with, but they're people I trust, who I've known for awhile on the migrant trails. Two of them told me that El Chilango is a typical coyote, hard to deal with and a pain just like the rest of them. They said that he had two run-ins with Don Fito. First, when he lost five migrants in Tierra Blanca because he was drunk while waiting for a train and his migrants decided to go on alone. The second incident was more serious. El Chilango wanted to fatten his wallet a little and stole two migrants from another of El Abuelo's coyotes. This is a serious violation in the coyote world. Each boss pays his *pollero* by the number of *pollos* he tends while they're in his zone. Stealing two migrants is what got El Chilango in trouble, and put him out of work. Don Fito himself had to call him and force him to give up all of his *pollos* in restitution.

They tear each other up. Coyotes fighting coyotes. Hardly any of them follow the rules anymore. They attempt to pacify the narcos, but it's like trying to tame a tiger in the jungle. They know what they're up against, but money keeps driving them. And El Chilango's case isn't unique.

UNKNOWN TERRITORY

In Ixtepec I was introduced to another coyote, Alberto. It was January 2008. Alberto was from San Miguel, a neighborhood on the east side of San Salvador, but had since moved to Monterrey in the northern state of Nuevo León, Mexico.

He was part of a network of luxury coyotes who don't work

with impoverished migrants overland. His clients paid as much as $7,000 per trip. The way it worked was that these migrants gathered on a designated day and hour in the central plaza of Tapachula. From there a driver picked them up and took them to a house to spend the night. At dawn the following morning the same driver would take them to a hidden runway in a remote canyon region. From there the migrants would fly to Monterrey, which is within a short drive of the Texas border. And that's where Alberto's work began. He would collect the migrants at the runway in Monterrey, arrange them in groups of no more than five, assign one coyote per group, and tell them the rules and the route they were to use in crossing the border.

The coyote group Alberto worked for would earn $35,000 for every five clients successfully ferried across. And they would usually cross at least four groups a month. Last month, however, they didn't make a single trip. Mexican authorities, in agreement with the US government, started trying to control the airspace around Tapachula in an effort to slow the flow of Colombian cocaine being flown in from Central America. Usually the smuggling flights are accomplished with Cessna aircraft, which can fly low and fast, and land on short runways.

Alberto, suddenly without income, said he couldn't wait around for the skies to calm. He went back to his former life and started riding the rails again. It had been three years since he had last worked as a standard coyote, and back then Los Zetas didn't exist. When I met him he was guiding three Salvadorans north on The Beast.

He was passing himself off as a migrant and seemed to me to be doing it pretty well. He gave instructions to his clients as we were playing soccer, like he was just giving them game strategies. Nobody suspected him of anything.

"It's because if another coyote sees me, I'm fucked. I'm not paying the taxes of the road," he explained to me when we were alone.

I remember thinking he was crazy. If they found him they

weren't just going to reprimand him, or ask him to pay a fine. Los Zetas only educate with pain. A few months after talking with Alberto, I met a Guatemalan coyote who showed me his cigarette burns and the scar on his lower back where Los Zetas beat him nearly to the bone with a paddle.

Coyotes already live on the edge, and yet they push their luck, risking everything.

HELP ME

I tell Father Solalinde about El Chilango's predicament. He says there might be something we can do. But then El Chilango doesn't show up again. He told me he'd stop by, and yet at dusk there's still no sign of him. We sit down for dinner. Maybe tomorrow, I think.

We can hear the train starting up, whistling its departure for Medias Aguas. For the past hour the conductor has been backing into unhinged cars and securing them onto the rest of the train, and now it's finally time to leave. It's a small group today, only about forty migrants. They'll all be able to find a spot on the lower platforms, which means they'll get some sleep and will be relatively comfortable. They've each also just finished a bowl of chicken soup, so they won't be traveling on empty stomachs. The priest, the other volunteers, and I have sat down to eat, but before finishing the meal I get a call. It's El Chilango.

"What happened? I was waiting for you all afternoon," I say.

"I couldn't swing it. The shelter is hot. Just wanted to call you before I lose the signal. I'm gonna take off on this train."

"But what if they keep following you?"

"That's why I'm splitting. There are at least three Zeta spies hanging around the shelter. And I know they know I'm somewhere here. Now they're looking for me."

"And the Hondurans?"

"They're coming with."

"But you're putting them in danger."

"Gotta run, man, before I lose the signal. I'll call you from Medias Aguas to see if we can arrange you know what. They're following me. And you know who they are."

I can see it clearly: I've just spoken to a man with a death wish. El Chilango has written his own epitaph: here lies a coyote who was killed by coyotes.

At dawn the shelter is empty. No trains arrive in the night. I don't expect a call from El Chilango. If he really wanted even the slimmest chance for witness protection, he wouldn't have left. But maybe he does have a chance. Maybe he can make it to the United States with the Hondurans, get paid, and then stay put a while up north.

Around noon my phone rings. I answer and hear the din of a market. Voices, the sound of something dragging along the ground, white noise.

"Heeey…" I hear. It's just a whisper.

"Chilango?" I say. "Chilango?"

"Heeey … Help. They got me. We're here in … Hey. Help …"

The call ends. I dial the number. It rings but nobody picks up. I try again. Try ten more times, then finally get a recording telling me that there's no signal, that the number I've called is out of service.

For the next year after that encounter I ask my contacts about El Chilango. I ask about him in each of the shelters, all along the trail, asking coyotes, migrants, prostitutes. I describe him, his huge jaw, his thinning gray hair. But nobody has answers.

In November 2009 I make my last trip along the migrant routes. I travel to Ixtepec on top of a train from Medias Aguas, to see if the shelter and the surrounding area are still hot. I ask again about El Chilango. Nobody has seen him. I try his number again, just in case. It doesn't even ring. There isn't even a voice to tell me it's out of service. There's nothing but silence.

8

You Are Not Welcome in Tijuana: Baja California

Finally, far from Tijuana, after searching for the once classic north-ward passage, we come upon a place where we can cross without paying a narco tax, without confronting desert bandits, and without being surrounded by the Border Patrol. And yet what we find in this desolate place frightens us. We left walled Tijuana behind, we passed by Tecate, Tijuana's wayward child, and then we stumbled upon the deadly trails of the undocumented. And we began to understand that even a border this long doesn't have space enough for everyone, much less for those who are last in line.

"I come here at least twice a week," Epifanio tells me, not break-ing his melancholic gaze away from the tops of the tall San Diego buildings, which he can see through the bars. We're on the beach in Tijuana and Epifanio, a migrant originally from Oaxaca, has spent the last three months trying to get out of here. He wants to get over there, to the base of those San Diego buildings he can see in the distance. He wants to get with his family. Hugging the salt-corroded bars, he hardly has anything left to do but look. For to cross over, to walk a few hours up the beach ... and give a hug to his brothers, Epifanio has come about twelve years too late.

The changes began back in 1997, when they started build-ing this wall. Epifanio, still skinny even in his thirty-third year, could easily slip through these bars. Yet he doesn't risk it. While we silently watch the horizon, a child crosses over to retrieve a ball that was kicked over the wall. On the other side of the bars there are train rails buried vertically in the sand, the milky-coffee-colored surf of the ocean, and then the distant view of the city. It's a beautiful view. A view that Epifanio has come to see at least once a week since he's come north in his attempt to cross.

He's imagined it dozens of ways. Some are simple: slip through the bars and race all the way to San Diego. Others are more complicated: take a deep breath, jump in the water, and swim for it. Or jump on a horse and gallop. Or ride a scooter over the bumpy desert and look to meet up with the hordes of other migrants on their way north. But he never works up enough courage. And he never will. Not here.

On the top of the nearby hillock, from what used to be called Friendship Park, at least two US Border Patrol agents keep an eye on the beach around the clock. There are also cameras, aquatic sensors, and horseback agents with binoculars. A child can slip over and get a ball, no problem. But to walk even fifty feet into their country, not a chance.

Places to hop over, like Epifanio had been expecting, don't exist in Tijuana. They used to exist, but not anymore. There are photographs from the 1980s in which migrants scaling the fence are received by Border Patrol agents in Santa Claus outfits. The Santas were handing out gifts to the kids, letting the migrants pass. In one photograph you can see migrants in what was then known as Zapata Canyon. There was another photo of migrants on the US side, eating chicken's feet in the dining hall known as "The Illegal." They filled their bellies and then moved on, another forty-five minutes or so to San Diego. There was simply no wall back then. In the pictures, it seemed, everybody was smiling.

According to a photo study done at Tijuana's Colegio de la Frontera Norte, in which borderline mounted cameras snapped pictures every few minutes, around eighty persons an hour would pass through this area back in the 1980s.

"I'm going over tonight," Epifanio says, snapping back from his daydream. "I'm going to give it a shot outside of Tecate."

Epifanio has been here for three months, day-working as a bricklayer to make money and constantly on the hunt for the best spot to cross, asking around. Where is it safest? Where can you steer clear of bandits? Where do the drugs go over? Where can you avoid getting kidnapped by the narcos? Where is there a spot left with no wall, no robbers, and no narcos?

Nobody has been able to answer this last question. So tonight Epifanio is going to try to cross outside of Tecate, where there is indeed a wall, where there are indeed robbers, and where there are definitely narcos.

He's going to risk it because after having been gone from Oaxaca for three months, he's starting to understand frontier reality. How the wall and new security technologies have enveloped and overtaken this border in the past twelve years. How everybody who wants to cross or get something across (migrants, narcos, and bandits) have been funneled to the few areas left where there are no walls and it's not too far to run to a city or a highway on the US side. This means that many (migrants, narcos, and bandits) are crossing at the same points. It's a game of chance, this border. Sometimes you get lucky and sometimes you don't.

Tijuana is where the wall starts its 1,800-mile trip. This wall is crossed by Mexicans, Central Americans, South Americans, and even Chinese. From here to Ciudad Juárez there are nearly 400 miles of walls, bars, or vehicle barriers, that funnel these people into the deserts. In Tijuana is where the routes that lead to some of the most violent cities in the world begin. And everybody (at least every migrant) is asking this one question: where is it safe to cross? And the answer is: nowhere. The US government has made sure of that.

Epifanio, without a word, turns again to stare at the gray buildings in the distance. Then he exhales and pushes himself away from the bars.

"Yeah," he says. "Tonight. I got to get moving."

It's his farewell.

He goes up the ramp to the sidewalk that runs along the beach, but there he stops. As I start walking away, I see him sit down on a bench and turn to look back again over the wall. He doesn't seem to notice the hubbub of the family picnicking beside him. Maybe he just wanted to get away from me, calm his thoughts, think of another way to get over without having to cross outside of Tecate. It's a nice thought, but it's an illusion.

TIJUANA—THE WALLED CITY

With the wall always in view, always snaking alongside the highway and climbing up the hills and flashing out between buildings, you have the feeling like somebody is turning their back on you. That somebody doesn't want you around. The wall in these parts has two variants: a flat metallic fence, and a tall prison-like parade of parallel bars.

The shorter sections of the fence were constructed in late 1994 with scrap metal left over from the Gulf War. Broken tanks, downed helicopters, pieces of whatever material was blown to shreds while US missiles rained down on Saddam and his troops. It was in the new spirit of recycling: converting war trash into something useful, like a border fence.

These short fences are only about six feet tall, which means they're pretty easy to jump. The barrier was installed to mark the sea change of border politics, stating that this is where one country ends and the next begins. And we, the fence also says, are those who control what and who crosses over. It was meant to slow, not stop, the crossing of migrants and drug mules, and to signal a permanent end to the era of Santa Claus Border Patrol agents.

But by 1997 politicians started realizing that a merely symbolic fence wasn't effective: the symbol needed to be reinforced with reality and technology. That was when the modern wall was born. Fourteen miles of twelve-foot-high bars, between which not even the head of a child could slip. It was an actual obstacle this time, not just a symbol. They also built a concrete canal for the Border Patrol trucks to drive through, plus stadium lights and cameras that are always on the watch. And still—the symbol intact—they left the old Gulf War fence in place.

This is how the deadly funneling started. The number of migrants getting caught in the Tijuana–San Diego corridor plummeted: fewer migrants and fewer coyotes were crossing there. One look at that new wall, and everybody started heading east. In 1996 the Border Patrol apprehended almost half a million people in this corridor. In 1997 the figure halved, down to 283,889. A decade later the number dropped to 142,104.

And yet the wall which led to the plummeting number of apprehensions had a bit of irony mixed into its steel. In 2008 a US federal judge fined Golden State Fencing, the subcontracted company that built large parts of the fence, $4 million for employing undocumented Mexicans and Central Americans.

What was a wire fence in 1980 was a metal wall in 1994, and then in that same year, with the promulgation of Operation Gatekeeper and Operation Hold the Line, the US government added floodlights, high-visibility cameras, and underground sensors, and tripled the number of Border Patrol agents. In 1997 President Clinton ordered yet another stage of construction, adding more sophisticated technology and more miles to the urban segments in California, Arizona, and Texas. Operation Jump Start, signed by Bush in 2007, bumped the number of Border Patrol agents from 12,000 to 18,000. Now, in 2012, there are over 21,000.

The evening is starting to come on. A cool wind picks up. About thirty migrants enter the Scalabrini migrant shelter, wearing thick coats. They've all been working as day laborers: bricklayers, errand boys, general handymen. Most of them, now sitting and waiting for their bowl of food, are Mexican. Almost none of them are going to try to cross. They've all been recently deported from the United States. Many haven't been in their birth country for decades. Some of them barely even speak Spanish.

Father Luis Kendzierski, who runs the shelter, has been receiving and sending off migrants in Tijuana for nine years now. He describes the new situation: "For years Tijuana has been a city of deportees. Before, they used to come here to cross. Now they're trying to figure out how to get back to their homes in Mexico."

By *before* he means "before the wall." Now he's dealing with a patio full of down-and-outs—Mexicans lost in their own country. It's a sight familiar to many who work along the border.

"Those who are planning to cross," Kendzierski says, "go up to the hills on the outside of town, toward Tecate. That's where the bandits are, the *asaltapollos* [chicken-muggers]. Just last week they killed a migrant in the outskirts of Tecate. These are some of the areas where you simply can't cross without carrying drugs over. It's all that's left of these corridors. Ten years ago, this zone was a lot less fortified. Now migrants get pushed into the most dangerous areas."

The funneling has changed everything for the migrants.

"Before," Kendzierski continues, "about 30 percent of the people in the shelter were deportees, and the rest were on their way to cross. Now, about 90 percent are deportees. A short walk to the United States doesn't exist anymore. Because of the danger, and as Tijuana is farther from southern Mexico than other parts of the border, hardly any Central Americans still come this way."

It's partly an argument of distance. From the Suchiate River, which marks the southwesternmost stretch of the border between Mexico and Guatemala, it's over 3,000 miles to Tijuana. But although Tijuana is farther than other crossing points in Texas or even Arizona, a lot of Central Americans have family in Los Angeles, just a few hours north of San Diego. And San Diego and Tijuana are divided by just a few feet—a few feet and a wall—the two cities sharing what is known as the "kiss on the border."

The proximity of LA is why, despite the difficulties and danger, some migrants still insist on crossing in Tijuana. Of the nine border sectors designated by the Border Patrol, the San Diego sector is the smallest, a mere sixty miles. Yet it has the third highest number of agents, around 2,500, and from October 2007 to February 2008 the Border Patrol apprehended 54,709 undocumented migrants on their hike north from Tijuana. Only in the Tucson sector of Arizona, which has the highest number of agents, were more migrants caught.

Receiving apprehended migrants from other border sectors as well, Tijuana has also become a city of deportees. The Mexican National Institute of Migration (INM) calculates that about 900 persons are deported to the city every day. The US Department of Homeland Security deports migrants to Tijuana (in what is called lateral deportation) because it supposedly deters them from reattempting to cross by separating them from their coyotes and support groups. But deportations don't just break up *pollo* and *pollero*. Even families are divided: a mother sent to Nogales, a father to Tijuana, an uncle to Juárez. Central Americans are usually flown all the way back to their country, which often means they have to wait a lot longer (sometimes months) in detention centers to get flown out and eventually released.

Those who still insist on crossing in Tijuana have to pay the price. Some pay a minimum of $3,500 for false papers, hoping to walk through the port of entry and fool a border guard. If they succeed, they'll take about ten more steps and board the trolley straight to downtown San Diego. If they fail, they can face up to two years in prison.

The rest, those who can't afford $3,500 (the bulk of those who make the pilgrimage north), risk their skin in the desert. They head to the outskirts of Tecate, especially to La Rumorosa, crossing the new paths that were forged when Tijuana was fortified. Esmeralda Márquez, director of the Coalition for the Defense of the Migrant in Tijuana for the past ten years, explains that the search for routes farther and farther from Tijuana brings high risks: "There have been migrants killed because they crossed paths with the cartels."

This is where confrontations reminiscent of war zones tend to take place. Two trucks packed with heavily armed men drive up to the borderline and drop off their drug mules in zones where sheer physical geography makes it nearly impossible to build a wall. The Eagle's Nest, for example, a narrow plain between two rocky hills, has been the site of fierce gun battles between three competing cartels: the Tijuana, the Sinaloa, and the Gulf. This is where bullets start flying in every direction. And this is where a migrant sometimes gets caught in the crossfire.

As Márquez explained, these bullet-riddled migrants don't have anything to do with the cartels or with their business. And yet they die like narcos, not like migrants. And if one of them makes it through alive, after witnessing a gun battle, they rarely file a report to explain that their dead friend abandoned in the empty desert wasn't a drug mule or a hit man, but just an unlucky migrant trying to get back to his family. That's because they're scared to talk.

More than 600 people were killed in Tijuana (a city of 1.3 million) in 2008, when they happened to get caught in the midst of narco gun battles.

It's a city of desperate crossings. You have to be crazy to cross here, migrants say. And with the wall, the Border Patrol, and the narcos all impeding a safe crossing, they might be right.

THE DOMINO EFFECT

At dawn, the photographer Eduardo Soteras and I decide to head to Tecate and look for crossing points. We pass the Tijuana suburbs, rows and rows of identical houses drifting east, compressed between the border wall and the highway for forty miles. These residential plains have been leveled by machine, the mountains carved out for the city to take over. The urban spill ties metropolitan Tijuana to the much smaller city of Tecate, which has a mere 100,000 people.

There's little to see in downtown Tecate: stray pedestrians, fast-food chains, plus dozens of Chinese and sushi joints, remnants of Asian migration in the nineteenth century.

This is nothing like the small border towns I've gotten to know in Chihuahua and Sonora where migrants crowd into the small plazas, waiting for coyotes or buying backpacks and last-minute supplies at market stands. Nor is it like the border villages where, if you're not a migrant, the minute you set foot in town everybody knows and assumes that you're either a narco or completely out of your mind.

We park and walk up to the wall, the same type of metallic fence constructed out of war trash that we saw in Tijuana. The top of a Border Patrol tower of floodlights and cameras pokes over the top. We can also make out two all-terrain vehicles perched on a nearby hill. Trying to cross in urban Tecate is as futile as in Tijuana, practically a voluntary surrender to the Border Patrol. It was this impregnable wall that kicked off the search for new crossing corridors, funneling migrants into more and more remote areas.

Working at a nearby taco stand we find a man who had been involved in protecting migrants in Tecate for nine years. He is the only person we find who's willing to speak candidly about the connection between migrants and narcos. Joaquín (not his real name) has lived in Tecate for twenty-five years and has witnessed the shift of migrant and *pollero* routes from Tijuana to the outskirts of his city.

It's the *polleros*, he explains, who find the new routes. They're like alpinists scaling a mountain: when one route doesn't work, they look for another one. And they even dig holes along the paths, leaving markers for those who follow behind. Since 2000, the search for safe or passable crossing points has intensified among *polleros*. Dozens of new routes have opened up, but each of them has an expiration date. The longest-lasting openings now only function for about five years.

The closing of these routes by the Border Patrol coincided with the closing of other routes by the narcos. At the end of the 1990s, the major cartels split into rival groups that started an intense turf war for the cross-border drug routes. And then, after September 11, 2001 the US government charged the Border Patrol and ICE (Immigration and Customs Enforcement, formed in 2002) to detain undocumented persons as potential terrorists. And then with the ugly upsurge in the fight against the narcos by the Mexican government, in which drug traffickers were some-times classified as terrorists, migrants were left with little space to cross the border in safety. The funnel tightened, with narcos and migrants vying for the same spaces.

Especially on the US side, the deserts, hills, and even the cities were guarded and watched over like never before, affecting migrants more than traffickers since the latter could afford tech-nology to evade detection, or simply buy off officials. And so the narcos took over the coyote trails, forcing the coyotes to find new ways to run their business.

"Now," Joaquín tells me, "some of the coyotes around here, when they see that there's no way to cross, they ask for advance payment from their migrants and then leave them in the lurch. Or sometimes they do them even worse. They ask for 500 bucks, put them in the trunk of a car, drive them south to Ensenada (a beach town about forty miles south of Tijuana), let them out and say, 'Go, run for it, you're in the US now.'"

And this is only one of the risks. Here in Tecate, migrants tend to cross in a zone known as "the mountain." Outside of the Jardines del Río neighborhood and far from the city center, here is where the narcos run the show and the bandits like to charge their migrant tax.

And the bandits are good at tax collection.

"They carry massive weapons," Joaquín explains. "It's not hard to get a high-powered rifle hereabouts. Just swing up to Calexico on the US side [opposite Mexicali], and there are stores where you can buy whatever you want, anything from a pistol to an AK-47."

Getting the gun back down into Mexico is just as easy. All you need to do is step through a gate that looks more like the passage into a supermarket than into a country. Joaquín himself has been offered thousands of dollars to go over and buy weapons. Just two days ago, two men were arrested around "the mountain" carrying AR-15 assault rifles.

Shoot-outs are common in these parts. Yesterday, again not far from "the mountain," a pickup truck approached a gas station where a police cruiser and a Ford Taurus were parked. Inside the cars were federal policemen César Becerra and Ulises Rodríguez. Six assassins jumped out of the truck and fired forty-five rounds into the cars. Miraculously, both men survived.

"Everybody's corrupt here," Joaquín explains. "Migration, the police, and the narcos are all in bed together, which makes the migrant routes really hot. They have to walk four days across the desert and they're still in bandit territory. The narco traffic has its own routes: a straight shot nine miles up to the highway. From there it's easy. They've offered me bribes to get in on the game, but I don't accept. Most people do, though. It's hard to turn down a stack of bills," he says, a bitter smile on his face.

We walk a few blocks from the taco stand to the Grupo Beta office. Grupo Beta is a government-run migrant aid organization charged with providing food and protection to undocumented migrants in Mexico. At the office we explain our intentions: to get to "the mountain."

The two young Grupo Beta agents glance incredulously at each other.

"Look," one of them says, "just don't go to any crossing point. Don't go into the Jardines del Río neighborhood or the surrounding factories, and definitely don't go to La Rumorosa. It's swarming with bandits and narcos and they'll spot you immediately."

The agent goes on to explain that even they only make one trip a day through those parts, in the early morning, and they ride in their big, orange, easily identifiable pickup truck. He also mentions that they hardly ever see migrants. They've simply learned, he tells us, not to attempt a crossing in these areas.

~

We head out to Jardines del Río. It looks at first like any other poor neighborhood of Latin America. In these narco zones, though, you can feel the tension. You often can't see it, not on first glance, but you can feel it. It's the art of a narco lookout to keep watch without seeming to be keeping watch. A corrupt cop doesn't wear a gang sign around his neck, and a *sicario* (hired assassin) doesn't wear his gun on his hip. These narco-controlled neighborhoods are calm, and seem calm—until they're not, and then they explode. If you don't witness a shoot-out it's hard to see at first glance that the neighborhood is run by the narcos.

On a side street in Jardines del Río, there's a migrant shelter that has been run by five nuns for the past twelve years. The sisters, understandably, don't want to comment on narcos, bandits, or the dangers that migrants face. Once in the shelter I see Vicente and Verónica, both Salvadoran, as well as Mainor, a Guatemalan. I first met them in the migrant shelter in Ixtepec. It seems miraculous to see them again on the complete other side of the country.

These three were fleeing the uncertainties of the road, hoping to find in Tecate, as they had been told, a safe spot to cross. Or at least a safe spot to lie low, while staying within driving distance from their families in Los Angeles. They'd recently picked up on a rumor, one of the many pieces of unreliable advice that passes from mouth to mouth on the tops of the migrant train. Old hopes or securities that change or fizzle as quickly as they are passed on. What they didn't know was that the same dangers and uncertainties of the road that they were fleeing still lay ahead of them.

"They told us it was easy to cross there," Verónica says, referring to the zone between Tijuana and Tecate. "But after only a day we started to see signs of narcos and bandits. So we asked around again and heard that there was at least one spot left that's safe, a hill called El Centinela." And that, a few days previously, is where they had gone.

From El Centinela [the Sentinel], with a compass pointing to Los Angeles, they started walking northwest, looking for the fabled hole in the border. They crossed La Rumorosa, but its bald rocks gave no hint of whether the route was free of narcos or not. Then the cold started working into their bones. At dawn they reached a small village that was covered in snow. None of them had anything warmer than a light spring sweater. There wasn't anything they could do. They knew they'd die if they set off into the desert. And so they turned around and came back to the shelter in Tecate.

"What about you?" Verónica asks us. "What do you know about crossing around here?"

We have nothing but bad news to deliver. For the third time, after traveling twenty-five days on the top of a train to this border, she realizes that she can't get across. And yet she tells us she'll keep looking for a way to get to Los Angeles. First she'll head back to Tijuana, to see if some relatives can help her there.

Tecate seems to offer little more than a dead end for migrants. There's not even a hole in the fence anymore. Crossing here is a kamikaze mission.

Despite all advice to the contrary, we decide to follow the route Véronica, Vicente, and Mainor had taken a few days earlier, to La Rumorosa.

THE HAMLETS THAT SCARE EVEN SOLDIERS

The highway snakes through the rocky hills in this vast, open desert. Only the Gran Desierto of Sonora and Arizona is as large. The hills here reach as high as 6,500 feet above sea level. And the huge cold rocks that cover them resemble Olmec heads, as though fallen in some long-past Biblical rain. These hills form into chains that stretch beyond the horizon. In the middle of this desolate landscape lies the small truck-stop town, La Rumorosa. It's a town of little more than gas stations, twenty four-hour restaurants, small cafés, and vacant lots where long-haul truckers like to pull off the road and doze.

La Rumorosa has a population of about 2,000, not

counting plenty of snakes, scorpions, and coyotes. This is where the Tijuana wall has been pushing migrants and human coyotes since 1997.

Here there's only one person who can talk about migration, the narcos, the holes in the border, even the bandits. It's Brother Pablo, a lay member of the Franciscan Aid Workers, in charge of a senior citizen shelter that recently started housing migrants. He is forty-some years old, but has the look of a man who's lived a long time in the desert.

A dirt road cuts through the rocky desert to the shelter. We introduce ourselves and explain our project to Pablo.

"It would be best if you waited for me. It's not a good idea to travel alone through these hills. There's the Jacumé ranch that's full of narcos. La Rosita and Chula Vista, if you make it there, make sure not to stop. That is, if anyone even looks at you, you better get moving. Microondas [Microwave], another town, don't even think about it. But if I go with you, and we go in the truck that has the shelter's logo, it'd be a lot safer."

Nobody seems to have anything good to say about La Rumorosa. We hear about a car chase the previous day in which the federal police arrested two men: José Gómez, a fat twenty-year-old with a shaved head, and Jimmy Bracamontes, a thirty-year-old with a goatee. They were both accused of being *asaltamigrantes* [migrant-muggers]. The police found a forty-caliber pistol and nine transistor radios with their chargers. Bandits in these parts seem to be well-equipped.

We wait a few days at the shelter with Pablo and some old men and women who are either abandoned or without a family. The rooms seem filled with sadness. The old people sit on the couches, staring blankly, apparently doing nothing but awaiting their coming deaths.

Finally we head out with Pablo, his brother, wife, and sister-in-law to the crossing points outside of La Rumorosa. Pablo says it's unwise to travel in a truck full of only men: the women will make us look less threatening. We enter into the desolate hills, approaching the border. A rattlesnake lifts its head as we pass. Next we spot a coyote, the animal, not the guide.

We arrive in Chula Vista, nothing but dirt and rock all the way to the border. The wall here is the same material and the same height as the wall in Tijuana. We're close enough to the big border city that the US government realized pretty quickly, after constructing the Tijuana segments, that migrants started crossing here. They sent their reinforcements: Border Patrol agents and construction crews.

The land, though, besides the wall, is completely empty. It's like a ghost town. When we approach the wall we see a few holes where someone tried to get through. Though if you even pop your head into the United States on this stretch the cameras spot you, and in about five minutes you hear the roar of Border Patrol's off-road vehicles.

Pablo's brother tells us a little about his own experience along this border: "I used to be a distributor for the little shops around here, but then the place filled up with bandits. They took over the stores, the streets, everything. I don't think we'll be seeing many more migrants passing through here."

We drive on toward another little settlement, Jacumé, amounting to a few houses clustered around a crossroads, but the feeling is that everybody has escaped. We don't see a single person in the streets. It's four in the afternoon and not even one child is playing outside, nor is a single store open.

We continue on toward this part of the wall and we see a Mexican military Humvee approach as if coming straight from the Iraq war. The vehicle is armored, topped with a submachine gun, and driven by a man wearing a balaclava and a helmet. The Humvee stops and six soldiers, all with bulletproof vests, jump out yelling: "Out! Out of the truck! This is a checkpoint!"

Eduardo Soteras and I step out of the truck with our hands in the air. The soldiers look nervous (and I wonder if the safeties of their machine guns are flipped off). The soldiers move all four of us men away from the truck before giving us a chance to take out our papers, which are in the truck, so they push us back to fetch them. They check them through and listen to what sounds like an unlikely explanation, that we're journalists and that Pablo is in charge of a senior citizen shelter where his brother occasionally helps him out.

"And what are you doing here?"

"We're going to see the wall at Jacumé," I answer.

"You're going to the wall at Jacumé?"

"Yeah, that's it. We just want to see where migrants are crossing."

"You're nuts. Migrants don't cross here. Even we don't go to the wall at Jacumé, not unless we want to get shot. It's narco territory. You can't even set foot there. I'm going to have to ask you to leave, for your own safety."

We're only 200 yards from the wall. Yet we can't go forward. It's incredible to see firsthand this explicit understanding between the narcos and the army. You can patrol here, the narcos say, but if you venture a foot over this line you're going to have a problem.

"That's fine," Pablo's brother says to us, "Let's go to Microondas. It's where more migrants are passing now, anyway. And there's less narcos there."

We finally come to a crossing point that's not swarming with bandits and narcos. Here in Microondas is the first area since leaving Tijuana where the biggest risk to a migrant is the weather, not other humans. From the road we're on we can even make out the faraway line of Interstate 8, the highway that runs along the border in Southern California. Most of the migrants are headed there, to meet up with their coyote-coordinated rides.

But after a while the road we're on veers away from the wall. We bump along, climb a hill, and then the road is impassable. We have a view, however, of the rocks and radio towers of La Rumorosa.

"Let's continue on foot," Pablo's brother says.

We get out and start scrambling up, rock by rock, climbing the steep pass.

"We've actually had to come here a few times to rescue migrants," Pablo's brother tells us. "They've had broken bones or gotten sick. It takes us at least six hours to get here."

The view from the summit is shocking. We see rocky peak after rocky peak trailing into the distance. We can even see, beyond more outcrops, the shadow of I-8 again. This is the only land that the narcos and bandits have left for migrants to cross in peace. This is where Tijuana spits out its unwelcomed travelers.

Rock after rock. Hill after hill these men and women have to cross. And then they have to navigate the dangers of getting caught along the distant highway. This is the first clear crossing point we've come upon, and we realize that it's just as dangerous for migrants as crossing through a narco zone. It's not a human hand here that kills the migrants, but the system that pushes them to walk this far.

Yes, there are other crossing points, other options equally as dangerous. Pablo points to the distant desert of Mexicali, the hill outside of El Centinela, or the white, salty expanse of stony desert known as La Salada.

9

The Funnel Effect: Baja California and Sonora

In this second phase of our trek across the northern border we leave behind the big cities, Tijuana and Juárez, that monopolize newspaper headlines. We travel through little-known towns like La Nariz, Sonoíta, Algodones, and Sásabe. Everyone in these towns—bandits, narcos, and migrants—struggles to carve a niche for themselves. A lot of them, we find, spend their time either assaulting or trying to escape being assaulted. Some give orders and others give in, and the migrants, as is almost always the case, carry the heaviest burden.

The military checkpoint is on the outskirts of La Rumorosa, in front of the hill known as El Centinela. In thick red letters a sign reminds the thirty soldiers who run the checkpoint: "Caution, mistrust, reaction." We ask the officer surveying our car to explain how the words are put into practice. "Be alert," he says, "even when you're asleep. Never trust anything that moves. And the thing about reaction, you get it, right ..." Then he makes as if picking up a gun, finishing his sentence with: "*Raca-taca-taca-taca-taca!*"

This checkpoint is the door that leads out of the easternmost tip of Tijuana and into the coyotes' backyard. This route, popularized at the end of the 1990s when the wall went up, is now the one most heavily trafficked by migrants. It's also the most heavily trafficked by narcos. That's why being alert, suspicious, and quick to react are smart commandments to live by for anyone walking this 400-mile-long stretch of border. Because it's not uncommon to hear that *Raca-taca-taca*. This is the "small-town border," away from Tijuana's wall and the checkpoints, the border of drug smuggling and bandits, the border that took the place of the "old border."

It's six thirty in the evening when we leave the checkpoint behind, turn left off the main highway, and duck onto a back road that leads straight to the border. The wind has turned from a whispering rumor to abrasive gusts of sand and dry leaves that feel powerful enough to blast our car into the sky. We're parked at the bottom of El Centinela, waiting for someone to walk by. Migrants, coyotes, narcos. Anyone.

To get here we had to drive forty minutes, leave the sprawling city of Mexicali and head north on a two-lane road that dies at the so-called "Normandy Wall" which stands only ten yards from us. The wall is made up of a series of three metal bars that look something like giant asterisks half buried in the sand. The vehicle barriers block cars from crossing, but can't stop a pedestrian willing to jump.

No one is around.

Back in Mexicali, Jorge Verdugo, manager of the traveler's hostel, Betania, explained the funnel effect to us. "This is the only crossing area left around here, the only one that's used anymore. The problem is that narcos also use it to cross their stuff." At this juncture in our travels, his line sounds trite. Over and over, the formula repeats itself: a crossing point on the outskirts of a city that will be heavily used by narcos, coyotes, bandits, and migrants alike.

Eduardo Soteras, one of the photographers in my team, takes a few pictures at the wall. When he comes back we walk over to the only three people in sight, three private guards standing outside a power station.

"Good evening, agents."

"Evening," the eldest responds. He looks apprehensive. He comes toward us as the other two stand back, eyeing our car.

"We're journalists and we're wondering ..."

"Come on over here," the agent says and turns to his coworkers, "I told you they weren't coyotes."

"No, we were just checking out the area. We were told this is one of those crossing points."

"That's right. They hurl themselves over here."

"Drugs too."

"That's right."

"But we haven't seen anyone since we got here."

"Well, you never know. All of a sudden people start coming and keep streaming across till morning. Sometimes trucks too. They park where you two were and five, ten people come out each truck. Then off they go."

"Just like that?"

"Just like that. Sometimes, like last week, if it's drugs, they send people to watch over the area beforehand, just like you guys. That's what we thought you guys were up to. They watch out to make sure no one is loitering around here, no migrants, no officials. And they check out the other side, too, with binoculars, to see if they can spot Migration. That's what we thought your buddy was up to when he went up to the wall."

After a while the other two guards come up to the car and join the conversation. We ask them about the third factor—bandits. We want to know if it's the same here, if everyone works on the same tiny piece of dirt, the mouth of the funnel. Some trying to cross, others robbing the crossers, and yet others telling the crossers when they have to clear out so that things won't look so conspicuous when they have drug loads to sneak over.

"They used to gather here, just over there," the youngest-looking guard says, pointing out a small grassy plot of land on this side of the wall. "Coyotes, their migrants, and bandits, all of them used to mix here. The bandits would be listening in, trying to find out where the coyotes were heading so they could follow them."

Behind us, about forty minutes by car, is Mexicali, its million inhabitants and its more than 200 Chinese restaurants. The

Chinese population in town is a consequence of the 1882 Chinese Exclusion Act, which was upheld by the US Supreme Court until 1904, and barred Chinese immigrants from entering the United States until its repeal in 1943. Behind us are cotton fields, worked by thousands of Mexicans who come from the southern regions of the country. But that's behind us. Here in this crossing zone, as happens in so many places far from Tijuana, there is only the dried-up desert funnel where everyone who can't legally get into the United States tries to cross. Here at El Centinela, it can be as hot as 122 degrees Fahrenheit in the summer, and as cold as minus five degrees in the winter. We're also relatively close to Los Angeles, where so many migrants are going. And all those factors have driven up the price of a coyote for a two-day walk to more than $2,000 for each attempted crossing, and that's with no guarantees.

"Many times it's the coyotes themselves who assault the migrants just a few feet across the line, or sometimes they're the ones who lead them to the narcos, who then force them into drug smuggling," is what Jorge Verdugo of the migrant shelter told us hours before. That's how it's been since the mid 1990s, when metal walls took the place of barbed wire.

This is where the bra tree myth was born. It's a desert tree literally draped with the bras and panties of migrant women who are raped by bandits along this border. Their underwear is kept as trophies. I refer to it as a myth not because it doesn't exist, but because it's not one tree but many. The rape of migrant women is a border-wide practice, from Tecate, passing La Rumorosa and El Centinela, to the neighboring state of Sonora. On this stretch of walled-off frontier, bra trees grow everywhere.

A volunteer at the migrant shelter in Tijuana gave testimony, the only personal account I've listened to so far, of a twenty-four-year-old Mexican woman's experience getting raped and having her underwear stolen in the desert. This is part of Sandra's story:

"I got to Sonora in August 2006 and started crossing the border to California. I rode in a truck with five other women, one who was thirteen years old, plus six men. We rode for hours, both by highway and unpaved roads. Then we walked for a long time until we got to a place where we saw a barbed-wire gate with a sign that read: 'No Entry.' From there we kept walking. I noticed a pair of black panties hanging from the gate on the Mexican side. As we went on we heard a whistle come from a group of men in the distance, squatting in some shrubs, then some others from another spot answered back with more whistles. It was daytime. Our coyote said: 'You know what, gals? There are bandits here.'

"He warned us not to resist, that if they asked for money we should give it up and that to save our lives we, as women, should cooperate in whatever they asked. We were in some shrubs and a group of armed men came up with their faces uncovered, they told us to give them money. They told us to take off our clothes. They sexually abused us. It's a sad thing. One woman was brutally raped. We couldn't help. They finished and we put on our clothes, but our underwear was thrown away, one woman's underwear was thrown over a bush. I don't know why, maybe it means something to them. All this happened on the Mexican side, and after that tragedy we just kept on walking."

DEATH OF AN OFFICER

For twenty miles, we drive next to sheets of soldered steel. As far as you can see, this rust-colored wall snakes up and down along the horizon. But then we pass Mexicali and, entering into San Luis Río Colorado, the parched scenery changes.

On the US side of the metal sheets the land starts turning green, starts looking more fertile. The border here isn't marked by a wall. There are nothing but vehicle barriers. You can see shoots of alfalfa and wheat growing in the US fields, which are all quadrangular and easily differentiated by their colors, brown or green.

The splashes of green, however, soon give way again to the desolate open desert. We approach what seem endless sand dunes.

This is one of the new crossing areas. Many migrants are currently crossing here, funneled outside of a little town called Algodones, though I doubt this point of entry will last long because of a recent death in the area

Of all the border towns I've seen, Algodones is by far the most friendly looking. The single-story houses are colorfully painted and have large front windows, and despite the town's proximity to the border, there aren't fences closing everything in. I even spot a few kitchen gardens, and rocking chairs placed on porches for residents to while away their afternoons. American retirees like to visit and sometimes even settle here, stretching their pensions a little farther than would be possible on the US side.

Algodones is on the Baja California side of the Baja–Sonora state line, abutting Yuma, Arizona, across the border. If you have the good luck to be able to cross legally, you can reach downtown Yuma from Algodones in twenty minutes. About forty dentists, ophthalmologists, podiatrists, and other doctors have set up shop in Algodones, to reap the profits of Americans looking to get cheap medical care. One American we meet tells us that "people like me, fifty-seven years old and without insurance, we can't afford to pay the bills back home."

On any weekend afternoon, on any day like today, dozens of young American couples flock to Algodones to eat tortilla soup or a few tacos, which are a lot cheaper than on the Yuma side of the line. Others head to the pharmacies to buy their pills, or even to the gas stations to get the cheaper state-subsidized gas. At night, however, stomachs and shopping bags full, most Americans return to their country.

A tall twenty-mile wall cutting through the city reminds those on this side of the border that a weekend afternoon shopping spree in the United States isn't possible. There are always at least four Border Patrol vehicles and numerous floodlights at the ready to catch any undocumented crosser.

To try to get more information about migrant crossings, I call the young priest, Father Ernesto, who runs a small church in

Algodones. I meet him in the middle of the afternoon, and I can see immediately that he's in a hurry. He changes from his sweat-stained lay clothes into his vestments, hurriedly preparing to give the three remaining masses of the day.

"Look," he says, "it's rare these days that you see any migrants around town. Sometimes you see them begging for food, but usually their coyotes herd them out toward the dunes. Things are too heavy here. There are even helicopters patrolling these days. What changed everything, what cut off the migrant flow, is that about a year ago some narcos killed a Border Patrol agent. That's when they locked down the border. Now nobody passes through."

The deceased agent was a thirty-one-year old Mexican American named Luis Aguilar. He was killed on January 19, 2008, at around nine thirty in the morning. A suspicious brown Hummer observed crossing into the United States was being chased by Border Patrol vehicles. Luis Aguilar was laying down a tack sheet to pierce the Hummer's tires when he was hit by the oncoming vehicle. Mexican authorities claimed that coyotes, not narcos, were driving the Hummer. The Border Patrol insisted it was loaded with marijuana, but, as the vehicle escaped back to Mexico, nobody was able to prove anything. Drug traffickers are careful to destroy any potential evidence. The Hummer was later found completely burned.

The following February the Mexican federal police detained a twenty-two-year old man, Jesús Navarro, in Ciudad Obregón. Jesús had been a coyote since he was sixteen years old. When he confessed to being the driver of the Hummer that killed Aguilar, he claimed to be carrying drugs that day, not migrants. Through his testimony agents discovered two houses where Jesús's bosses supposedly lived. In the subsequent raid they found false visas, high-quality printers (to make the visas), ammunition, and drugs. The group was obviously working to transport both drugs and people across the border. It was further proof that the two businesses have merged. Organized crime will try to make money however it can, smuggling whatever can be smuggled, whether drugs or people.

Later on I spoke with the Border Patrol press officer of the sector, Esmeralda Marroquín, who is of Mexican descent. After Aguilar's death, she said, they applied to Washington for reinforcements. Before that, this sector was one of the least patrolled of the border. "We had to respond vigorously," she explained, "to show that we were going to be tough on these kinds of crimes. It's one thing to smuggle drugs across the border. It's quite another to kill a US agent."

And so they were sent two new helicopters, ten off-road vehicles, plus some thirty extra officers. Coyotes soon learned to avoid the area. If that Hummer had missed Aguilar, Algodones would have been a very different place today.

An agent dies, and the FBI comes screaming in. It's quite another thing when a migrant dies. On April 28, just outside of Mexicali, two migrants died and eighteen were injured as Border Patrol agents chased them. The nineteen-year-old coyote, Héctor Maldonado, trying to outdrive three BP vehicles, flipped his Chevrolet Suburban. Despite the crash and his injured passengers, Maldonado tried frantically to escape, stealing a Border Patrol vehicle while the driver was attending the victims, and speeding back into Mexico. He was eventually caught by the Mexicali police. When he was presented to the press, his face was completely swollen from the blows they'd dealt him.

But then there was almost no follow-up. The two dead were undocumented. They became an anecdote, nothing more. Nobody called Washington. Nobody called the FBI. Nobody raided any house for more information, and no reinforcements came.

So what's left for the migrants—bottlenecked into the desert—are the dunes. Crossing within city limits is like walking straight into Border Patrol custody. Nobody bothers to try anymore. Instead of the quick jog into Yuma, migrants now have to walk as much as three days across the desert. And the desert doesn't just mean risking heatstroke and dehydration. It also means crossing paths with the narcos.

This is what's come of the funneling: those carrying a change of clothes and the hope to find work now have to walk the same paths as those smuggling guns and drugs.

THE GREAT FUNNEL

When we leave Algodones, the metal wall reappears. Metal plate against metal plate. We'll see it go on like this for the next fifteen miles, until the man-made line gains distance from the highway, as we drive into the open vastness of the Great Altar Desert.

These 714,556 hectares without horizon are considered one of the most inhospitable and arid areas of the world. A desert of brown rock and hard limestone pocked with jutting silhouettes of cacti, loose sand dunes, and a large volcanic reservoir, El Pinacate. It's a wonder that once upon a time someone with a native eye was able to qualify and differentiate these seemingly faceless natural landmarks, naming one hill El Alacrán (The Scorpion), another Cactus Blanco (White Cactus).

We reach Sonoíta, the western entry point into Sonora, a state that in the last few years has become a major crossing zone for migrants. Because of its small collection of suburb-like towns sparsely spread out along the border, the area is now also a smuggling corridor for narcos. Nogales is the only big city nearby. This rural scene is the perfect environment for the narcos, who don't have to negotiate with high-level authorities and can instead focus on buying rural sheriffs and municipal police. There aren't many big cities or police squads on the US side of Sonora either. Lukeville, for example, is a tiny border town with a population of one hundred (seventy of whom are of Latin American descent), and with nothing in its downtown but a gas station.

Authorities of the Mexican justice system are known to call the stretch of border between Sonora and Arizona "The Golden Gate." Between the desert and the so-called Golden Triangle—an area of high drug production, just southeast of Sonora—lies the money-laden paradise of drug smuggling. Most of the narco-tunnels that have been uncovered along the US–Mexico border have been in the seventy-two municipalities of this area.

Little by little, however, military barracks have been put up beside these towns. A couple of weeks ago a military unit took three days to burn two tons of marijuana seized at a ranch. The air of Sonoíta reeked.

Father David receives us in his parish. We need to ask him for help in getting to La Nariz, which is an hour away from this city, with a population of 10,000. "Sure," he says. "It's better to go with someone you know, because narco hawks are always there, watching from the hills. And as soon as you get to La Nariz, right at the entrance of the town, go to the little store and ask for Doña Baubelia. Tell her you're there on my behalf, and that you need to be put in contact with Pancho Fajardo. He has all my trust and is an honest man. Just make sure not to miss your turn, and go directly to La Nariz. If you miss the right turn and still try to walk into town, you'll be in for it."

But directions like *straight ahead*, *right*, or *left* are of no use on this dirt road. It's pure desert, and choosing a route means trying your luck. We end up taking a wrong turn and find ourselves in the calm emptiness of the narco desert. There are just a couple of signs in sight, pointing to some ranches lost in the nothing of the desert scrub. Not one living thing. Nothing but silence and desolation. The complete emptiness is how we realize that we've picked the wrong path. We turn around.

Doña Baubelia eyes us suspiciously when she receives us. Her sons are known coyotes, and she doesn't like journalists. But soon Pancho Fajardo shows up. He'd been working on his tractor. Hearty, sixty-one years old, and with a leathery complexion, Pancho is the stereotype of a rancher. He's lived over half his life in this suburb of thirty houses, built in 1979 thanks to a growing market for wheat and alfalfa. But those were other times. Now most residents live off migrants. Most, as they say here—a sort of nod to the obvious—live off "who knows what," or "best not to ask." And a minority, like Pancho, live off their cows.

"I'll show you guys the area. Everyone knows me here, and they know I don't mess with anyone, that's why the *mafiosos* don't touch me. I just hope no one sees you guys alone and gets to thinking you're deep into something else."

That "something else" can lead to a particular and horrifying situation. Four months ago, the body of Pancho's nephew-in-law was found a few yards from his ranch. The body had five nine-millimeter impacts. One of them right between the eyes. He was "deep into something else."

We pass by a suburb called División del Norte, where five military personnel play football in a store and a group of migrants sit waiting for nightfall, when they'll make for the border line.

We walk into the desert.

"I'm going to take you to the military's hiding spot," Pancho explains. "It's close to one of the military offices right next to the line." He knows the place like the palm of his hand because of the rounds he makes on his pickup, keeping an eye on his thirty-five cows as they graze on desert shrub.

We pass two slumping, battered homes in the middle of the desert, surrounded by nothing. There's no grass, no water, no roads.

"Those two houses were dismantled by the military a couple of months ago," Pancho says. "Used as a hiding spot for *clavos* [drugs] before the loads were smuggled across. One of them was the home of a relative of mine, until a man who wasn't from here came and bought it. Not much later they found the house filled with drugs."

Such houses are deliberately scouted out by criminals because they are in the middle of nowhere, far from any military. Migrants, at least those who know, walk as close as they can to a military unit, so as to avoid invading the mafia's turf.

Pancho turns out to be an excellent guide. Some 300 yards from the military office, without saying anything, he climbs down from his pickup and walks into the scrub. In a couple of moments we hear his hoarse voice: "Good afternoon, gentlemen."

Hidden among the thorny bushes, huddled in a bunker of dried branches, there's a group of four Mexican men and one Guatemalan woman. They've been there two days, they say, waiting for their moment.

A forty-year-old man, making his second attempt, explains: "One group left early today. The groups make sure to leave one by one. We're giving them their space before we head out."

The greatest obstacle here is not the border wall, which is only good for stopping vehicles, but the narcos and bandits hidden on the American side, near Organ Pipe Cactus National Monument.

This desert, it seems, is too big to be corralled. There are about 370 miles of border that still have unmonitored breaks, allowing narcos and migrants through. Areas that by the same token—not a person or a town in sight—imply a treacherous walk for the migrants. At a good pace, one has to walk seven nights to get to Tucson. That's what the wall has left us.

One of the sheriff patrol squads is in charge of keeping an eye on the US side of the border. On that side we see a coyote (the animal, not the person) terrorizing a herd of donkeys only a few yards from the spot where the migrants are bunkered down.

Pancho later invites us to a meal of beans and coffee at his house. A rancher from División del Norte stops by for a visit and gets started on the current situation. Pancho had been reserved, but his friend speaks with resounding anger.

"We used to live comfortably here," he complains. "Only familiar cars with familiar people drove around here. Now it's big trucks that pass by at night and nobody knows who's driving them. Migrants used to cross in peace, without having to mess with anyone. Now that the mafia's trying to move their drugs, the migrants come back all beaten up. They hit them with base-ball bats to make sure they don't take over their turf or heat it up or anything, attracting migration officers. Or the mafias get hold of any bandits working against them and break their legs. The narcos have even started warning taxi and bus drivers not to bring any *pollos* this way whenever they have an important load to cross."

Night falls in Sonoíta and we find ourselves drinking beer with two Oaxacan coyotes who are guiding a group of five migrants. They've decided not to take their first-choice road through Altar, which is some miles to the west.

"The mafia is charging too much: 700 pesos a head just to let you walk up to the line. It's not like they don't charge over here, but it's 500 and there's a lot more room," explains the leader, who's young and very small, with tight, clear skin.

Tomorrow they'll pay what they have to pay. They'll pass La Nariz and they'll walk close to one of the military units and they'll go on, so the coyote guesses, for six nights until they reach the Tohono O'odham Indian Reservation, where they'll be charged another $3,000 to be piled into a van and driven an hour away to Phoenix.

"We would've walked less through Altar, but things are too hot over there. It's not like there isn't mafia here, it's everywhere, it's just that there's more of it over there."

Morning breaks and we walk toward Altar.

THE CRABWALK VILLAGE

I've visited Altar five times now, and each time I think that things couldn't get worse. And each time I've been wrong.

The migrants don't have much of a choice. If they're in Altar it usually means that they've backtracked to Altar, that they've been pushed here by the narcos, that they've had to turn back. They've had to crabwalk. This used to be a village where you could get a cheap ride, where you could start your walk to the United States in peace, on an easy road to the border. There wasn't even a wall, and there weren't narco taxes. The open desert was wide enough for everybody who wanted to walk. Now migrants seem to wait around in Altar for nothing more than bad news.

We talk with Paulino Medina, a taxi driver who has lived here for the past twenty years.

"It's all gone to shit! All to shit! They just upped the price again. Now it's 700 pesos a head to get to El Sásabe. They're saying they need more because the peso fell, or maybe the dollar rose."

When I was last here, six months ago, the price was only 500 pesos a head and Paulino was busy hunting for migrants to take to the border town, El Sásabe. Now he doesn't bother. He only does service between Altar and Caborca, which is a small migrant launching town about a half an hour west.

After strolling around for a few minutes I run into Eliázar, who I know from my first visit here in 2007. Back then Eliázar worked as something like a coyote agent, receiving $200 for each migrant he could convince to join up with the coyote he was working for. But now he too is having to adjust to the new laws of the town. He recently went back to his home state of Sinaloa to ask for official permission to work the main square. In Sinaloa he had to convince his boss to pay off Minerva,[1] the municipal policeman in charge of collecting bribes from the coyotes. Minerva then grants permission for the agents and coyotes to work. He also provides security to make sure nobody who hasn't paid is herding migrants. Minerva charges $150 dollars a week for each coyote-agent to work. There are fourteen of them. This works out to $260 dollars a month in bribes for the eight municipal policemen, and that's on top of their official salaries.

Eliázar receives a call as he explains the new setup. When he gets off the phone he says everything's in order. The plaza is, for the next few hours, his to work.

---

1   Minerva is the officer's code name. All municipal and federal officials work under a code name.

"I gotta run," he says. "I don't get twenty-four hours to work like before. Now we have to take shifts. Six in the morning to six at night. Then the night shift takes over."

The plaza is the best place to swindle migrants. One classic stunt is to sell a migrant's information to the people who work in the "call centers." Coyote agents, who are typically pretty chatty guys, like to squeeze names, numbers, destinations in the United States, and any other info they can out of migrants. They listen in, build up trust, redial phone numbers, whatever it takes. The call centers pay 1,000 pesos for a family member's phone number. They call migrants' families and tell them their loved one has been kidnapped, and is going to be beaten or killed unless they wire 5,000 pesos through Western Union.

It's a cutthroat money game here. There are no sales and no special offers. It's like the whole town and all the crossing zones are being taken over by parasites, by anybody who can leech off the system. The whole package to cross costs $2,400 and includes a grueling seven-night walk across the desert. If the migrant is a Central American, the coyotes charge an extra $600, just because they can: because in Mexico most Central Americans have nowhere to go but north. On top of this each migrant has to pay the seventy-dollar narco tax once they get over the line. There's usually another tariff as well—one hundred dollars for the marijuana farmer or cattle rancher who lets the groups cross through their land.

In the morning we have a meeting set up with Grupo Beta. It's in El Sásabe, which, as Paulino tells us, might be a problem. Our car has plates from Tijuana, and El Sásabe is run by the Sinaloa Cartel whose lookouts (hawks, as they're called) don't like to see unfamiliar faces coming from Tijuana, faces that could mean the Tijuana Cartel is making inroads.

We make a call to a friend, Father Prisciliano Peraza, to see if he can clear the way for us, if he can tell the right people that we're journalists interested in migrants and not narcos, and that we don't want to make moves on anybody's territory. He responds to our plea: "Okay, okay. Let me see what I can do."

Everybody has the number of the head boss here. You have to call him to let him know you're coming to town, or a new group of migrants is passing through, or something unusual is happening. Even the priest has the number, but that doesn't necessarily mean that he's in the game. It just means that he follows the rules of Altar. In other words, everybody follows the rules of Altar.

Driving by the gas station on the road leading to El Sásabe, we realize we'll be fine when the young attendant steps out and signals us to stop. "You guys are the reporters, right?" he says, before we've opened our mouths. "Going to El Sásabe to write about the migrants? Just make sure to take the turnoff at Sáric, it's smoother than the dirt road."

He is the first of many lookouts. We're being watched, we know, and we're also being covered. The narcos know who we are and are giving us instructions, telling us to play by their rules. "Take the road to Sáric," they tell us. "Twenty-nine miles on the pavement and thirteen on the dirt."

Our hope is to find out from the Grupo Beta how effectively they practice "the protection of migrants" in a zone completely run by narcos. Once we arrive, it doesn't takes us long to learn the answer.

The normal turnover rate for Grupo Beta officers here is one month. That's because nobody wants to bring his or her family to this place, and nobody wants to stay. When the commander (who prefers to remain anonymous) ends his shift at six in the evening, he explains how they work here.

"We seal ourselves in. We don't even leave the office to go out to the store. It's super dangerous. The smartest thing is just to keep a low profile."

We try to negotiate with the commander to get a quick tour of the crossing zones, but he says no and won't budge. The best he'll offer is to show us La Pista, an out-of-the-way crossing point hardly used these days, or so he tells us. We want, however, to get a look inside the funnel, to see the intermixing of drugs and migrants, to get to La Sierrita, El Chango, or La Ladrillera, but his response is firm.

"They don't let us work around there."

"Who doesn't let you work?" I ask.

"You know very well who. Pretty much everyone's in the business here."

The commander says that the narcos don't let them work in El Tortugo anymore either. It was there they used to stop trucks, count migrants, and warn them of the dangers of the desert: the climate and the animals. It was the Good Samaritan work of Grupo Beta. But then they were run off. Or so the commander's story goes.

I hear a different story. A trusted source tells me that Grupo Beta simply got a better offer. They explain that Grupo Beta officers used to charge 200 pesos a head on the migrants who were passing through El Tortugo. But when the narcos got wind that the government was using some of their own strategies, they got jealous. So they offered the agents a monthly salary to lay off the crossing tax. The officers accepted. I hear the identical story from a driver as well.

Before we leave El Sásabe, the folks at Grupo Beta want to offer us something. It's the least they can do, they say. They take us to another semi-active crossing point, far from El Tortugo. There, unexpectedly, we catch a peek inside the funnel and come away with a good idea of why the high-rolling narcos like getting involved with poor migrants.

Two pickup trucks pull up. One has fifteen migrants. The other has twenty-three. In fifteen minutes the narcos collect more than $2,500 in tax. And that's without trafficking a single bud of marijuana. It's roughly the monthly salary of a hired hit man. The coyotes are carrying a veritable gold mine in those trucks. And if they succeed in getting all of their clients across, they'll earn at least another $84,000—more if any of the migrants are Central American. We hang out for a few hours, passing the afternoon and the early evening, and in those few hours we witness more than ten trucks pass through.

CLOSE TO JUÁREZ, FAR FROM JUÁREZ

A forty-minute drive from Altar, still deep in desert terrain, lies another town with a name often mentioned on the border: Naco, a town with a population of less than 5,000. It's another one of the flashpoints that cropped up in the 1990s, and to this day it's a town that doesn't cultivate or manufacture a single thing. People here work as bandits or coyotes, or they have a small hostel for migrants or restaurants specializing in cheap food. Naco serves as a pit stop for those who are crossing as well as those who have just been deported. It's one of the slots through which disoriented Mexicans are shoved back, deported to a country many of them hardly know.

The problem is that in the past couple of years the twenty-mile radius surrounding Naco has become a tight bottleneck, and the narcos, as they have everywhere on the border, have since laid out their rules: the hill known as Gadiruca, where it would only take two nights to reach the US town of Sierra Vista, can only be used to cross drugs. So now Naco shares another route with Altar, but migrants there have to pay an even higher price to be packaged into trucks and taken north.

Benjamín is a well-known coyote agent in Naco. He spends his time loitering in the small plot of concrete where the deported get dropped off, waiting for clients who can't imagine a life in their native country and so decide to go back to the United States. When I walk up to him he seems willing to talk. A coyote agent isn't regarded in these parts as a delinquent, but rather as a necessary laborer in a widely accepted commercial framework.

"They say crossing gets ugly around here," I say.

"Fucking hell."

"Because everything's under surveillance on the other side?"

"No, it's not that. They do keep guard, but only here in the city. We have an easy time over there, out in the hills where we cross. The thing is that the bosses don't let us work it over there because there's so many loads the bandits have, and they're in charge. So we have to go look in Altar."

"And that raises the prices, I imagine."

"What can we do? We're asking for 3,000 now."

Some agents can't count on a steady stream of migrants willing to pay to be taken to El Sásabe, and so they've had to start relying on the infamous kidnapper express. They tell migrants they'll cross them over, but instead they lock them inside a house and get their information to call their families back in the States, and demand $500 to $1,000 in fast deposits.

This is an example of how the border keeps mutating due to the funnel effect: one tightening route drives migrants to new routes already saturated with narco-traffickers and coyotes, and the whole border, little by little, becomes tighter and tighter.

Our journey continues. After two hours of highway driving we arrive in Nogales, the only Sonoran city split down the middle by the border, with half on the US side and half on the Mexican side, both halves with the same name. We've only come here to quickly check out the terrain, thinking we won't find anything new. The story of migrants getting pushed to the outskirts of a city has been the same at every point throughout our journey on the northern border.

Nogales seems to grow assailants. The Buenos Aires neighborhood that hugs the urban shell around the border wall is the most dangerous part of the city. Every night it's crawling with dealers and drug mules ferrying their cargo of marijuana to the other side. The idea is to attract the Border Patrol there, leaving the hills free for bigger loads to pass unnoticed. This neighborhood is dominated by the Los Pelones gang, who are in an open war with Los Pobres. They are mostly underage boys, willing to kill in order to show they're worthy of being recruited by a bigger cartel.

We're received by Commander Henríquez, the head of Grupo Beta. Henríquez, known for his order and discipline, was part of the military and a judicial police officer in this area until his body became proof of what happens on this divisive line. Fourteen years ago he was shot three times while walking the migrant routes: once in the chest, once in the abdomen, and once in his right tibia, which is now metal. He says it was narcos who aimed at his chest, and a larger group of bandits was responsible for the other wounds. He survived and now works for the migrant aid organization.

He takes us to the Mariposa arroyo, a bed of dry dirt that's the only open pathway in these parts for crossing over to the United States. Both sides of the creek end in coffee-colored hills and valleys that continue steadily and in uniform as far as the eye can see. From here we can spot the last sections of the wall and the start of an area so rugged it's unnavigable, even by an ATV.

In a quarter hour we get a decent look at the stage and have even met a few of the actors. A black Suburban pulls up and fifteen migrants, their *pollero*, and a drug mule get out. All of them are following the same route. They're going to a small town, Río Rico, which is a three-night trek away. A US Border Patrol officer watches the movement from behind the wall, and from the top of one of the brown hills on this side of the line two narco hawks watch the patrol. Today is a load-carrying day. Everyone against everyone, migrants caught in the middle.

Migrants tend to walk these dry, crumbling lands until they get to the hill, El Cholo, and from there they duck into the desert, leaving the best roads open to the narco-scouts. Grupo Beta has to search these inhospitable expanses to find the bodies of those abandoned along the way—migrants who've died of starvation or who were shot by bandits, as well as any bandits shot by narcos.

"It's impossible to know how many have died here," Commander Henríquez says. "Sometimes, because animals eat the flesh, we only find skulls."

~

We've quickened our pace. The border repeats itself down the line. In about four hours of highway driving we'll get to Agua Prieta, Sonora. That's the closest point to Juárez, the most violent city in the world.[2] Agua Prieta is where all of the migrant routes on the western side of Mexico end. It has the most scattered and quickly tightening funnels. Beyond that, there's only Palomas left, with its small suburb, Las Chepas, but because the cartels of that area have been in perpetual war for the past two years both towns have been abandoned as crossing points.

There's a rule in these parts for the coyotes: Juárez might be close, but it's off limits. There are simply no migrants crossing on foot anywhere near Juárez anymore. In the best case, a lucky migrant can get away with paying $3,600 for a fake visa and a ride to El Paso. That's if Border Patrol's laser technology doesn't detect them first. It's advance payment only and, of course, there's no guarantee.

Agua Prieta is not quite a town and not quite a city. It hasn't stopped being the one, and is just starting to become the other. It's full of one-story houses that look built for a Hollywood stage set, with shops that sell only cowboy boots and billboards picturing tough-guy laborers with cigarettes hanging off their lips, amid neon-lit nightclubs and horse-drawn carts ambling between cars on the two-lane streets.

In the late 1990s, laborers would go over to Douglas for a day of work and be back in Mexico by six in the evening, in time for dinner with their families. Mexicans knew Border Patrol agents and would greet them as they walked by. Now there's a wall with metal bars over two yards high, surveillance cameras,

---

2 According to both Mexican and US news sources, violence in Juárez has considerably dropped since. See Jesse Hyde, "'The Broken Windows' Theory Worked in Juárez" *Atlantic*, March 26, 2013, theatlantic.com/international/archive/2013/03/the-broken-windows-theory-worked-in-juarez/274379/ and Lorena Figueroa, "Juárez Now Ranked 19th Most Violent City" *El Paso Times*, February 8, 2013, elpasotimes.com/juarez/ci_22545964/ju-225-rez-now-ranked-19th-most-violent.

and flood lights. No one waves to anyone. Instead people are caught.

According to Grupo Beta, until two years ago Agua Prieta was characterized by its coyotes guiding large migrant groups. When coyotes caught wind of the growing number of Border Patrol facilities in the area, they rushed to cross large groups all at once, knowing that soon they'd have to face what so many others were starting to face along different routes. They were like cowboys feeling a storm approaching, galloping to bring the cattle in.

Two Border Patrol officers outside of Douglas apprehended a group of eighty migrants walking across the prairie in late 2008. Ten vans were needed to take them to the detention center, escorted by a helicopter and a troop of officers on horseback, making sure no one escaped back into the desert.

Then the arrangement started to crumble because of two events, one that happened four months ago, the other only three. The first was when a van, while trying to escape, failed to clear a ramp that was set resting against the border wall and got stuck, dangling on the edge of the wall. The patrol crew complied with the rule they had been given: if it's not the mafia, it's not anyone. They lit the van on fire and shot into the air as the people inside fled.

The second event was when two drug mules were detained by a Border Patrol officer who took them for migrants, and didn't ask for backup. He got out of his car fingering his gun. One of the drug mules grabbed the pistol that the agent had left in the passenger seat. He fired into the air, disarmed the agent, ridiculed him, and fled with the agent's weapons. The agent was later discharged for violating protocol, for being over-confident. And then Washington got yet another letter from the Douglas sector, requesting forty more officers, who now patrol the area.

It's five-thirty in the evening and we pass by a crossing point some seven miles from Agua Prieta, known as the green bridge. Again, dry brown hills and plains full of thorn bushes. We're 200 yards from the military checkpoint on the highway, hidden from the soldiers by the curve in the road.

Suddenly, one by one, fifteen migrants and their *pollero* show up. They quickly gain distance from the checkpoint and crowd into the thickets. In a few minutes, another group of twenty-four runs to catch up with the first. Five minutes later another group shows up, this time thirty strong. All of them jog rigidly, like a military garrison. They don't pay us any mind, but we watch them until we can only see what looks like ants trudging up a distant hill. Eventually they'll take cover and wait for nightfall.

Here are three different groups, each with their *pollero*, out to take advantage of the last quickly fading rays of light. They run, trying to evade the military closing in on them. They get so close to the agents they almost crawl inside their noses, risking being extorted or detained. That's the only way to avoid narcos and bandits.

But they break all the rules that a good *pollero* would follow: don't take a group larger than eight; don't travel with other groups; give them at least a day's worth of walking space; don't get too close to the military; and the best route is the one least taken by others. But today's border isn't fit for following rules. The only rule now is to hurry, before the wall closes altogether and only leaves space for the narcos. It doesn't matter that Border Patrol agents are waiting up ahead and that they've probably already seen you. Nothing matters except running, running like someone trying to reach a slowly closing door. There's nothing to do but run.

10

The Narco Demand: Sonora

After visiting this city for the third time, I've only now started feeling comfortable. It wasn't easy finding the principal migrant- and drug-crossing zones the first few times. Two cartels were fighting to control the passage, but then one of the cartels won, and everything changed. Now people at least know which bosses to ask permission from to approach the border. Now the undocumented know how much and who to pay. And now the coyotes know, because it's still fresh in their memory, what the consequences are of slipping up. Even though it's more expensive these days, it's a lot simpler and more peaceful when there's only one cartel in command.

The last time we talked, he was trembling. Nineteen months ago when we met in the hotel room he had hand-picked, Mr. X was shaking, his voice was cracking, and every few seconds he'd glance at the closed blinds, hoping he wouldn't glimpse the shadow of a man with a machine gun. But not today. Today he's not shaking, nor is he jumping at every noise or asking repeatedly if I work for the narcos. He's calm, even smiling.

When I first met him he made me go through a process that seemed overkill for a tiny border town like Altar. He had instructed me to come alone, arrive at nine on the dot, and then knock three times on the door before we could talk for thirty minutes. After our talk, he told me to get in his car so he could drop me off at a street behind a church. Not until he drove away should I begin to walk toward my hotel. This was what Mr. X made me go through back in May 2007.

Today our meeting is at the same time, nine at night, and again we'll meet in a hotel room, but this time that's all there is to it. Meet and talk.

Outside of the hotel, Roman candles are lit and firecrackers explode in celebration of the Virgin of Guadalupe Day. I watch Mr. X get out of his truck. When he takes off his thick brown coat I see his black norteña-style shirt with flashy buttons and gold embroidery on the sleeves. He enters the room and surprises me by calmly asking, "How are we gonna dance this time?"

"You should know," I say. "I want to talk about the same thing we talked about last time. About migrants and their situation with the narcos. I'd like to get an idea of how things have changed in the past year."

The last time we talked, more than a year ago, he was jumping at shadows, mistaking them for assassins. Just before we met there had been a mass kidnapping of 300 Mexican and Central American migrants. They were holed up in a narco ranch not far from the border. Nobody except for the priest, Prisciliano Peraza, knew anything of their whereabouts. Prisciliano negotiated the release of 120 migrants with an unnamed narco. Most of them were beaten black and blue and had had their ankles broken by a bat. "Of the rest of them," the other 180, the priest later told me, "I don't know a thing. They refused to give them up."

The 120 were released by the truckload. And all of them soon got lost, fled back to their houses or to other border towns where they wouldn't be recognized. Nobody filed a single report. No official denouncement was made. And nobody ever learned the fate of the 180 left back at the ranch.

This is how it works: if a narco (one of the unnamed narcos) doesn't want to give up 180 migrants, he doesn't give them up. That's it. That's how the game plays out.

THOSE WHO KNOW DON'T TREMBLE

Mr. X knows a lot about how the dirty work gets done in Altar. He's someone who since he was eight years old, in order to survive, has tried his hand at everything. He isn't a narco. Despite looking like one, with his big truck and gold embroidery on the cuffs of his black shirt, he really isn't a narco. All the same, the deal we made back in May 2007 is that I wouldn't reveal who he was, what job he had, where he was from, what he looked like, how I found him, or anything at all about anything he does. "Anything about anything," that's how he put it. We agreed to baptize him as Mr. X.

On that day in 2007, narcos kidnapped a whole bunch of migrants who were traveling on various buses and vans heading toward the small, nearly hidden desert town of El Sásabe. The town, which is now a primary crossing point for the undocumented, sprawls right in front of the nearly ten-mile-long wall the US government began building in late 2007.

The migrants were kidnapped because it was to be a high-traffic day for drug crossing, a day of fat loads or *paquetes bien ponchados*, as they say around here, and they were sick of migrants heating up their turf. Drug mules, almost always young men between sixteen and twenty-eight years old, are in charge of carrying forty pounds of marijuana on foot to a particular stretch in the Arizona desert, where another employee picks up the packs for distribution to vendors in the ultimate drug market: The Northern Giant, or, as they say in Mexico and Central America, *El Gabacho*. The USA. A drug mule makes $1,500 per journey of two or three nights.

Getting the place hot—or fucking it up—means attracting the Border Patrol or the Mexican army. When they turn up it's not to ask questions but to start shooting. The last battle was just a month ago, when the army and the narcos went at each other right near the turnoff to El Sásabe. Two of the drug mules are now behind bars at the Nogales penitentiary, three hours from Altar.

What gets narcos angry is that migrants attract enough attention to force authorities to look like they're doing something about a situation that, as long as no one heats the place up, happens daily without anyone blinking.

Mr. X sits on a bed in front of a closet mirror with his boots propped over the brown tile floor. Now he gets that I want to talk about the same things as last time, and I wait for him to start quaking.

"Sure," he says, "lay it on."

He's still, calm. We start talking. He doesn't answer with the truncated short phrases I remember. He seems to be a whole new Mr. X.

"I remember," I said, laying it on, "that drug traffickers charged van drivers 500 pesos per migrant to go to El Sásabe, and that the tax was forked out by migrants. I remember that if any driver lied about the number of people he had with him, a narco would burn their trucks, sometimes kidnap their people, and force them to sneak across drug loads. I remember seeing three burned vans on the dirt road going to El Sásabe. Is it still like that?"

"Yeah," he answers, locking my gaze.

"I was told this afternoon that narcos are thinking of raising the tax."

"Look, when they hit, they hit. And in this business that's what they do. They've already planted the fear and locked in their fee, which is how it's going to stay. That's how it is everywhere, they're demanding fees, it's just that here the price is locked. So now van drivers have more peace. They say it's better this way, that the rules are clear, that they know what to do. They know they have to pay *los mascaritas*, and they pay them." He readjusts himself on the bed, remaining cool.

Los mascaritas, the little masks, are the guys in charge of counting the passengers in each van and collecting 500 pesos per head. They're narco-employed and take the 10,000 pesos per van to their boss who takes it to his boss who takes it to his boss, until it gets to the hands of the narcos in charge of distributing profits. The little masks have to work in Altar's central plaza, in front of the church and City Hall where fifteen or so vans are parked, one after another, their drivers waiting for them to fill up. They need to get twenty migrants into a van before they can move an inch. The guys are called the little masks because, simply, they always wear masks and are known as such by Mr. X, Father Peraza, the local priest, and the old women who sell roast beef cooked in salsa in front of the plaza. Because everyone in town sees them working with masks on yet they don't take any other precautions.

"But you seem very calm," I say.

"Look, last we talked, the narcos had just showed up. Now they're more organized than any other business in town, now they have fees and they handle things pretty calmly. They don't want any more than what they get. They have their business set up. They know how to get what they want from migrants and they know they can't be given more. That's it. Everything is peaceful. I'm telling you, van drivers say they're better off with them, they say the narcos can charge whatever they want, but that they at least know how the business is and that it works."

Nineteen months ago, everything was just getting settled. Kidnapping was necessary. The narcos needed to hit hard so that the town, the guides, and the migrants understood that the fee demand was serious, that the fifty-five miles that separate Altar from El Sásabe was narco property, and that on their property a fee has to be paid or there will be skin to pay. Stories had to be sowed in order to harvest good fear. Now everyone understands. Talking about the narco's fees is as common as talking about the rise in the price of tortillas, which, indeed, has spiked the price of tacos at the street stand, El Cuñado.

Altar exemplifies what's happening all along the border. When migrants and narcos cross paths (and they always do, because they're both chased down ever-tightening routes) the same thing happens, all the way from the Suchiate River to the Mexico–US border: the migrants pay. This has been happening in Altar since 2007, but people were scared then, and that fear fueled the perception that something might change, something might explode, that things could still turn to a less extreme normal. But no, the only thing that's happened is that those who were once princes have now become kings.

Van drivers warn everyone seeking out their services, they stress it without lowering their voice: "Yes, I'm going to El Sásabe, but you have to pay me 100 pesos and another 500 in fees." And if they're asked who the fee is for, they'll put it one of two ways: it's for "*el narco*," as the organized crime scene is referred to, or it's for "*la mafia*."

And though they're inconvenienced by having to wait hours to find twenty migrants with 600 pesos in their pocket, they don't complain. They have to take it as it comes, as Mr. X says. They make less money now, but they know what they have to do to not get their car or their face burned.

But some, like the taxi driver Paulino Medina, do complain a little. Still others try to outsmart the system.

NOTHING BUT A TANTRUM

Paulino, fifty-three years old, is always grumbling about something. Since I met him in 2007 I've heard little but complaints come out of his mouth. This whole town is a disaster, he says, it's full of crooks, the smugglers don't get that if they don't stop messing with migrants the whole business is going to collapse. The difference now, as opposed to a year ago, is that there are more than enough problems to justify Paulino's tantrums.

Paulino has been working in Altar for twenty-three years. He started as a taxi driver and worked up the ranks until he was appointed municipal secretary of transportation, a position he held for a month. As secretary he tried to work with the narcos. He tried to maneuver a deal between them and the van drivers, so that the latter wouldn't keep getting exploited. But the narcos didn't like somebody else trying to organize them. Their organization, or lack of it, was their problem. As soon as word of Paulino's attempt at fostering a deal with narcos got to the mayor's office, they sacked him.

I see Paulino again at a taxi stand in front of a church in the central plaza. He's wearing the same old glasses, has the same gray mustache, and the same old pair of cowboy boots. He used to always greet me with an anecdote of some sort, and today is no exception.

"We all know that you gotta pay, but then there are some tough guys out there who think they're all that and try to swindle the narcos. Just two weeks ago some van driver reported that he had eighteen migrants with him. He paid the fees to the little masks, but then stuffed two more migrants in his van to pocket an extra thousand pesos for himself. He didn't even get to El Sásabe. A few armed lookouts pulled him over on the road, called him a son of a bitch and asked him where he'd picked up the extra passengers. Hell no, he didn't get away with it."

How it works is that the little masks write a code on a piece of paper and give it to the drivers. Say, for example, "birdy" is the code for twenty migrants. Then the lookouts waiting on the hills stop the occasional van to do a quality control check. If "birdy" doesn't match up with twenty heads, then the driver had better start explaining.

Paulino continues: "You see how it got all normalized here. They don't kill you or burn your van anymore. Now that the place is theirs, it's all about business. As long as you pay your fine. But like they say, if you don't fork over the 120,000 pesos a week, they're going to stop by and visit you. I have a friend who needed to sell his van to pay them back."

Altar has changed. There's less fear now, but there's also less work. Back in 2007, Paulino used to make as many as three trips a day to El Sásabe. His beat-up '87 Hyundai bumped along at least five hours a day with one to six passengers. The trips cost the same, 1,200 pesos, no matter how many were riding. He even bought another car and employed another driver, Artemio, a retired coyote who could also usually fit in three trips a day. Paulino was living large, eating huevos rancheros at the local restaurant Las

Marías every morning, even leaving a nice little tip for the young waitress.

Now Paulino eats at home every meal, pinching every penny. These times are, as the local phrase goes, skinny cow. "A lot of good people left the place," Paulino tells me. "They couldn't afford the narco taxes here. But now I hear they're raising taxes everywhere else too."

Altar has become little more than a market for migrants. Here is where they'll pick up their coyotes and here is where the coyote agents rake through the plaza looking for prey sitting scared on the sidewalks. There are about fifty clothes sellers too, pitching warm outerwear in the winter and visors in the summer, hoping migrants decide to outfit themselves for their five- or six-day hike through the desert to Tucson. Some thirty van drivers, forty telephone booth operators, and fifty hoteliers (who will rent an unventilated room with a stained mattress to fifteen migrants for as little as thirty pesos) are eager to capitalize on migrants' last-minute needs. The same goes for the countless food stands, the two cantinas, and the eleven currency changers, all on the lookout to make a buck from a migrant. And all have very few other clients. Even the eight policemen in town try to make a buck off migrants. Though they never confront the narcos ("They're not idiots," comments Paulino), the police do wield their clout, or their pistols, to extort 2,000 pesos a week from coyote agents.

For a migrant, passing through Altar is no cakewalk. It's not as bad as some places, and it's not quite the frenzy that it used to be, but it's still the launching point for maybe as many as hundreds of thousands of people a year. The numbers have recently dwindled because migrants everywhere along the border have started spreading away from the traditional crossing points.

In 2007, the Tucson sector of the Border Patrol apprehended 378,339 migrants. In 2008 that number dropped to 281,207. Esmeralda Marroquín, public relations officer for the unit, explains that this drop doesn't necessarily mean that fewer people are crossing, just that they are looking for new places to cross.

When I visited Altar in 2007 I saw that some of the agents and coyotes were moving to work in Palomas, a city in the neighboring state of Chihuahua. They told me it was the new in thing, that there were good pickings there. But in 2008, when I went to visit Palomas, I didn't see a single migrant. The National Institute of Migration stationed in Palomas was even ready to transfer the four Grupo Beta agents, whose supplies of tuna cans and bottles of water were waiting untouched in warehouses.

"It's all on the move," Mr. X had said. And he was right.

The constant shifting is why Paulino keeps complaining. He throws his tantrums because in this damn town the narcos (and their taxes) are on the up and up, while the number of migrants keeps hitting new lows. And with the scarcity of migrants, the drivers face tough times. Paulino is no exception.

"Those pricks charge me 1,500 pesos each trip, 1,700 if I take more than five. There's no way around it. I have to go where they tell me, have to report my count to the little masks. So how thrilled do you think I am paying both the fee and the taxi tax?" Paulino hasn't made a single trip in a month and a half.

He poses a legitimate question. What group of migrants is going to be able to afford 1,500 pesos for the narcos, 1,200 for Paulino, and 15,000 for the coyote—almost $1,300? A few. Not many, but certainly a few. If nobody could afford it there wouldn't be thirty folks still baking like lizards under the sun in the central plaza.

Paulino's regular taxi work has plummeted as well. His two drivers work from dawn till dusk and still they've only managed to earn two fares, each taking a woman to her house for fifty pesos. That's a hundred pesos, less than ten dollars, for Paulino and both his drivers, one of whom is trying to support a family.

A lot of the coyotes have started lumping the tax they have to pay to the narcos into the fees they charge migrants' families, which means that most migrants can't afford taxis anymore. They hardly ever, Paulino explains, come in groups of six anymore. They prefer to each pay their 500 pesos and leave the complications of a group behind, hoping that their coyote will take care of the narco tax for them. And Paulino tells me that he's heard through the grapevine that there might even be more changes on the horizon.

"You won't believe the shit going down. They're saying that they're going to raise the taxes on the vans, to a thousand pesos a head. How are the poor *pollos* going to afford that?" Then Paulino throws in another local saying: "If you pull a finger and it doesn't let up, you're going to end up pulling the whole arm with it." Who's going to resist the mafia here?

What Mr. X said—they've already made their hit and now they're satisfied—might not exactly be true. The narcos know that nobody can resist them. And what they also know, as the priest Peraza told me, is that no one is going to resist if they squeeze a little harder.

THE PROTECTION OF THE CROSS

Narcos from any cartel—Gulf, Sinaloa, Juárez, Tijuana, Beltrán Leyva, or Los Zetas—seem to have no qualms about killing police, justice officials, migrants, military personnel, and traitors, but it's a different story with priests. Narcos were supposedly responsible for killing 5,600 people in 2008, and not one of these victims wore a cassock. That gives Father Peraza a space to talk that no one else enjoys around these parts. It doesn't mean he can drop names or file reports, just that he can complain in a little more detail than most, and he can mention the names of a few places.

When I met Father Peraza in 2007 the situation was tense after a fresh kidnapping Mr. X told me that a city official from Altar had reported a kidnapping at the Attorney's Office in Sonora. The guy had had the guts to pick up the phone and call the Justice Department. It took him little time to realize that the narcos weild the power of both the balance (the official judiciary system) and the sword. They called him up, asked why he had just made that report, and then warned that if he continued being so brave, they'd have to deal with him directly. It was after hearing this that Father

Peraza started getting a better feel for his place in the scheme of things. He can talk more than the rest, but he can't cross the line. The crucifix around his neck doesn't mean he's completely untouchable.

We meet at his parish close to the central plaza. He founded the migrant shelter in Altar, but it's so far out of the way, hidden on one of the many small dirt roads in the vicinity, that few take advantage of it. Despite the shelter, he's more of a community priest than a migrants' rights activist. He oversees two other parishes and is up to his neck in leading Mass and conducting confessions, baptisms, and first communions.

Before we get started I give him the option of speaking off the record, but, as I said, he knows his limits and will talk within them.

"I've always understood that I don't have to get too involved," Father Peraza explains. "If I get them to let one hostage go, that's enough for me. The ideal would be if these groups just didn't exist, but what can we do? What they least want is journalists around or for the place to get hot, not because they'd get caught, but because the fees would go up. A report's been filed, their logic goes, so they're going to have to charge you more."

He's referring to his ability to do what migrants can do, without going out on much of a limb: get the place hot, get the narcos hot, and get Altar in the headlines. And he knows that damning headlines would raise the price mafias have to pay to the authorities in order to be protected. Of course, if Father Peraza heats the place up, they won't break his ankles with a bat. He's a priest, and if they kill him, they'll be the ones responsible for getting themselves in the papers. He has a theory similar to Paulino's theory. He thinks the rubber band will keep on stretching, but then it will have to snap.

"Sure, this has been normalized, and no one goes to El Sásabe without paying the set fee, but that doesn't mean everything will end there."

When the priest says that no one is exempted from the tax, he's not being precise. He himself is exempt. He doesn't pay, but he does have to give advance warning. He shows his cell, held in his right hand, and shakes it from side to side as if there's something inside it. And there is. A narco's number who the priest has to call whenever he goes into town, so he won't be confused somewhere along the way with a clever dick trying to dodge the fee, which could mean he'd be greeted by a hailstorm of machine-gun fire. "I don't know who it is," he says with a toothy smile, "I only know I have to call this number." He shakes his head and gives me a look like he's goofing around with a child.

"I have friends who are paying the fee to keep their convenience stores from harm. They've heard it's about to go up."

Raising the 500-peso fee per migrant on the vans to 1,000, that's the song Father Peraza started hearing. He explains what's driving the price spike.

"There was a turf war about four months ago," Father Peraza says. "Two separate fees were being charged because two narco groups were operating at the same time, until a fight broke out between them and one of them won. The group that had been in power before had contacts with the authorities, as well as a few soldiers. Not much more was heard about this. The double fee lasted two months. So now, since the other group has gone, the one that stayed knows that people can get used to paying 1,000 pesos, and they're wondering if they should run with that rule again."

The group that stayed is made up of the leading members of the Sinaloa Cartel, the most powerful cartel in Mexico, led by Joaquín "El Chapo" Guzmán Loera, who's at the top of the US list of most wanted. As Mr. X explained, at least six local narcos pay Guzmán's organization to protect them and let them rule over, and rent out, a few miles on the border.

Despite the current tension, Father Peraza is sure Altar will survive. It works, he says, like everything else: by supply and demand.

"The flow has thinned in Altar, as it has everywhere else on the border. Some 300 people show up daily [though a 2007 study calculated that the daily flow of people was up to 1,500]. Many are going directly to houses that they know will take them in, because they come with coyotes who guide them there. The norm is changing. They don't stay around the plaza like they used to. If we go to one of those houses, I promise you it will be full. If we go to El Sásabe, some seven loaded vans will pass us, and if we go at night, it'll be thirty. But a lot of this flow is moving to Algodones, because the fees are cheaper there, and the place hasn't yet been exploited."

Algodones is that small town close to Mexicali, on the border with California and Arizona.[1] It's about 150 miles west of Altar, and it wouldn't show up on the map of 2007 migration routes had it not gained popularity thanks to the advantages of its outskirts. Narcos are just getting settled in there, so the fees are lower, and there's no desert to cross, which means less environmental hazards, except for the mountains. Pros and cons.

It was about twenty days ago, Father Peraza says, when he was coming back from Algodones, that he realized something. Getting out of his car in the small town square, he heard two voices in chorus saying, "*Padrecito.*" Little Father. He turned and recognized two *polleros* from Altar. "What's going on?" they asked him. "Did you decide to move here too?"

The priest uses this anecdote to explain that people are getting tense about there not being enough work or resources to go around, so they're looking for new territory, and if the narcos pressure their workers too much or raise their taxes too high, they'll be the ones responsible for losing control.

"Remember that the groups of *polleros* are also strong and organized. If they have trouble doing business here because the fees are so high, they'll look for other routes, like through Algodones, where they'll have to pay less to the mafia. And when they go, you'll see just how much supply and demand reigns. The

---

1   We saw the situation in Algodones months later (around April 2009) as described in the previous chapter.

narcos around here will end up lowering the fee, and then the *polleros* will come back. That's how this works. Always changing."

Supply and demand. I'll rob you less than that guy. But in the end, whether the fees go up or down, the ones who pay most in Altar are the migrants: they have to pay taxes all along the way for that one service they seek, that journey north through the desert.

The coyotes and narco agents have to be ready to adapt. If the meat gets overcooked, they'll move on. But right now the meat's still juicy enough to keep them milling in the central plaza. El Pájaro, El Metralleta [The Machine Gun], José, plus some other veterans, like Javier from Sinaloa, who sits at my table in the restaurant, they're staying put for the time being.

THE ROUNDUP AND THE MULING

Originally from Sinaloa where some of the toughest narcos come from, hardened like the best of the coyote agents, and having done time in US prisons, Javier is proud to be alive after working for so many years. He introduced himself to me just as I was leaving the church, mistaking me for a migrant (it's not uncommon) and offering me his services.

"Eight hundred bucks and we're off, brother. Think about it. Food, clothes, a room, all included. We can leave tomorrow."

It often starts as low as $800, but it always jumps to at least $1,200. And that's what street vendors are good at, hooking you in at a low price and then squeezing you dry. The agent's job is just to get you on board, and turn you over to the coyote. They get 200 bucks for each catch. It works so the guy who has to explain that the price is higher than advertised isn't the same one who first hooked you in. That is, they don't raise prices on you until you're already on the move.

Javier first came to Altar after being deported in late 2007. He had just finished serving three years in a Texas prison. They caught him back in 2004 with fifty-seven kilos of marijuana in the trunk of his car. Back in Mexico again, the first thing he told himself was that he couldn't stay. He asked around and heard that the best way to get back over the fence was through Altar. But without family to help him out and no money of his own, he had to start working, fast. He found a job selling chickens (actual feathered *pollos*, not migrants). But anybody with street smarts in Altar can find much better-paying work than in the food industry. A coyote, noting Javier's smooth tongue, decided to try him out as an agent.

"It's not great work. The bribes for the fuzz always come out of my pocket," Javier complains as we sit down at the table. I told him I'm a reporter and he's agreed to talk about his work. He talks with me for a while with no other motive than to chat, or maybe to see if I can throw a little business his way.

In a village of narcos, the agents are usually the most honest of the whole chain. That's because the police, or the fuzz, as Javier calls them, are always looking to extort them. Javier has to pay 2,000 pesos a week to the police. It may sound official, but it's nothing more than one man paying another man, the fuzz, who has a gun. If the agent doesn't pay, he doesn't get to work. That simple.

"They keep fucking with you here. Never letting you work in peace. It's like they did to Eliázar a few months back, they locked him up for pulling a grasshopper (trying to go into the business alone). They kept him tied up for thirty-six hours, wouldn't let him go until he paid who knows how much. That's why I make sure to pay my dues every week. That's the only way to do it, keep slipping them their dues."

Eliázar, who I met back in 2007, didn't pay, so he justified it to me, because he simply didn't have the money. The plaza was crawling with migrants and Eliázar decided to jump the line, to pull a grasshopper. But they found him. After that experience, he decided to go back to Sinaloa to pick tomatoes with his cousin.

People ask around here, "Who's got your back?" and the answer, I've found, is not the authorities. In my brief conversation with the mayor of Altar, Romeo Estrella, when I asked him if he knew that his police charged the coyote agents to let them do

their illegal work, he poked at his tortilla and responded, "Yeah,
I know, but what am I going to do about it? If the agents want
to pay the cops, that's their problem. Who am I to tell them not
to do it?"

Javier and the others prowling in the central plaza are proof
that the narco taxes are here to stay, and that it hasn't put a stop
to the flow of migrants. Hondurans, Salvadorans, Guatemalans,
Nicaraguans, Mexicans, and even the occasional solo Ecuadorian
are still passing through. And I see Javier constantly checking his
phone, waiting to hear when the money will be ready and where
to drop off his two *pollos*. He hasn't hit his target of eighteen
today, but it's December, a slow month, and he's earned $400 by
lunchtime.

We finish our coffees and stand up from the table as soon as
we see one of the many buses that pass through the city reach the
plaza. Javier, jittery as usual, hovers around the door of the bus,
waiting for potential catches. Three migrants get off, but it turns
out that they already have a coyote. Javier still waits, hoping his
luck will improve. Minutes later two pickup trucks, crammed with
young men, pull up behind the bus. The passengers jump down
and start raucously shouting and milling about. Then they all
jump back in and the trucks peel out. Javier throws up his hands
and murmurs, "Fucking hell. They're all mules."

He's right too, the young men are all drug mules from Sinaloa,
expecting to earn $1,500 in four days of work. Today they'll eat
and sleep at different houses around Altar, and tomorrow morning
they'll set off. A *pollero* will guide them and their loads out into
the desert. A narco hawk will also follow them, to see that if they
don't make the delivery it's because they were caught by the
Border Patrol and not because they sold the drugs for themselves.

The presence of the ant-like flow of mules is the deciding
factor for most migrants in their choice to go through El Sásabe.
Sometimes the little masks show up by the plaza vans not to collect
taxes but to tell migrants they'll have to wait another day to start
their trip. Because if anybody went today, the crossing zone would

get overheated. And if a migrant compromises a load of drugs, you can't imagine what they do to him.

The ant flow stays steady all year round. Cargo always needs carrying. In September 2008 the Border Patrol in the Tucson sector decommissioned eighteen tons of marijuana. And they always say—both the Border Patrol and the mules—that what is found and decommissioned is only a fraction of what gets through. If that weren't the case, the danger simply wouldn't be worth it.

Though it's only five o'clock in the afternoon, dusk is already beginning to settle when I arrive at the church migrant shelter. Within half an hour of my arrival I watch sixteen people come in after me. Fourteen of them are migrants. Two are mules. The two mules are set up in a shack about fifty yards from the shelter where thirty other mules are already staying. I figure them to be the young men I'd spotted earlier in the pickups. All of them are planning on crossing tomorrow to deliver their loads, but today they've been given the day to do as they please. The two men I saw enter were hoping to save some money by eating a free meal at the shelter.

I sit down with the two mules just as the cook starts to stoke the stove. A man from Veracruz, who was deported after walking three days in the desert, and another quiet migrant, both looking to cross again, join us at the table.

The older mule, who is twenty-three, hardly says a word. He asks me if I have a joint and after I tell him no he shrugs and doesn't open his mouth again. The younger mule, who is twenty, very short, and has a Red Sox hat sticking out from under his red hoodie, talks without a break. I get the feeling he's sniffed a line or two of cocaine. His pupils are widely dilated, all of his gestures are a little wild, and he fills any pause between his words with onomatopoeic mumblings: "The thing is, is you got to put it all out there, and, um, mum, mum, give it your all, yep, pep pep, without stopping, no stopping until you're done."

I find out that this is his fifth trip as a mule. He started when he was eighteen, as soon as he realized he had more of a future muling dope than picking tomatoes in Sinaloa. The last four trips he hoofed with the typical forty-five pounds. Three of the trips were three-day walks, the most recent was five days. Tomorrow, now that he's proven himself to his boss, he'll walk with over seventy-five pounds on his back.

"Tomorrow we're going to head out. We're going out in groups of six and eight. Setting off at night, shhhwooo, so you hear nothing but the wind. All the way to Highway 19, on the Tohono Rez. There we're gonna, woop, deliver the goods, and then, vroom, get the fuck back out of that country."

Fifteen-thousand Native Americans live on the Tohono O'odham Reservation that runs along the southern Arizona–Sonora border. Tohono O'odham means, literally, people of the desert. Living on their own reservation gives them certain degrees of autonomy, including their own police force and even their own laws. Even the Border Patrol needs to ask for authorization to work on their land. The narcos, however, just need to pay.

Tomorrow, the young mule tells me, they're going to give the red light to all the migrants. Because tomorrow, like on that day when 300 migrants were kidnapped, a major shipment is going through, and the narcos want the trails as quiet as possible. "They already gave the notice to the van drivers," he tells me, and he seems proud, like he feels he's taking part in an important event.

When I step back out into the evening I see two migrants on the patio of the shelter, one young and the other in his forties, sitting on their backpacks and chatting. The older one gets up when I walk out. I go and take his place.

The young migrant, Mario, is a Honduran who has been working for the past two months in the neighboring state of Chihuahua. As soon as he realized the border wall spanned much of the state, closing it off from New Mexico and Texas, he crossed over to Sonora. But the thing is, he tells me, the situation here isn't much better.

"There, at least," he says, referring again to Chihuahua, "I could get right up to the wall and see if I had a chance to cross.

Here I can't even get out of Altar. Without 600 pesos for the ride and the narco tax, I can't even get close to the wall. My plan was to walk with the will of God instead of with a *pollero*, but how am I even going to try if I can't at least get to El Sásabe?"

There's little that Mario can do here. Altar is still the principal crossing point in the state, but it's also been turned into a toll road with strict rules. It's not like it used to be. Now there's nothing but migrants with money, those who can afford to pay, no exceptions made. Because along this border, as Mr. X said, as Father Peraza explained, as Paulino grumbled, as Javier confirmed, and as Mario came to realize, there are always taxes. And if you dodge them you're playing with your life. The taxes in these parts are sacred.

So for a migrant without money there seems to be no one left who can answer Mario's question: "Where can I at least give it a shot?"

11

Cat and Mouse with the Border Patrol: Arizona

I remember what the photographer Edu Ponces told me at the end of this trip: "The story about the Border Patrol is more myth than reality." It turned out that the bad guys of this story aren't so bad, and that the border, with its wall, its radar, and the constant patrolling, is still porous, though in reality it makes way for drug traffickers far more than it does for migrants. Undocumented migrants aren't high on the Border Patrol priority list, and so the chasing of some counts enough for the ones who get away. And getting caught, what migrants call failure, is looked at by some Border Patrol agents as winning the game. A game that is played again and again, every hour of every day.

One of the twenty-three revolving radar systems located on these 220 miles of desert border flashes a signal. Four dots appear on one of the screens at the Control Center Headquarters. The radar system, located near the town of Arivaca, hovering over one quadrant, has stopped revolving. It has detected movement and has focused on one of those small red circles projected on the monitor.

The game has begun.

At least three patrol SUVs have received the signal on their screens. The four dots are moving. The SUVs make their way to a surveillance zone. They park on top of a mound overlooking the plain. The same message blares from sixty Border Patrol radio transmitters: "We have movement."

Twenty minutes pass after the radar first flashes its signal. The agents fail to come to a consensus. They don't know who to go after. From the radio of the patrol car we're riding in, we can hear the confusion swelling when those four red dots meet up with another four that have just appeared on screen. It's three in the morning and down below, in the middle of the desert, there are eight people walking through the deadly December night.

The uncertainty on the radio goes on: is it two groups of migrants? Two guides mixing their groups together? Are they drug mules meeting up with the guides who will lead them to a drug stash?

Esmeralda Marroquín, the border agent we're with, decides to get closer. She steps on the accelerator of her SUV, crosses Arivaca, passes ranches, and turns off at a road that goes to the town of Amado. We stop before a hilltop. We see the agent who was most talkative on the radio, glued to his infrared-vision binoculars. He observes the mound from the roof of his truck and signals the three patrol agents who have gotten out of their cars to go look for the migrants or traffickers—the eight red dotted silhouettes on the viewer: "One eleven, one nine, from your position heading northeast."

Three agents leave on foot with a screen that lets them see in real time what the agent on the car roof is seeing through his binoculars. The silhouettes disappear and reappear. "Look for a kite stuck in one of the broken parts of the wall."

The task isn't easy. Whoever those walkers are, making their way across the Tucson desert, they have changed direction three times in half an hour. They come in and out of tiny of pockets of lower ground that provide shelter from surveillance. They probably don't know that an entire technological system is focusing in on them. They probably don't know that some fifteen agents are following them.

Agent Marroquín warns: "On this job, patience is key."

Meanwhile, the five patrol agents standing at the foot of the car with the mounted agent and his binoculars are chatting over coffee and cigarettes. They talk about coworkers, kids, the weather. "How's Michael?"

The others are still tuned in. "We haven't spotted them," the patrollers report.

"They were going northeast," the one with the binoculars says, "but then changed direction and I lost them. Locate the kite and I'll direct you from there."

"We're there, but we don't see anything."

It's been over an hour since the ground surveillance radar flashed, since the agent at the control room in Tucson communicated the signal to the patrols, since these officials alerted the rest of the patrols by radio, since the agent glued to his binoculars jumped up to the roof of his SUV, feeling the bite of the cold despite his gloves, hat, and heavy jacket stamped with the name US Department of Homeland Security—Customs and Border Protection.

It'd be impossible to see anything from this mound without infrared technology. The only thing that can be spotted, in spite of the huge, full moon, is a dark lopsided plain, some desert bushes, and the shadowy scrub. The only thing that can be heard is the whistle of the wind whipping against our skin. My lips are chapped, and when I open my mouth to stretch my jaw I feel as if my skin might break like an old rubber band.

The agent with the binoculars and those deployed over the ground check in to tell each other the same thing: "No contact." "Nothing here either."

Simple logic tells us at least one thing: the operation is complicated. Maybe one of the thirteen OH-6 helicopters will appear behind Diablito Mountain and flood the plain with light, letting the three agents on foot move more easily and take off their infrared goggles to spot those eight red dots that would turn into either eight scared people hiding in a thicket, or eight narcos dropping their load and running back toward Mexico.

But here routine is routine, and the rules of the job are applied the same every night. The agent gets down from his SUV. The three trucks are started and Marroquín tells us we're leaving.

Edu Ponces and I look at each other, surprised. These fifteen agents have been following those red dots with all their technology for over an hour.

"Where are we going?" we ask.

"To see what else there is," Marroquín answers.

But she realizes that neither Edu nor I understand what's going on, that we've forgotten what she said earlier: "We have to get used to losing at this game. Sometimes we win, sometimes we lose. It's like that every day and every night."

She warned us of this some twelve hours ago, when we met at the Tucson headquarters. They're not going to let fifteen agents hunt the same target for two hours. This desert fills with too many targets every night. That's part of the game.

TRACKING

"Ready to play?" she said. It was the first thing Esmeralda Marroquín, a dark, short, and partly indigenous-looking Mexican-French-American said to us when she came through the station doors at the Border Patrol headquarters in Tucson, Arizona.

We didn't respond.

She insisted. "Ready to play cat and mouse?"

Esmeralda Marroquín and the other 18,000 agents who guard the US borders are, of course, the cats. Those who carry thousands and thousands of pounds of marijuana and cocaine, as well as the estimated 3,000 undocumented migrants trying to cross the border every day, are the mice.

We arrive by three in the afternoon, twelve hours before we would start the chase between Diablo Peak and Diablito Mountain.

The planning for this ride-along took a long time: two months of telephone calls and emails, negotiating back and forth. The Border Patrol offers ride-alongs every month, during which reporters visit a few migrant crossing corridors, interview a few patrol agents, and then call it a day. "Tours," the press agents call them. We, however, asked for an atypical tour. We wanted to see the full routine, how agents work on a daily basis. Only after consulting the Border Patrol center in Washington DC did the Tucson sector give us the go-ahead for a full shift tour.

We first started calling the Border Patrol after we'd already gotten to know some of the busy crossing points on the Mexican side, which included Ciudad Juárez, the most violent city on the continent, where one in every four of the 5,600 narco murders occurred in 2008. We had also spent time in Nuevo Laredo (on the Mexican side of the Rio Grande from Laredo) where drug traffickers, mostly Los Zetas, control the migration routes and direct the kidnappings that take place in the southern part of the country. Then, besides Tijuana, we also got to know Altar and Nogales (the closest Mexican cities to Tucson), where since the 1920s Mexican marijuana has found easy entry into the United States. And where, since 2005, more undocumented migrants have been crossing than at any other point along the border.

The question we wanted to see answered, on the US side, after witnessing all of these Mexican sites controlled by narcos, was if the wall, the helicopters, the cameras, the underground sensors, the horses, and the off-road vehicles were sufficient to control a border that had thousands of people wanting to cross it every day. We wanted to know if the message from the US government was for real.

Is your wall really unpassable? Is your wall (in all of its forms) sufficient to stop the waves of people and drugs?

Michael Chertoff, the secretary of homeland security during the Bush administration, often emphasized that the border situation was "an enormous challenge that couldn't be solved in thirty minutes." Yet he also repeated numerous times that the government efforts to secure the border would herald a "final victory," the "definitive blocking" of the flow of drugs and undocumented migrants.

We wanted to know if the declarations made by the suits in Washington were making any actual difference on the desert dirt.

~

The agent we were paired up with was a ten-year veteran currently working on the busiest sector of the entire border, the Tucson sector. Esmeralda Marroquín, thirty-seven years old, daughter of a French father and a Mexican mother, was born in Arizona. Her mother came to the country legally, she told us, with papers. When I asked her why she had wanted to work for the Border Patrol, she responded emphatically: "For the love of my country. To give back to something that has given me so much."

For the love of her country she spent six months in training, as well as taking Spanish classes and doing physical conditioning. For the love of her country, she affirms, she also spent two years on Operation Disruption—a team working to break down the coyote networks responsible for locking up migrants in safe houses for ransom. Though Marroquín doesn't speak very highly of coyotes, "those traffickers that trick a migrant and leave them stranded in the middle of the desert just to make a buck," she has a better view of undocumented migrants, considering them simply "people looking for a better life." Yet the constraints of the job remain at the forefront of her mind. "I can't let them pass," she says. Then she adds, leaning back toward her natural sympathies, "I know how poor a lot of these people are. My grandma was indigenous. I know how they live."

Marroquín switched on the radio transmitter and our night began. "We're going to look for some action," she said. "We'll scout for migrants first, what we call tracking. But as soon as we hear anything on the radio we'll jump on whatever it is. Sometimes we get a lot of drugs and no migrants. Sometimes a lot of migrants and no drugs."

She drove with her head jutting forward, her gaze fixed on the passing asphalt. Half an hour in, and the radio hadn't made a sound. Marroquín resorted to telling anecdotes.

"I remember the only time I had to draw my weapon. It was in my first year with the agency. I came across seven drug mules. When I approached, one of them picked up a big stick. I flipped off my safety and thought, here we go. But thankfully the guy dropped the stick and booked it. We're only allowed to open fire if someone has the intention and possibility to cause harm or death. It doesn't matter if it's a rock, a blade, or a firearm. If I think my life is at risk, I can open fire."

We drove in her SUV for miles and miles, cutting through the desert. The sun beat down and the cold wind whipped in through the open windows and against our skin. Nothing seemed to be moving.

Agent Marroquín, her hair pulled back in a loose ponytail and tied off with a bow, kept giving us warm smiles, trying to diffuse the silence around us. "It's often like this," she said. "Sometimes there's a lot to do and sometimes you don't hear a thing in the whole desert. But don't worry, any minute and we could see some action."

"There," she pointed as we arrived at the checkpoint between the small towns of Amado and Arivaca, "is a pickup spot for *polleros*. We've detained a lot of migrants waiting to catch a ride along the side of the road here."

The only difference I noticed between that and other desert spots was that three Border Patrol agents (two of them of Latin American descent) had marked it off with fluorescent cones. These hotspots aren't recognizable except to the eye of experts. *They* know that six miles straight into the desert from this road there is a trail that is out of reach of Border Patrol cameras, where migrants can walk at ease without even having to climb any hills.

But despite agents' sensitive noses, which can help them pick up on migrant trails, it's still mostly a question of luck. "There's simply not a pattern to this," Marroquín explained. "You can't say where they're crossing. Every day we find new routes."

We chatted with one of the agents at the checkpoint for a few minutes, asking him if he'd seen any action. "No. We've got nothing today so far," he responded. The popular idea of the border created by film, music, and popular myth looks nothing like the reality we were seeing. The area did not look like a war zone, and we learned it would be rare to spot uniformed men haring after ragtag Latinos or narcos in pickup trucks firing machine guns. This area of the border was, more than anything, empty. Empty and silent. In the Tucson sector there are 275 miles covered by 3,100 agents who take turns patrolling the seemingly endless plains, hills, mountains, and thickets. In these hundreds of miles of border there is always movement, but it's rarely seen. There, that day, between the towns of Amado and Arivaca, the agents were reporting a whole lot of nothing.

And Agent Marroquín took it in her stride. "That's how this game plays," she said.

We continued on our drive. "We'll head towards the Nogales wall. There they sometimes ferry drugs over at night." She drove for an hour before we finally arrived and parked in a lot filled with trailers.

Agents often spend an entire boring night inside of their SUVs, with nothing but coffee and cigarettes and the still desert out their windows to occupy them. And then sometimes an agent gets killed, as happened to Luis Aguilar on January 19, 2008, run over while laying down tire-puncturing strips. Aguilar is the last agent to have died in the line of duty.

The parking lot we reached was empty except for seven trailers and a lone agent on a bicycle who reported movement shortly after we arrived. The lot sat on top of a tall hill from which you could see thirty miles of wall dividing northern Nogales from southern Nogales, the United States from Mexico, houses on one side from houses on the other. All of it separated by the blank gray of the wall, by twenty-five-foot bars driven and locked by cement five feet into the ground, much of it constructed from leftover war material. Combat material put to a new use. In the Tucson sector there are sixty-six miles of wall and over 160 miles of vehicle barriers.

Marroquín chatted for a minute with the agent on his bike, then took his binoculars. She peered toward the Mexican side. "There they are," she said. And there they were, two men, camouflaged and hunkered into a bush, shaking with cold. They were watching us the same as we were watching them.

"They're hawks for either narcos or migrants, watching for movement on this side, trying to decide when people should cross or when they should ferry the drugs."

Marroquin's game started becoming clearer to us. The migrants, they're waiting to cross. And the agents, they're waiting to catch them. And the two groups look at each other, waiting. Those on the Mexican side get to make the first move.

CALM INTERRUPTED

"It's about to get dark. That's when the movement begins. They know how to wait," Marroquín explained, before suggesting we continue driving along the wall.

It was 5:40 p.m., the sun casting its last orange flashes and the radio starting to sputter directions. With the efficiency of a factory, everyone immediately responded to the orders coming in on the radio. The next thing we heard was: "We have a small car trying to cross near Sásabe."

And then: "There's a chase close to Abraham Canyon. It's two different groups."

Marroquín, glued to her radio, explained that all the action was far from Nogales. "This is a peaceful season. Other months around this time, it seems like every Mexican and every type of drug is trying to cross." The comment seemed to have urged the radio on. The transmissions poured in.

"They're launching drugs," said a crackly voice, "in virtually every nearby location."

"That one is for us," Agent Marroquín said, stepping on the gas.

Another patrol car was parked on a street running parallel to the wall. The line of houses between the wall and the street prevented the narco hawks on the other side from spying on the Border Patrol. With the lights turned off and the radios set at the lowest volume, two patrol cars followed two agents on bicycles sent to intercept packages thrown over from Mexico.

"The seizures by the wall are always dangerous," Marroquín whispered. "Sometimes they shoot at us from the other side, trying to stop us from catching the pickup guy on this side."

An agent came down the street. He was sweating. All of the patrol agents have twenty-pound belts around their waists, to which they strap their pistol, tear gas, flashlight, water, firearm magazines, and pocket knife. The agent set a package down on the ground: a backpack covered in electrical tape.

I stuck my head out the window and asked one of the bike agents what had happened to the narcos seen trying to collect the packs.

"They ran off," he responded, as he started pedaling back uphill.

Sure, they'd run off, but I didn't see anyone go after them.

"That's how this game is," Marroquín insisted. "We don't endanger ourselves with a chase that involves risks. If we seize the drugs but they run and get to the other side, we let them go. We don't know if they're armed. We take care not to get involved in any shoot-outs and not to follow anybody who could be armed."

The border agents came back with two more backpacks, twenty pounds between the two of them. It's hard to understand why the guys on the other side throw any packages around this area, knowing that most of the Border Patrol's surveillance cameras are set up around the wall, but everything has its explanation in this game. There's a strategy to it all.

"Sometimes," Marroquín explains in whispers, "they throw their drugs around here and in two other key places to tie our hands and distract us from other sectors where they're crossing with vehicles. It's the same tactic used when drug traffickers send large migrant groups for us to catch, so we'll leave another sector empty while we take that group to the station. But what can we do? Even if we know this happens, we can't let these packages cross. We don't even know how to get to the empty sectors where they're supposedly crossing bigger loads."

It can be a gamble trying to differentiate between getting work done and walking into a trap. As Marroquín said, sometimes it seems that all of Mexico's drug loads are being thrown over the wall and all of Mexico and Central America is trying to cross. And the SUV radios blare on.

7:12. Escaped subject now picking up packages thrown from Mexico, feet away from where his previous pack was seized.

7:21. Two migrants detained some miles from the wall. One of the screens flickers with a man seen on the Mexican side walking away from the wall with two backpacks identical to those just seized, apparently deciding to hold off on crossing until the scene cools down.

7:24. At checkpoint on Interstate Highway 19, five undocumented Mexicans discovered hiding under a truck's false floor. Driver, upon seeing the checkpoint, flees.

8:03. Man jumps over the wall in downtown Nogales. Classic desperate attempt. He tries to hide in a crowd, but two border agents follow him.

"They're almost never successful crossing like that," Marroquín says. In the same area, some young men throw more drug packages.

8:31. Fifteen pounds of marijuana seized.

"And the drug mules?" I asked.

"They escaped, they walked into those woods," an agent explained, pointing to a thicket of trees ten feet away. "They got back into Mexico."

Rather than a deadly game, the activity here is one of routine. A routine with many interruptions. If drug smugglers escape, they escape. If they lay a trap in order to divert agents, agents have to fall for it, even when they know they're going after bait. Marroquín said it well—in a game, the same player can't win every time. The goal is to hinder the drugs, not to stop them.

"That's impossible," Marroquín said as we left the site of the backpacks. "If we build a wall ten feet high, they'll make an

eleven-foot ladder. The Border Patrol's mission is to gain operational control over the area. We know they're always going
to come in. You have to learn to lose. After 9/11, our mission
changed. Now the priority is to detain terrorists. Migrants have
been demoted to second priority."

What is surprising, however, is that they've never reported
the detention of a single terrorist along the US–Mexico border.
That is, if by "terrorist" we understand what the United States
usually defines as a terrorist: a bin Laden–appointed individual, a
member of Al Qaeda, an Iraqi insurgent who works for Muqtada
al-Sadr and has dedicated himself to combating the foreign
soldiers in his country.

But the definition of a "terrorist" is always changing. "Of
course we've detained terrorists. Narco-traffickers are terrorists,"
Marroquín argued without taking her gaze off the highway.

"They live off breeding terror," Marroquín continued, sound-
ing like a Border Patrol spokesperson, while on our way to to the
Tucson detention center. "And we don't want them to do here
what they've been doing in Mexico. That's why we have 18,000
agents on the border and why we'll keep raising that number."

As an example of what "they've been doing in Mexico," she used
Mexico's southern state Michoacán, where, on September 15, 2008,
two grenades went off in the central plaza of its capital, Morelia,
where thousands of people were gathered for the Independence
Day celebrations. Eight died and scores were injured. The attack,
almost certainly committed by Los Zetas, was considered revenge
for the recent seizures of their drug loads.

It wasn't too long before the SUV radio transmitter blurted
out a more concrete example of what the Border Patrol avoids on
this side of the wall. A message from one of the sector's coordi-
nators requested border agents to temporarily abandon the area
surrounding Nogales, in order to let a group with firearms pass.
US informants on the Mexican side—probably anti-narcotics
agents—had communicated that there had been threats by narcos
to execute Nogales police officers. Sometimes, as in this instance,

hit men try to flee into the United States, and the Border Patrol counters by calling off standard patrol agents and mobilizing special units to handle the situation.

It's impossible to know how much the Border Patrol's new prioritization has affected the traffic. It's impossible to know, while more narcos have been ferrying drugs, whether fewer migrants have been crossing. What we do know is that the statistical data confirms Marroquín's take on things.

Between 2005 and 2008, this border area registered a decline in migrant apprehensions. The 439,079 detained in 2005 became 281,207 in 2008.[1] But the 221 tons of marijuana seized in 2005 rose to 236 tons in 2008. It's understood that whatever is seized is at least proportional to what is successfully crossing. This follows a simple logic: if more drugs are seized than are successfully crossed, business wouldn't be viable for the narcos. If more migrants are seized than those who cross unnoticed, then that business wouldn't be viable for the coyotes.

At night the desert turns into a mysterious territory, an immense darkness where a twig's movement can look like an oncoming person. The light of the moon is deceptive. We drove through that landscape, down Interstate 19, with the radio transmitter blurting: "Another vehicle entered. Ten miles from Nogales. Receded when it saw the patrol car. It's still making rounds, trying to come in."

"We go on like this," Agent Marroquín said with a faint smile, "chasing them all the time." And she started telling stories that made her laugh, though they involved drug traffickers, desert bandits, and coyotes. She told them like she was remembering the mischief she used to make as a kid.

"They're very creative," she said. "We've found three false

---

1   As of 2012, Obama's administration has deported 1.4 million undocumented migrants. PolitiFact.com, "Has Barack Obama deported more people than any other president in U.S. History?" August 10, 2012, politifact.com/truth-o-mter/statements/2012/aug/10/american-principles-action/has-barack-obama-deported-more-people-any-other-pr/

border patrol agents among us, trying to smuggle drugs. Of course, when we radio them, ask who's there and don't get any response, we know they're a lie. Oh, I remember," she smiled, shaking her head, "one eighty-five-year-old woman who was taking sixteen migrants in a van that said: Church of Love." But Marroquíns face became grave when she recalled that a month ago one agent bumped into three smugglers. "One had an AK-47."

"And sometimes," she went on, resuming her friendly tone, "they're more ingenious. Especially the narcos. One time, we detected a van but only because they hadn't covered it completely. On the screen at the control base we only saw a tiny red dot that couldn't have been a person or an animal or a vehicle. It looked as if it were floating through the desert. When we got closer, the agents realized it was a vehicle full of drugs covered in a metal invisible to infrared light."

This is the stuff of movies that we were expecting. The traffickers had obtained a type of fiberglass or metalloid, germanium or the like, and covered almost the entire car. "They accidentally left just that one spot uncovered that gave them away." Marroquín hit the nail on the head as we drove into Tucson: "Everything you could imagine, they've done. They've done it and more."

Back at headquarters, some agents were taking fingerprints, others were easing the cuffs off a recently detained migrant. Four agents stood as they always do, day and night, watching the thirty-eight monitors that show images of the desert and the wall. Two big computer screens showed tiny red dots. People were moving through the mountains.

In one of the detention rooms I saw seven undocumented migrants wrapped in military blankets, lying down on a gray slab of cement.

"Those are the ones that have criminal charges," Marroquín explained. They've entered more than once without papers, or they raped someone, robbed someone, or drove drunk. Whatever it is, all of them will testify before a judge who will decide whether they'll be deported or incarcerated. "Those over there," Marroquín pointed, "are the undocumented without any charges." I saw three disillusioned men in another room, hunched quietly on the bench or lying up against the wall.

"This is sometimes full, but usually not until morning. Most people try to cross at night," Marroquín said, as if trying to justify the nearly empty rooms. "Sometimes one wins," she repeated her refrain, "sometimes one loses." Whoever was here was a tally on what she considered the winning side.

For the first time, now after midnight, we prodded Marroquín. We'd been making rounds for nine hours without undertaking a single migrant detention operation. We wanted a border agent to report a migrant group crossing. Then we'd be able to see just how unrelenting the Border Patrol is in this daily game. Then we'd be able to see just how a group of undocumented migrants with no water, little food, and such bodily exhaustion confront a group of agents in this sector who can't complain of a lack of equipment: twenty-eight helicopters, including three AStar B3s, considered the most capable machines at ground-level flights and landings in inhospitable areas; nine Cessna planes; 140 horses; 1,800 motor vehicles; and a slew of cameras, radars, and land sensors that can't be named due to security reasons.

Marroquín said she'd fulfilled her promise, but couldn't do much more. We'd seen the daily routine. The minute by minute that is sometimes exciting and sometimes silent.

We all piled back into her SUV. Marroquín was determined to join a "tracking" squad, following the trail of a group of migrants walking in the desert.

"Let's go to Bear Valley," she said. "If someone's moving there at this hour, they're up to something illegal."

We drove toward Montana Camp, which is in the middle of Bear Valley, a landscape of trees and dirt roads. When we arrived at the mobile base, there was nothing to report. The agent had lost sight of a group a little less than an hour ago. "I didn't see them again," he said. And at this juncture, they'd probably already slipped into the valley or disappeared into the open desert.

"Let's go down again." Marroquín was stuck on finding someone tracking.

It was then, driving down those irregular paths, bordering a gorge, that we heard a transmission coming from Arivaca. It was one twenty in the morning when agents launched a chase between Diablito Peak and Diablo Mountain. We'd started tracking.

The ground surveillance radar had flashed its signal. But then they lost the dots. Minutes later they saw them again, meeting up with another four dots in the desert. The agents climbed up Mount Amado, took out their infrared binoculars, and sent three agents to scope out the area on foot. The dots changed direction. "They're going south." "Now north." And then, in the middle of the chase, fifteen against eight, the game was over.

"Sometimes you win, sometimes you lose."

The agent with the binoculars got off the roof of his car. He stopped looking for them. It ended. Here we are.

TO WIN OR LOSE, A QUESTION OF LOCATION

"This is the way it is, all day and all night," Marroquín says as she gets back in her SUV to seek out another incident.

Here in Arivaca, the shadows have won. Another 240 pounds of marijuana will hit the US markets. Or, if they were migrants instead of drug mules, eight men or women will cross and start looking for jobs, opportunities to send money back to Mexico or Central America. They're still somewhere out there in the desert, not yet knowing that they've won, that they can stop hiding, that the border agents, for now, have gone away and let them be.

This is the pattern the Border Patrol has to accept, in Marroquín's words: "learning to lose." "What we want," she explains, "is to have operational control along the border." It's all that's possible. To seal the border is a pipe dream that politicians sell from their offices. Here, maintaining control, ceding space and clamping space, is all that can be done. And they're doing what they can.

You don't need to witness an entire night of tracking to understand how the cat wins and the mouse loses, or vice versa. Those who lose are the ones who take a single false step, who enter into the field of vision of a pair of binoculars, or light a cigarette at the wrong time. If the mice avoid these mistakes, then they win.

Marroquín keeps on. "We're going back to I-19. Around this time at night, groups are looking to catch their pickups."

It's fourthirty in the morning when we arrive again at the highway checkpoint and see the other side of the coin.

At least for these two migrants, the game is over. They couldn't avoid the traps. They took a false step. Now they're loaded into the back of a truck, the small paddy wagon of one of the Border Patrol SUVs.

Two Hondurans. I can't make out their faces behind the green blankets they've been given. They sound like youngsters when they respond that they don't want to talk to us. They sound, unsurprisingly, let down. They thought they were about to make it. But they became separated from their group. They ran to the highway to try to thumb a car, the agents explain to us. On seeing the SUV with emergency lights on the roof, they ran back into the desert but were quickly caught.

When dawn finally comes we find ourselves on the highway between Tucson and Phoenix, a destination city for a lot of the migrants still wandering this desert. On each side of the highway you can see nothing but cold, endless, December desert. It's been fourteen hours since we first got in the SUV with Marroquín.

The two Hondurans are uncommunicative. They tell Edu that they don't want photographs taken either, at least not of their faces. They just want to be left in peace. I'm not surprised. We're standing right at the checkpoint manned by Border Patrol agents whose job it is to stop people exactly like these two men. This checkpoint is the last on I-19. Everybody knows that if you can get past this point, you've probably won the game. It's this checkpoint, and ones just like it, that sharpens creativity: trucks with false bottoms, migrants hidden in the most unlikely spaces in a car, like inside the dashboard, drugs riding in the tires, in false ceilings, or deep inside the driver's clothes.

Marroquín is yawning after her marathon shift. She has some sympathy with the Hondurans' silence, knowing that this stage is a low point for those who lose. She takes off her glasses and rubs her eyes, saying, "What a pity. If only they hadn't come out on the highway, we never would have got them. It's supposed to be a rule: don't stick your neck out on the highways!"

This isn't pursuit unto death. Marroquín already admitted that most of the migrants are just looking for jobs. Yet the agents are just doing their job as well. And their job is to apprehend, not to play a game. Because of this, because we're not dealing with friends or enemies here, but rather with roles, she can drop a line like: "If only they hadn't come out to the highway."

But they did come out, they made a mistake, and the agents had to act on it. And now three other agents are out in the desert looking for the rest of their group. "It's how the game plays," Marroquín repeats. "The same, day in and day out."

12

Ghost Town: Chihuahua

Even the poorest of migrants have to pay for the journey, which means that where there are migrants there are jobs. We learned this in the spectral border town of Las Chepas, which sits in an old crossing zone in the middle of nowhere. The few remaining residents we found were hesitant to speak to us, worried that they would be seen as delinquents. But after getting a little used to our presence, and with the help of a bottle of tequila, the stories of how everything used to be better, and then how the narcos ruined everything, started spilling out, one after another, onto the table.

It's like they've stopped existing. The people talk about these empty desert borderlands as though they were nothing but barren fields. Like there was nothing here at all, not even a reason to come. Like they were ghost towns.

And one's first impression is that they're right, that there's nothing here and no reason to be here.

There's a half-mile of border wall to go before we reach Las Chepas, the biggest of these tiny towns. Up ahead I start to make out what appear to be white stains in the desert. They look like walls, and it seems unlikely that they would be houses. There's not a soul in sight. Desert to the left, desert to the right, a thin wall of metal separating Chihuahua and New Mexico. The only sound is the wingbeat of the occasional swallow and the slight rustling of the breeze.

If it weren't that the hill blocked the road from continuing straight, it would be easy to pass by Las Chepas without even noticing. But soon we realize that those few white walls must be our ghost town.

Edu and I stroll up one of the sidewalks. Dirt roads lie in front of the fifty or so crumbling houses, the wind flapping the steel sheets on their roofs. A brown horse, grazing behind one of the walls, spooks as we walk past. The door of one of the houses swings open, blows closed. Peering inside, we see a thin layer of dust kick into the air. There's a large broken window, an abandoned church, a school pavilion under which grows a thick tangle of weeds. The only sound is the wind. Not imagining that we'll discover anything here, we decide to go to Ascensión, the municipal center, and see what we can learn.

After another two hours on the road we arrive at Ascensión. What's nice about towns this size is that there's less bureaucratic runaround than in state capitals. Formal records requests are replaced by simple telephone calls. In just a half an hour we already have a meeting set up with the municipal secretary, Alejandro Ulises Vizcarra.

Vizcarra is a stereotypical Chihuahuan desert dweller: thick mustache, cowboy boots, jeans, and a belt with an enormous silver buckle. He's an expert horseman and each summer he participates in an annual desert roundup. In the last decade he himself was a migrant (with papers) in the United States. Living in Palomas and commuting to New Mexico every day, he was a supervisor at a shipping company that exported products to Mexico. For the past year now, back in Mexico, he's been municipal secretary of Palomas.

"I know migration because I was a migrant," he explains, following this pronouncement with a few rather trite statements: "These days migrating is difficult," and "It's risky to cross the border in these deserts." What we want to talk about, however, are the ghost towns.

"Ah, yes," Vizcarra exclaims, "the phenomenon of the ghost

towns. Well, speaking again about migration, most of the towns' residents have left for the United States. Only some older folks stayed around to forge a living by helping out the crossers. They weren't *polleros*, though. There was a lot of flow through here for a while. Good opportunities for business. Some folks were selling soda, others food, some were renting rooms, some even selling medicine. Migrants were a boost for the local economy. But then when the flow stopped, communities like Las Chepas were almost completely deserted. The few who remained did so only because it was their only property. Now if people don't start coming back around, those towns are going to be history."

So, we realize, there still are some people in Las Chepas. It seemed, in the short time we were there, completely abandoned, and yet inside a few of the buildings there was life.

Vizcarra doesn't think anybody is going to get back into agriculture in Las Chepas; it's only a matter of time before the outlying ranches die out for good. "Winters are hard," he says. The freezing desert winds destroy anything that's not a bush, a cactus, or well protected.

But even Vizcarra admits that the departure of the migrants wasn't the first step in the towns' decline. Nor was winter solely responsible. "The extreme vigilance of the US government after the September 11 attacks made crossing here very difficult," he says. "Up until 2007 the US Army with all their high-tech equipment started patrolling around here. Compared to all the migrants you used to see, now there's nobody."

But something seems to be off with his logic. Neither 9/11 nor Al Qaeda had much to do with the upsurge in border vigilance in 2006. He was hesitant to talk about it, but finally he went there. "Another aspect that influenced this part of the desert was the arrival of the drug fighting. The cartels came to wage war over control of the drug routes. That set off a red light for the US government, who responded by reinforcing vigilance."

And then, which is rare considering the topic, Vizcarra continues: "It's a fight for territory, a fight for the whole package, the passage of drugs and the undocumented, which together bring in a flood of money. We've been in the midst of this war for a few months now, which is why all the migrants left, leaving the place deserted. Nobody wants to cross here anymore and it's nearly impossible, in the midst of the war, to find a *pollero*. We don't think a group has yet established definitive control, so the fight probably isn't over. Las Chepas," he concludes, "is about to die."

And then he excuses himself, in case his words come back around to haunt him. "But I don't like to talk about it. My own safety is at stake. I don't really know anyway. I don't know who's on one side and who's on the other. Our task at the Municipality is not to do intelligence work. We only know what we know because our residents tell us. The narcos don't show their faces ... They could be my neighbors ... I really don't know."

Las Chepas, we learn, is in the middle of a Bermuda Triangle: the cartel war, the lockdown of the border, and the fleeing of the migrants.

There's not much chance of getting lost en route to the ghost town. With a bewildered look, any Palomas local will say: "Just follow the wall along the dirt road until you get to the hill." And then most add: "But there's nothing to see over there." We would find out, however, that there is something to see, for people still live there.

The wall that guides us to Las Chepas starts in Palomas. For the first mile it's made up of thick bars, three yards high, between which not even a child's head could fit. Then, for the following few dozen miles it's a steel fence, a yard high, that works to deter vehicles. The word *wall* is a mere four letters that signify much more: the constant presence of agents, cars, helicopters, motion sensors, surveillance cameras, horses, all-terrain vehicles, reflectors, and then, of course, the actual physical wall itself.

Two people are riding in a Grupo Beta truck (*mueble*, or piece of furniture, they call it in these parts). They're both young. We make signs for them to stop, but they accelerate. Then, some fifty feet ahead, after eyeing us and deciding that neither Edu nor I are drug traffickers, they slam on the brakes. Our conversation is short. They can't talk, they assure us, not without prior authorization. And there's nothing to talk about anyway, they say, there are no migrants and nothing else worth mentioning in Las Chepas, the ghost town.

These Grupo Beta agents are in charge of walking the area, looking for any disoriented migrants and, if they find them, handing out water and pointing out north from south. They don't do much else. To let us shadow them to Las Chepas we'd have to go through a mess of calls, letters, and signatures sent to the National Migration Institute headquarters, located 1,000 miles from this wall. "But nothing goes on here anyway," one of the agents repeats.

The road that takes us to where nothing goes on is a bumpy strip of dirt and rocks surrounded by desert on the Mexican and the US side, with the exception that on the latter grow small patches of peppers that can withstand the hard winters thanks to the laborers, fertilizers, and machinery of the Johnson family, who own a big farm here.

The road is a washboard, and a city car like this one would fall to pieces if we drove faster than fifteen miles per hour. Ten miles turns into a forty-five-minute drive. We get used to the idea that we're traveling parallel to a wall we could easily hop over and be in the States. For migrants, of course, the difficulty lies in getting deep into the country, not just nudging it with a toe.

We see signs of life.

The official name of this ranch town is Josefa Ortiz de Domínguez. Josefa was a Mexican heroine who fought on the side of the Creoles against the Spanish. But everybody here calls it Las Chepas, The Humps. Of the fifty houses, only about fifteen are still completely standing. We knock on three doors before one opens.

A woman of about sixty answers. On the doorframe is a Coca-Cola sign and a small bell. Evelia Ruiz looks us up and down and asks what we want. It's a hard question to answer. How do we start: by asking if everyone else in town is dead, if she's the last one left, if even the migrants and narcos have jumped ship? The rare visitors to town have a reason to be there. So, unable to think of anything else, we ask if she still sells Cokes.

"I think I got a few," Evelia responds, inviting us into her small front room and closing the door. She ends up having five Cokes left, plus three bottles of water and a few dozen little candies.

Evelia tells us her basic story. She's lived here for thirty-two years. That is, she came five years before the Mexican government offered, in 1971, eight hectares to any family willing to take a shot farming this unforgiving land. Evelia explains, in few words, that back in 2007 there were seven stores in town. Now there are two stores, both of which sell "about one or two things a week" to either Grupo Beta workers, or soldiers who appear out of nowhere hunting narcos among the rubble.

She tells us that when the migrants were passing more regularly through town, in 2005 through early 2007, she would sell more in a day than she sells now in a month. And, she says, when she sells the last of her stock she's going to close up shop.

As we're speaking, her older sister, who also lives in the house, watches us from a back table. It seems obvious that Evelia doesn't trust us.

Besides Coke, the other name brand flashing around town, though with an antiquated logo, is Fanta. We decide to go to the Fanta store, which is next to the derelict, roofless school and about four blocks from Evelia's house. After we ring about twenty times, an old, lonely looking man opens the door. This time we ask to buy a bottle of water.

When seventy-five-year-old José Ortiz returns through the wooden door with the water, he asks, rather shyly, "What are you looking for here?" We explain ourselves.

"Migrants?" he responds. "No. They're none left. They

moved on. Sometimes one passes through, but not often." We ask how much longer he's going to run his store, but he interrupts. "This isn't a store. It used to be. Now I just live on my pension. Sometimes I'll sell a lamb in Palomas, but I'm just selling off the little I have left."

It seems hard to believe that he's still getting rid of what's been stocked up for two years.

"Well," he explains, "back in June about forty-five soldiers set up in the old school to make sure drugs weren't passing through. Business surged a bit when they were here."

He's referring to the federal program known as Operation Chihuahua, which sends the army to drug-trafficking hot zones. It started in 2005 when the governor of New Mexico, Bill Richardson, complained to the governor of Chihuahua, José Reyes Baeza, that narcos and their drugs, as well as *polleros* and their undocumented migrants, were launching crossing expeditions from shacks on the Chihuahua side of the border.

Speaking in Las Chepas in 2006, Governor Baeza qualified it as "a problem of public security," and Richardson approved. That year, detention of undocumented crossers shot up 36 percent in the hitherto little-patrolled New Mexico sector. Seizures of marijuana reached an all-time high: more than fifty-six tons.

"Now there are only old folks here," José Ortiz says. "Sixteen seniors left in Las Chepas," he specifies. "There was life here before, though. It used to be good business selling to the migrants passing through."

In 1986 Las Chepas had its highest historical population, a total 486 inhabitants. Taking advantage of governmental agriculture incentives, residents started cultivating sorghum, corn, alfalfa, and wheat. The US government even offered to legalize everyone in town. That was the first big migration. The younger residents were especially content to be legalized, and many of them worked on the large Johnson farm on the other side. But half of the residents, mostly older, stayed behind. Then in the 1990s government assistance waned, eventually petering to nothing, and at the start of the new century there were only seventy-five people left in Las Chepas, most of them finding ways to continue to farm.

But the *before* referred to by José Ortiz, as he was leaning against his doorframe, was before 2005 when the flux of migrants, Central American and Mexican, found a nearby crossing route and started coming by the hundreds. With this bonanza the stores reopened, farmers had money for fertilizers, and the harvest came back to town. The townsfolk even held a celebration meal.

"Now they say that this is a ghost town," José tells us. "We who are left have roots in this ground. Nobody is going to buy us out, either. We don't want to give away or leave behind for the wind to blow away what we worked so hard to put together. Now nobody comes through here. Just take a look at the shape of the road from Palomas."

Two years ago, that same road looked very different. A neighbor of José, a man originally from Michoacán, would charge a tax to the buses full of migrants on their way into town. At least ten buses came every day, each of them carrying about sixty migrants. The man from Michoacán ran his thriving business from a sidewalk. Now he lies below one of the fifty crosses in the town cemetery, which lies a half a mile straight into the desert.

"They killed him a year ago. The mafia came and machinegunned him in his own house. It seemed like he had some business with them," José remembers. "Now nobody pays this street any mind at all."

We ask José where we can find more people. He points us to the house of Erlinda Juárez and we say goodbye to José, promising to return.

This house is the tidiest in town. We don't even have to knock more than once. Erlinda, who is sixty-eight, had already spotted us through her window, where she commonly spies for prowlers. We explain ourselves and, under her suspicious gaze, chat for a minute on her doorstep. Then she decides to invite us in for a coffee.

Her dining table, built into the wall up against the window, as well as the pastel curtains pulled aside to let in the afternoon light, give the room the air of a dollhouse. The interior of her house contrasts sharply with the rubbled exterior. Halfway through our coffee, Ignacio, Erlinda's seventy-year-old husband, returns from the fields. He is still sweating from a day of baling hay, which he'll later try to sell in Palomas.

Hesitant to talk about migrants, Erlinda does admit that *los chepenses*, the locals, have been accused of trafficking both people and drugs. To a Salvadoran man who came into town with bloodied feet a year and a half ago, a few chepenses gave a pair of shoes. And to a Honduran woman who witnessed her traveling companion die of dehydration on a day when the temperature overshot a hundred degrees, a few chepenses gave food and assistance. That's all, or that's all that people say.

"This isn't even a good place to cross," Erlinda reasons. "With sandstorms in the winter and the infernal heat of the summer, there's no easy season. Plus the Border Patrol is always on the alert now. They have a balloon in the air that they use to watch over the hills. Plus they have horses, ATVs, helicopters, and highway checkpoints."

The checkpoint is on Interstate 10, the US highway that runs from Las Cruces to Tucson. For a migrant to even reach the highway from Las Chepas, he or she needs to trudge over forty miles across the desert. And despite Erlinda's claims, this is without doubt one of the main routes for the undocumented to reach pickup points from where they will be ferried to Los Angeles, Houston, or San Francisco. But it's more than a question of distance these days. Since Governor Richardson complained about Las Chepas and the Mexican army moved in, migrants have more than just the desert to contend with.

"Plus," chimes Ignacio, "there's the mafia."

The mafia. It seems that everywhere on this border there's the mafia, the narcos, organized crime. There's no longer a crossing point along the border where you can avoid talking about the mafia. And it is the mafia that brings our talk to an end.

"You should get going before the sun goes down," Erlinda tells us. "At night here there's no traffic. Nothing but crooks and robbers watching you from the hills. And they'll definitely spot your unfamiliar car."

We start on the road back to Palomas, pausing for Edu to take a photograph. We see a white Nissan Pathfinder halfway up on the shoulder, right against a guardrail. When we approach we find that both its doors are open, and the windshield is riddled with bullet holes. We later discover that it's been there since last October 6, when an Army Humvee tried to stop it for a traffic check. The driver of the Pathfinder didn't want to stop. He speeded up, but only made it as far as this ditch. The driver and single passenger, according to the newspaper *El Siglo de Torreón*, escaped on foot, leaving a cache of weapons in the vehicle: three Kalashnikovs with twenty-one cartridges, a grenade launcher, two shotguns with seventy-nine shotgun shells, two grenades, three pistols, two rifles, 4,168 pistol and rifle cartridges, eight bulletproof vests, ten military helmets, a gas mask, nine pistol holsters, plus a few AFI uniforms.

So the migrants may have gone, but the narcos have stuck around.

As we inspect the bullet-riddled Pathfinder, a Border Patrol agent in his SUV, parked just beyond the vehicle barriers, watches us from the US side. After a few minutes we take off.

The sun rose six hours ago. Again we're driving over the rugged, washboard road on the way to Las Chepas. There's nothing but the wall, the wind, the wall, a few swallows, and again the wind, and the wall, all the way until we arrive.

We knock on the first door we come to, the store that is no longer a store, owned by José Ortiz. No response. We try Erlinda and Ignacio's house: same thing. It's like on our first visit, when all we found was the whistling wind and a huffing horse. It seems we're seeing Las Chepas on its deathbed.

But no. The only death that day was that of Gonzalo Apodaca Ruiz. He died of cirrhosis twenty-five days after his father, Francisco Apodaca Ruiz, expired in the same house. One more empty shack. Fifteen inhabitants left.

At forty-nine, Apodaca was one of the two young people in the community. His father died at seventy-nine. The younger Apodaca hadn't been seen for a few days. They say he shut himself in, as he often did, to drink tequila. Only this time he never came out, not until José Ortiz found him dead.

Every single chepense went to the cemetery to see Apodaca buried, and they were now driving back through the desert in the vans of the Juárez and Quintana families. The Quintana family, with its three members, makes up one fifth of the population: Arturo, the sixty-three-year-old father, Margarita, the fifty-two-year-old mother, and their son José, who at twenty-two years old is now the only young person in the community that his grandad founded, along with Erlinda and Ignacio. José is a chubby, cheerful young man with a thin mustache. The Quintanas' older son didn't want to stick around. Now he lives in Palomas.

Yesterday, before we left town, José waved at us as he was coming out of his house and stopped by our car to chat. He soon became tense, looking sidelong at a green backpack sitting in the back seat. Not paying attention to anything we were saying, he stared at it as if trying to guess what it contained; he couldn't know it only held photography equipment.

When we put his mind at rest he grinned and said, "You guys looked suspicious to me. I saw you in that tiny car and with that suitcase in back." He laughed, then invited us to his house for coffee.

The Quintana family, Erlinda, Ignacio, and José Ortiz are seated at the table when we come in. They've owned the house (where a lamb is dozing in the corner) since 1971. Though José Ortiz hardly speaks, Margarita takes it upon herself to chatter away everyone's stories.

Las Chepas appeared in some Mexican newspapers in 2006, when surveillance in the area started increasing and all the chepenses were described as coyotes or drug traffickers. Margarita is the most outspoken in defending Las Chepas. She was the one who, in 2006, stood before the tractors that the governor of Chihuahua had sent to demolish the community.

"We're good people here," she says, "living off cattle and whatever we get sent. We all have family on the other side—thanks to that law they passed in the eighties. The papers have made me out to be a *pollera*. But that's nonsense! Migrants make me anxious, they leave so much trash everywhere, and sometimes the cattle eat it and get poisoned."

Arturo, her husband, quietly observes and smokes one cigarette after another as Margarita chatters on. He has US papers, and works as a welder and bricklayer on the other side every time his union finds him a temporary job with a US company. When he chips in he's an outspoken northern-style man, who always sounds as if he's scolding you.

"What happened here," he grumbles, "is that they put too much pepper on the beans, that's what. They put the military just the other side of the wall, only paying attention to Las Chepas, even though there are so many other little towns around here."

Sure, there are more towns: like the community of Los Lamentos, where last we heard only Don Pascual was left. Or Sierra Rica and Manuel Gutiérrez, other tiny places farther out, of which no one here has any news. More ghost towns. With roads snaking up the mountains, where it's impossible to travel without a four-wheel drive. And as it's mafia turf, chepenses don't recommend the trip. Margarita warns: "That little car you guys have would be easily flagged by the mafia lookouts."

When George Bush approved operation Jump Start in 2006 (which ended in 2008) 6,000 National Guard forces were sent to the border. Since then, and up until a few months ago, soldiers entrenched on the nearby mountain were the nearest neighbors of Las Chepas.

Arturo, Margarita, José Ortiz, and the young José do not look like coyotes to us, and we say so. It's hard to imagine that Arturo at his age could stand the long walks a coyote signs up for. And José, who's young but overweight, works at the customs office in Palomas, and seems too good-natured to fit the profile. After reassuring them with these impressions, the Quintana family pulls out more stories.

"Well, people would come, money in hand," Margarita recalls, "so some of us worked driving buses, others had fast-food carts. Up to 300 migrants came every day."

But when I ask if they wish the migrant flow would come back, Arthur takes the floor: "No, no. You couldn't live in peace." And his wife chimes in: "Gringos used to come over here to pick on migrants, they'd jump over the wall to chase after them, and there's no justice to that." With the migrant flow came unrest: migrants died, and so did a resident of Las Chepas.

"It was Don Apolinar," Margarita says. "We rented him that small house across the street." I look across the street but see only rubble—four crooked walls surrounding heaps of trash and bed fixings left over from passing squatters.

"On their way to the US all the way from Honduras!" she says about the squatters. She adds, "Don Apolinar warned us about a gringo who would jump over the wall and threaten him. Don Apolinar was crossing migrants then. That was his job. One day in 2006 as he was crossing a group he stopped by my food cart for a bite to eat. A little later, three of the young men he was guiding from Honduras came by again, and told me a big white guy with blue eyes had killed Don Apolinar."

All that's left of him, this dead man, is a cross on the hill, marking the spot where he fell.

New Mexico and Arizona are the two states with the most civilian-run border militias hunting migrants. The Minutemen, describing themselves as patriots, are the ones who gave new currency to the idea of civilian vigilantes.

~

We finish our coffee, and José, the youngest Quintana, decides to go with us to the cemetery, where we want to photograph Apodaca's grave while it's still light. The back road we take is in even worse shape than the washboard of a path we'd traveled on earlier, and the cemetery we find is little more than a handful of crosses in the middle of the desert hills. It's already getting dark when, as we're about to start heading back, we notice the puddle of transmission fluid under the car. There's no other option but to hoof it. Hiking through the brush and the burs on the way back to Las Chepas, we chat with José.

He's warmed up to us by now, and gives us his view of the ghost towns. "I want to get out of here," he says, "but my pop says I need to stay, because he needs help with the house. My brother already lives in Palomas. They let him leave when he got married. But I'm young still, and there's nobody but old folks here. And nothing happens. I need to go out for drinks once in a while, go to bars, have a life."

Palomas, though, isn't much more than a small highway town either. It has two restaurants, five cantinas, and a few unpaved roads surrounding its small central plaza. Compared with Las Chepas, Palomas is a big city.

Back in town, the Quintana family offers to let us to stay the night in their house. Arturo has already towed our car with his pickup, and we plan on seeing if we can get it running again tomorrow. They serve us a dinner of beans and potatoes and tell us about life in rural northern Mexico. Their stories sound surreal to us, as if they're from another century.

Trying to describe the feel of the region, Arturo reminisces about a murder in Los Lamentos. A cowboy, rounding up his cattle outside of town, approached a ranch house and asked the owner if he could use his stove to heat some water for his instant soup. The rancher showed him in just as another cowboy came to ask the same favor, to heat some soup. The second cowboy ended up using the first's hot water. There was a discussion; the second cowboy suggested that the first cowboy merely heat more water;

but, his pride wounded, the first cowboy took out his gun and shot the second cowboy in the head.

"That's desert people for you," Arturo explains, opening a bottle of tequila. "Rough."

After Arturo pours a round and Margarita leaves for bed, we ask him again if he'd like the migrants to come back to town. And maybe it's the tequila, or because the family finally believes that we're not coyotes ourselves, but he admits something we hadn't heard before: that it was the departure of the migrants that turned this place into a ghost town.

Arturo tells us that up until the end of 2005 his son José didn't work with customs, he drove a truck for migrants on their way from Palomas.

"There were sixty each trip," José puts in. "Each migrant paid fifty pesos. That's almost five dollars a head. And, only spending about one hundred pesos on diesel, I was taking home about a hundred dollars a day, plus what the owner of the bus gave me on top."

Now José earns twenty-five dollars a day as a customs guard, sometimes having to work as long as forty-eight hour shifts.

Arturo serves another round of tequila. We wonder about Margarita.

"How was it for her?"

"Oh, it was gooood," Arturo sings his northern-accented response. "I tell you, back in those years," 2005–6, "we never had less than 300 people passing through every day. Sometimes there were as many as 600. Some of us would be renting out rooms, others, like José Ortiz and Evelia Ruiz, working their stores, then Erlinda and my wife selling lunches, and then some others who aren't around anymore worked transporting people, taking them up into the hills. The whole place was a big market. Each migrant put fifteen or twenty pesos into the town. Sometimes my wife would make as much as 6,000 pesos a day."

After such nostalgic musing, he pours the last round of the night.

"Yeah," José chimes in, "my pop even bought himself a truck. Isn't that right, Pop?"

"Yep, but that's history now," his pop responds.

When Arturo went to the States, we learn, to buy and legalize his truck for transporting migrants from Palomas to Las Chepas, it was almost 2007. Governor Richardson had already asked the governor of Chihuahua to put a stop to the migrants flowing out of Las Chepas. Bush's Operation Jump Start had already sent National Guard troops to the border to assist the Border Patrol. The flow of migrants was already dwindling.

Arturo had taken a risk. He usually made about $1,000 for each job his union found him in the United States. His son convinced him that a new truck would be the best investment he could make with his savings. Back then José was forking over sometimes as much as 7,000 pesos a day (almost $700) to the owner of the truck he was driving.

"And then," Arturo says, putting a cap on the night, "everything stopped. Las Chepas stopped existing. We're not even on the maps of Chihuahua anymore."

It was getting cold. The wind outside was whistling through the ruins of the town.

The next day, thanks to the family's help, we fixed up the car—a few taps of the hammer and some soldering—enough to get us back to Palomas.

As we thanked the family for their hospitality, Arturo held out his large calloused hand to us, and said, in all sincerity: "If you see some migrants in those parts, tell them to come back."

13

Juárez, Forbidden City: Chihuahua

Why, we asked ourselves when we first arrived in Juárez, has such a long-standing crossing zone, so close to El Paso, died? Yet after just one day in this city known as the most violent city in the world, our question was simplified. What the hell is going on here? Thanks to anonymous testimonies we were able to sketch out an answer in the form of a travel journal. A day-to-day log marked by gunshots, the wall, the narcos, the dead, the deported, as well as the few and frightened Central Americans who still come to this deadly city.

FRIDAY, OCTOBER 31

El Paso del Norte International Bridge, better known as the Santa Fe Bridge, spits out dozens of deported Mexicans. It's a busy day. Every Friday at five o'clock in the afternoon, airplanes from all over the United States land in El Paso, Juárez's sister city. Undocumented migrants are unloaded from these planes and driven down to the bridge that circumvents the border wall. They emerge disoriented, with a plastic bag in hand that holds a copy of the papers ordering them out of the country. Some hardly speak Spanish and use Spanglish to ask how to reach their hometown, which they may hardly remember. Some have no family in Mexico at all.

"Seventeen years over there," says one young man, turning, stupefied, to look down Juárez Avenue.

There's an immense difference between one side of the bridge and the other.

Grupo Beta agents offer the deported men and women transportation. A volunteer driver suggests going to a shelter run by Dominican friars. I can tell that for a few of them, it's hard to take those first few steps away from the Santa Fe Bridge. They stare into the distance, into their home country. A few, however, dressed like *cholos*,[1] plow forward with confidence, swaggering in their bright sneakers and loose pants, decked out with earrings and huge, swinging chains. The few sporting gray pants and a gray sweatshirt have just been let out of prison for serious felonies, such as attempted murder. Others are in field laborers' garb, thick long-sleeved button-down shirts and cotton pants. These guys have been caught in the act of trying to cross, and it's rare that they're younger than forty. The minority group is made up of over-fifties who came to the United States in the 1980s or early 90s, when there wasn't yet a wall. When Juárez wasn't what it is.

Some 6,000 Mexicans are deported every month by the El Paso customs office. On Friday evenings it looks like a school parking lot at the end of the day, with people rushing out the doors or waiting for their ride.

Currency exchange dealers mob the freshly deported migrants, hollering their offers. They circle the migrants as if they were tourists at a market, knowing that any money they have left from *el otro lado*, the other side, needs to be changed into pesos. Rodrigo, one of these dealers, dresses in orange, just like the Grupo Beta agents, to try to confuse migrants who are looking for advice. The three young women who work for him, wearing tiny shorts and shirts that show off their dark legs and belly buttons, take migrants by the arm and walk them to the exchange house.

"We only charge you 3 percent, we do it to help more than anything else," Rodrigo lies as he pockets 8 percent as tariff.

Still, on this street, options have to be measured by their degree of evil; the corner shop keeps thirty of every hundred dollars.

---

1   Originally a derogatory term for members of a lower-class Latino subculture, the term is now used by many as a badge of ethnic pride.

But the technique there is more sophisticated. The fat woman responsible for luring migrants in tries to convince them that it's the only place to get pesos. "They're all swindlers who bribe the authorities," Rodrigo complains, suspiciously eyeing the shop. The owner, a tall skinny man with gray hair and an enormous, hawkish nose mounted on his gaunt face, films us with a small video camera.

"He always does that," Rodrigo explains. "It's to intimidate us so we won't work this corner." The giant's threat has nothing to do with showing the video to authorities, at least not for legal purposes. Rodrigo has a license to do his work. The threat is more along the lines of, *I'm going to show your face to so-and-so and he's going to smash it if you keep taking away my customers.* Rodrigo has already suffered two beatings: one from the police, who accused him of resisting arrest (though he asserts that they came up to him already intent on attack), and another from a group of gangsters who waited for him on a corner a couple of blocks away.

"Beware of the police," Father Jose Barrios, director of the Juárez migrant shelter, warned Edu Ponce and me as we parted ways a few hours ago. "And beware of the thieves who roam around here. They're in it together. They're the ones robbing migrants."

When people talk about the danger in these parts, they don't mean a young man who tries to snatch a purse away from an unsuspecting passerby. The fear here is sown by the police and by the drug traffickers. No one can trust anyone. Three hundred city police positions were taken over by national military forces this past October. Only those few agents who passed some obscure test of trustworthiness are still working. And, according to Father Barrios, people should still be wary of them, even though most do nothing but act as chauffeurs for the military.

There are no city officers in sight today. Instead, nine military officers armed with AR-15 assault riffles watch over Juárez Avenue, which ends at the bridge. At least seven businesses in the area have shut down this month. Pharmacy owners, bar owners, and restaurant owners have chosen to leave the area rather than pay the monthly 20,000-peso tax that some of the drug cartels currently fighting over the area demand. The Juárez Cartel and the Sinaloa Cartel, two of the largest organized crime groups in Mexico, are battling for control of the border zone, all in order to win more for their side: more people, more streets, more authorities.

They're not gangs and they're not corner hoodlums. They're organizations that cross hundreds of tons of South American cocaine and Mexican marijuana and methamphetamine to the United States. The Juárez Cartel was the largest in Mexico during the 1990s. Back then it was led by Amado Carrillo, known as El Señor de los Cielos, The Lord of the Skies. Carrillo was something like the Mexican version of Colombia's Pablo Escobar. He earned his nickname because he used his Boeing 727 to cross loads of cocaine every week, sold at 200 million US dollars. The Mexican government alleged that an unrecognizable body, found in 1997 in a clinic specializing in plastic surgery, was Carrillo's. Since his death or disappearance his relatives have led the Juárez Cartel, but it has been weakened by the Sinaloa and Gulf Cartels' power surge.

The Sinaloa Cartel has its hands in both Central and South America. This cartel is led by the most famous Mexican narco-trafficker, Joaquín "El Chapo" Guzman Loera, who wants to strip the Juárez Cartel of its last bit of armor in the city that gives it its name. El Chapo became a household name in 2001, when he escaped from a maximum security prison by supposedly hiding in a crate of dirty laundry. Now he wants to snatch the throne that the Lord of the Skies left empty.

Ciudad Juárez is now considered the most violent city in the world. According to many newspapers, Mexican cartel warfare has left some 4,550 people dead, 4,000 in Juárez in 2008 alone. Since late 2008, there's been a self-imposed curfew in town. At five in the afternoon, as soon as dusk sweeps over the city, everyone recommends doing one thing: "Lock yourself in." Already today, four people have told us to do the same.

Under the bridge, the lights hung along the six-foot metal wall dividing Mexico from the United States give a glow to the borderline. On the US side, two Border Patrol SUVs are making their rounds. The recently deported crowd into the shelter or into Grupo Beta vans. They stare sidelong at Juárez Avenue. The military is on the alert, and people walk hurriedly to leave the area or make their way to customs to cross over into the United States. Where they feel safer, I imagine.

This is how night falls over the Santa Fe Bridge in Juárez, the city that went from receiving thousands of departing northbound migrants to receiving thousands of southbound deported migrants; the city where everyone watches their back. The militarized city. The war in Juárez provoked increased border militarization, to prevent the violence spilling over to neighboring US cities. Yet, despite the heavy military and Border Patrol presence, the outskirts of Juárez is still a major drug crossing zone.

This is one of the many faces of Mexico's northern border. This is Juárez, a frontier hot spot and, at the same time, a city that little by little has been vanishing from the migrant map.

SATURDAY, NOVEMBER I

A body lying on the Juárez pavement can be one of two things: it can be an execution or it can be a murder. The stabbed body of a man found in the suburbs, briefly mentioned in yesterday's papers, represents a murder. The body of the man found downtown in his white truck, punctured by forty-nine high-caliber rounds, represents an execution. That is, if a man dies in a bar fight or is stabbed in the street, he was murdered. It's very different to what happens when a cartel, or the mafia, executes somebody. When a cartel kills, you know it.

In recent years Ciudad Juárez has developed its own whispered vocabulary, words that carry meaning from the streets: *muro* (wall), *rafagueo* (machine-gunned), *malandro* (bad guys), *ejecución*, *mafia*, among others. As night falls, everything shuts down and the words come streaming in, telling stories, giving warnings.

"Here's where they executed the owner of the funeral parlor. Twelve shots. He was involved," a taxi driver tells us on the way to our hotel. The driver adds: "He was a friend."

When in a city of 1.3 million there are thirty-seven police murdered in the last year, twenty-two stores torched for not paying narco-taxes, thirty-eight businessmen kidnapped, 10,000 cars stolen, and fifty-two bank robberies; when 5,000 families move out of the city for their own safety, 2,500 soldiers move in, and 521 small gangs are active, all allied to various cartels, then we need to emphasize a few words in particular that may help describe the situation.

Fear. A worker at the migrant shelter (whose name I won't reveal) tells me that he is scared to use a public restroom, in case he finds a decapitated head. It sounds at first like he's paranoid, or crazy, but it's happened to him twice.

Lockdown. The woman who sells us lunch on the street says she's been living in lockdown for the last six months. She's been in Juárez for twenty-two years, and says that ever since "the war" (as people call it) started at the end of 2007, "you can't go out for a beer, you can't go to a movie, and you can't go out dancing," because you don't know when things are going to explode, if they're going to light a place up with machine-guns, or drop off another human head. "From home to work and back, that's it," she says. Just a month ago she witnessed her most recent execution. She points to the pink house opposite her shop: "Over there a truck pulled up and someone blasted some guy with bullets. It was in plain light of day, around eleven in the morning."

Get out of town. This is what the only Central American staying at the migrant hostel told us he wants to do. He's a twenty-six-year-old Honduran who came to Juárez with intention to cross. He had tried in Ojinaga, about 200 miles southeast of the city, but it was flooded by the Rio Grande. That's when he came to Juárez, "*a lo burro,*" unthinking as a donkey, without knowing what he was getting into. And now he just wants to get out of town. "What with the wall and the crime, it's not even worth trying to cross here," he says. Nor does he have a chance to "work a little to make a bit of cash, because everybody says how dangerous it is to even step outside the door."

Tax. According to the owner of a bar nearby the Santa Fe Bridge, taxes have put an end to Juárez night life. Hardly any clients come anymore. When we met him at about ten at night, he was sitting completely alone at his own bar, bored and drinking a glass of wine. "As owners we wanted to close because even though nobody was coming to drink anymore, we still had to pay the tax or fear for our lives," he explains. The bar was very popular, he tells us, just a year and a half ago. "This is the worst I've ever seen the city." He received a notice saying that he'd have to pay $500 a month if he didn't want the place burned down. The last bar to go up in flames, four months ago, was just down the street. Five masked men showed up one night, armed and carrying drums of gasoline.

SUNDAY, NOVEMBER 2

"Let us ask God to forgive the politicians who created these walls," Armando Ochoa, a bishop from El Paso, says in prayer. We watch him—through the wall—from the Mexican side. To his left is the fence that divides the two countries. To his right, the desert. In front and in back are thirty-eight double reflector posts, six motion-detecting towers, and five chunky Border Patrol vehicles.

Some 200 faithful from the United States and 500 from Mexico are attending this binational Mass in Anapra, the last crossing zone left in the Juárez area. This is the last haven people have, and yet it is nothing but desert, thirty-eight double reflector posts, six motion-detecting towers, etc.

It's not a very good idea to cross here. Those who do try must not know any better. The Border Patrol divides the 1,500-plus miles of border into nine sectors. The sector that has the most agents is Tucson, followed by this area close to El Paso, which includes parts of New Mexico and Texas. 2,206 patrol agents looking for drugs and undocumented migrants over 267 linear miles. The numbers might be different now: this data was taken from the last stock of official information written in October 2007, before Operation Jump Start (with its 2,000 agents stationed along the border) came to an end. Also, more cameras and motion detectors have been set up. And out of the nine sectors, this is one of the six fortified with a wall, or fence, or whatever you want to call it.

The Border Patrol doesn't build walls or install reflectors to stop migration. Right now, the top priority is drugs. And El Paso is the second-most-guarded sector.

"They come at dawn," explains a man whose house faces the wall, "but not very often these days. Since the beginning of last year, this zone has been heavily patrolled because so many drugs were coming through." His house is in a low-income residential neighborhood on the outskirts of the city, where every dwelling is made of aluminum, cement blocks, thatch, or car parts. It's really more of a gaggle of houses than a neighborhood—a makeshift settlement on land where only thorny shrubs can withstand the blistering sun and cold nights.

Narco-trafficking warrants surveillance. That's the logic that reigns in these parts. The Border Patrol informs us that they'll continue to build up the wall until the end of the year. It'll be ready by next year, depending on whether or not US legislators slash the funds for those operations that have already been approved.

When surveillance increases, migrants leave for increasingly remote areas. Such as Anapra, the settlement out in the desert, far away from Juárez's urban shell. From here one has to walk for four nights, skirting highways, to get to Las Cruces or El Paso, the closest cities where one can find water, bread, transportation, or a telephone booth.

"We'd have a row that reached to the sea if we wanted to put up a cross for every death in the desert," says Bishop Renato León in his sermon.

There are no absolute numbers here. Each institution or expert has their own estimate. No one tallies by area, nationality, gender, or age. The dead are dead. Dead in the desert, the rivers, the hills. Dead migrants. The number that US humanitarian rights groups use when counting the deaths of migrants in the desert is 4,500 since 1994, when the first border operation began. Most bodies found are reported as "Dead Unidentified Migrant." The organizations that compile this information refer to it as "limited calculations," "conservative numbers," or "incomplete data."

Two tables are spread with consecrated bread and wine. They stand flush against the border wall, one on each side. The friars give communion by sticking their fingers through the holes of the wall.

Mass is over, and so is our sense of peace. Five migrants, either Mexicans or Central Americans, wait for the Mexican-side table to empty so they can scramble on top of it and over the wall. A futile attempt.

One after another they jump, only to be scooped up by a couple of Border Patrol agents who promptly stuff them in their cars and take them away. Edu Ponces runs with his camera rolling, but the scene is short-lived. From this side of the wall the faithful sing their chorus: "Let them go! Let them go! Let them go!"

If this was their first attempt, they'll be back in their country of origin within a week, whatever country that may be. If one of them is a repeat offender, he just got himself five to seven months in prison.

This crazy jump seems to be one of the few ways left to cross from Juárez. Last year, two people at this same Mass tried and were met with the same poor luck. The US authorities have promised to put a stop to it. But I can almost see how, what with the wall and the 2,206 patrol agents screening this zone, that cat-jump off the Eucharist table can seem like a reasonable option. The other option is to pay $8,000 at one of the currency exchange houses along the Santa Fe Bridge, for a fake visa, and hope not to get caught by customs, or be prepared to pay the consequences—up to two years in jail for falsifying government documents.

The congregation continues with Mass until the soldiers tell everyone on the US side that it's time to pack up.

MONDAY, NOVEMBER 3

Three more Hondurans showed up last night at the migrant shelter here in Juárez. The rest of the folks—there are forty in total, all spread out on cots—are deported Mexicans. This is the most well-furnished shelter of the twelve I've seen across the country. The male and female areas, for example, are separate, each with bathrooms and showers. The eating room is large and well-lit, and the whole shelter is contained within a large concrete-block building behind the priests' quarters. In the sleeping rooms the bunks are tidy, each equipped with a thick blanket for the cold nights. There's a projection room with a large screen where you can watch TV in the afternoons, and every night there are volunteers who make the food, which, we discover, is hot and delicious. It's not uncommon for them to serve meat.

One of the Hondurans who showed up last night came for the same reason as the man I met a few days previously: the crossing points of Nuevo Laredo were unpassable. The heavy rains had swelled the Rio Grande, making the currents even stronger than usual. The man decided to follow the river upstream to see if he could find a spot to cross. The only place he kept hearing about was Juárez. Certainly, though, he must have heard it from people who don't know the city.

Smoking with me out on the patio, he says he realizes he made a mistake. "There's no work here, and it's just too dangerous to be around town. Plus, there's nowhere good to cross over.". But then a forty-one-year-old Mexican, who's been at the shelter for three nights, convinces him to attempt it with him tomorrow in Anapra.

According to the Mexican sitting with us, deported after twenty-two years in the United States, if you climb up one of the barren hills you can jump the fence and cross an empty section of desert where the Border Patrol doesn't go. He himself crossed there twenty-two years ago. But back then Juárez wasn't a war zone, and it did not have a wall separating it from El Paso, nor were there thousands of Border Patrol agents guarding its gates. Back then, the Mexican explains, it was an easy four-hour hike to El Paso.

The other two Hondurans at the shelter are determined to get out of town, reach Sonora, and try crossing through the Altar Desert. After Juárez the Altar Desert is the most watched sector of the border, but the difficult topography, including sections only accessible on foot or on horseback, makes it hard for the Border Patrol to catch so few crossers. The Hondurans are only here in Juárez because they too were tricked. A fellow Honduran told them he knew how to get across in Juárez and asked for $200 apiece for fake visas, but once he got the money they never saw him again. When traveling for the first time across this country, before you've learned the number one rule—which is not to trust anybody—it's easy to fall into these kinds of traps.

I ask if they've already gotten a feel for what it's like here in Juárez. Their response tells me that they have: "We're too scared to go out. Everybody says that there's a lot of bad guys on the streets, and nobody knows anything about crossing over." The few Central Americans who have found this shelter, I realize, have all lost their way.

The argument this Honduran makes is that Juárez is simply not the crossing zone it used to be. It's not a place for migrants anymore. It's a cartel war zone, which in turn has increased US border vigilance. One thing leads to another—violence and then vigilance—and the migrants bear the brunt of both.

THURSDAY, NOVEMBER 6

Today we return. We spent Tuesday and Wednesday outside of the city, getting to know the outlying desert. Life in Juárez continues on in its frightening normalcy. Typical headlines over the past two days: "Three more murdered." "Businesses complain of police extortion." "Over 500 reported vehicles burned in 10 months." "Their business burned." "Their house a wreck." "Threatened with being bombed." "Body hanging from bridge causes outrage."

We get a call from a Juárez journalist working for *El Diario*. "There's been another execution," he says. Edu and I make our way out of the downtown district. At a small farm nestled between two roads, lies a man, shot nineteen times. The journalists, three of whom have just arrived, look for the best shots. Little else seems to matter. This man is another body. One of the photographers summarizes the scene of the crime as he dips into a bag of candy: "A car came and out piled three men and that was that: pum, pum, pum."

When they drove off, the shooters allegedly yelled: "Thief had it coming to him!"

A group of kids play around the farm while the forensic team wraps up the body. The neighbors spend the evening chatting on the front stoops of their homes. No one is shocked. The narcos have killed again. As common as a car crash.

Last Tuesday, the same day that a decapitated body was found hanging off a bridge, another body was found crucified on the balcony of a shopping mall, with a pig mask over his face and two gunshot wounds in his chest. Last night there were thirteen executions. When the mafia kills, you know it. They leave a signature.

This part of the border is racked by a madness akin to civil war. In the Chihuahuan papers the SAO lamented, "We weren't designed to face this scale of threat."

As Rodolfo Rubio, a researcher for the Colegio de la Frontera Norte, put it while on the phone with me: "It's not strange at all that the flow [of migrants] has gone down in this area." In the 1950s, between 12 and 15 percent of all Central American and Mexican migrants chose this area to cross. In 2000 these numbers started plummeting. Now only 2 percent of the undocumented detained by the Mexican Migration are apprehended in Chihuahua, despite being one of Mexico's largest states and the one that has the most miles of border.

Few migrants arrive having studied the landscape. They play a game of chance, clutching to the roof of a train that will take them to some new and unknown destination. Still, Rubio thinks there's a vox populi on the migrant route that tells many which course to follow. Not an exact route, but a vague knowledge of where it's best not to try. It's the voice of the coyotes, who sprinkle some of their knowledge as they move northward. They know, not from official documents, but from living in the desert, in the hills and along the Rio Bravo, where there's more surveillance, more Border Patrol cars, horses, motorcycles, agents, and motion sensors.

The interviews Rubio conducted with recently deported Mexicans on the Santa Fe Bridge revealed that most—some 72,000 every year—crossed at another part of the border, but that the US authorities deported them here with the goal of making reentry harder, knowing full well that this is one of the most dangerous spots to cross.

Rubio sums up the difficulties people face: "It's almost impossible for a migrant without help, with nothing but his will, to pass through Juárez. This land is controlled by organized crime, so much so that it's only possible to cross if migrants contract narcos to guide them through these areas."

It's always the same story on this route. Migrants as well as narcos search for areas far from state control. Some to cross, others to smuggle. The undocumented migrants will go on walking narco turf without permission. And narcos will go on showing that without payment, no one comes or leaves this place unpunished.

It's six o'clock in the evening and María stops running every which way, then sits down to talk. Needless to say, her real name isn't María. She works close to the Santa Fe Bridge, selling half-price bus tickets home to the recently deported. She has an agreement with Grupo Beta to offer these discounted tickets. Much like the scammers and delinquents, she's been working this corner every day for the past year.

In her words, Juárez and the sum of its circumstances always mean the same thing: fear plus corrupt officials plus US surveillance add up to one maxim. "Be very careful."

"As soon as you step onto this street you're being watched," she says. "By now you guys must be closely monitored."

I tell her we've been here many times, and so far nothing has happened to us.

"Sure," she responds," because you haven't done anything to upset them."

To upset who?

But this is a dangerous question to answer in Juárez. Upset the scammers? The corrupt police? The cartel minions? The military? The bar owners? The prostitutes who lie to the freshly deported, in order to lead them to some dark corner where someone will assault them? Who isn't there to upset?

María isn't exactly sure who we should be afraid of. She's been running in circles with the deported, and barely has the time to drink a glass of water. She suffers this situation firsthand. "They come to threaten us twice this week," she says. "I'm not sure if they're from the mafia or if they're *polleros*. They don't like it when we take away their migrants. The first time they threatened us by phone. Then a man in a hoodie came to tell us, in so many words, that we needed to shut down the business." You either shut it, you sons of bitches, or we set fire to your business, this was the message to María.

The mafia's pattern is no longer surprising. They attack when they don't get paid. They've burned a number of businesses on this street. It's a common problem, but the *polleros?* What are they doing here, if hardly anyone is trying to cross?

"Look," she explains, "there are lots of *polleros* here who are trying to hook deported migrants, some of them Central Americans, who are going around asking for help. Of course you won't see them in the streets, they're inside exchange houses, hotels, and bars. These *polleros* take them to other states to cross."

Migrants in Juárez, though their numbers are so small, still mean business.

SATURDAY, NOVEMBER 8

We cross over to El Paso, leaving the city to fly to Laredo, Texas, and from there cross over to Nuevo Laredo, Tamaulipas, to see how the undocumented are crossing the Rio Grande. On the plane I read Juárez's newspaper, *El Diario*. On page 11A there is a letter perfectly expressing the feelings of many in the city. It's a petition, a desperate plea to those in charge:

> Dear Hit Men,
>
> I'm a citizen who is tired of our useless, good-for-nothing politicians. This is why, in all respect, I'm writing you, not wanting to be another statistic. I suggest to you the following: I'm willing to pay you a fair tax and I'm willing to respect your business and not involve myself in it either for good or for bad.
>
> I'm willing to accept you as the authority here. And in return for this respect, I ask of you the following: that you help us not to pay taxes (which we'll be paying to you) to our useless government. That you respect reporters. That your shoot-outs take place outside of the city, so our children and loved ones can be safe and so that we can walk the streets without fear of being attacked or getting hit by a stray bullet. And that you execute only people who have harmed society.
>
> If politicians can't manage, you help us and we'll help you.

14

Dying in the Rio Grande: Tamaulipas

To cross the Rio Grande you either pay a coyote or you drown. The bloated bodies trapped along the rocky banks, and the flailing attempts of migrants trying to make it upriver, prove how desperate people are to cross. Some of their plans are as rudimentary as dive in and swim. And then we meet Julio César. He's a Honduran who shows us that patience and sacrifice are the difference between letting the currents decide your fate and taking fate by the horns.

The Rio Grande spat out two more bodies last week. They were found washed up on the rocks by a fisherman in an area known as El Resbaladero (The Slide). Nobody knows how long ago it was that they drowned. Their bodies are swollen and their flesh soft and pale. Tied around the waist of one of the corpses is a plastic bag that holds a few personal effects and a passport. The drowned man was Honduran. A migrant. He died trying.

The bodies first bobbed up in one of the bends in the river that is a typical crossing spot, just behind the migrant shelter in Nuevo Laredo. If the Hondurans had successfully made it to the opposite bank, they would have reached Laredo.

The Rio Grande runs 900 miles of the 1,900-mile border, but Nuevo Laredo, Tamaulipas, and Laredo, Texas, are the sister cities that people talk about when they talk about swimming this river. The waters are deep and a churning green here. The currents are strong and swirling. And the thick brush on the US side makes it difficult to climb up but easy to hide. The river in these parts acts as a natural wall. Many who try to cross it turn out swollen, soft, and pale.

In Nuevo Laredo the difference between having knowledge of the river and not having this knowledge is a matter of life and death. It's the difference between swimming out at a random deep bend, and launching with a raft in a shallow area with just a few swirls. It's the difference between arriving in the United States, and ending up as a lump of rotting flesh.

It's a fall November afternoon, five o'clock, and migrants are just starting to pool around the shelter run by Scalabrinian priests. The migrants are returning from their day jobs loading sand onto trucks, putting up drywall, or selling newspapers at traffic lights. Shelter rules only allow people to stay from four in the afternoon until seven in the morning.

There are about sixty of them today. Most from Honduras, plus a few Guatemalans and Salvadorans. The black, skeletal man sitting apart from the rest with his shoulders hunched and his head hidden between his knees is the only Dominican at the shelter. The others suggest I go talk with him. "He tried it yesterday, stupidly, and the river almost took him," a young Honduran tells me, laughing.

The Dominican's name is Roberto. He's thirty-two years old. He has a wife and three kids, aged eight, five, and three, waiting for him—and for money—back on the island. His family is eating nothing but beans. He was a bus driver before leaving his country a month ago, earning some $120 a month. Out of everyone here, he's traveled the farthest. A group of his friends lent him the money for a plane ticket to Guatemala, where visas aren't needed for short stays. From there he migrated like many Central Americans: on third-rate buses, on foot, on top of cargo trains, until he arrived in Nuevo Laredo after being assaulted six times, five of them by the Mexican police. His journey almost came to an end yesterday, coughing up mouthfuls of water as he fought the current, briefly made it, and then returned to the Mexican shore, exhausted, the sun setting behind him.

The irony of Roberto's story is that he decided against migrating to Puerto Rico—the more prosperous neighboring island—because he didn't want to risk drowning. The Mona Passage, an eighty-mile strait in the Atlantic, divides the two countries. Dominicans cross on small, speedy motorboats, often lugging too much weight on board, and sometimes end up shipwrecked.

"Your plan failed you yesterday?" I ask

"Hell! I didn't have a plan," he says, and quickly falls into the story of his attempt.

"I'd been here three days already, and was tired of selling newspapers from seven in the morning till three in the afternoon to earn six pesos [less than fifty cents] a day, and so yesterday I took the plunge. I went down to the river behind the shelter with thirteen other people. It was maybe five in the afternoon. We stood there just watching the other side a while, until I started praying. And then I jumped in to swim. The others followed me. And the current dragged me a few yards. It was tough, but I got to the other side. Then when I looked up I saw one of those police officers turn on a light and shine it on us, and so I jumped back in the water. But I was too tired then and I almost drowned on my way back. I thought I wasn't going to make it. I swallowed a lot of water."

Pray and swim. That was his strategy to reach the United States.

"And what happened to the others?" I ask.

"Three of them went ahead. They were probably caught. The rest were dragged away by the current. Farther than I was. And I never saw them back on the shore, and I haven't seen them around here either."

Maybe the Rio Grande will soon spit up more bodies.

According to the Center for Border Studies and the Promotion of Human Rights in Reynosa, more than seventy bodies have been found along the shore each year since 2005. Representatives of the center, which is dedicated to gathering data from multiple migrant shelters along Mexico's northern border, acknowledge that those numbers are estimates, and that the real figure is probably much higher. The river passes through many miles of uninhabited shoreline where brush can easily hide bodies.

The shelter in Nuevo Laredo, like many of the migrant shelters in Mexico, seems like it's in a war zone. A young Mexican man walks into the front room with a bandage around his head and a black eye. He was recently deported from the United States, and after his parents wired him $1,700, assailants stole the money and pistol-whipped him in the head. The Salvadoran man next to him is rubbing cream on the ankle he twisted earlier in the day on the riverbank.

Julio César lights a cigarette, his three children playing in circles around him. The first time we met was in Ixtepec in southern Mexico, about 1,250 miles from Nuevo Laredo. That was over a month and a half ago, and neither Edu nor I thought he had a chance of getting even close to the US border. Julio is a twenty-five-year-old brick worker, traveling with his wife Jessica (twenty-two) and his three children: Jarvin Josué (seven), César Fernando (five), and Jazmín Joana, who was born on the trip north two months ago. She almost died on the first adventure of her life, when she slipped out of her mother's arms on the roof of a moving train. Luckily Julio César was able to catch her before she fell. And now here they are, all five of them.

From Ixtepec the family rode north by bus. "I wasn't going to put the baby at risk again," Julio César explains. Making sure to take out-of-the-way and shorter stretches to avoid immigration checkpoints, they took fifteen buses to arrive to Nuevo Laredo. Julio is a very thorough man. He draws maps, marks up potential routes, asks questions, and knows how to wait.

These days he's been studying "the flow of the river." He's already crossed twice from Nuevo Laredo. In 2005, like the Dominican, he swam it alone. But the Border Patrol picked him up as soon as he hit the opposite bank, and promptly deported him. Agents tend to hide in the thickets on the US side, so that people will at least give the crossing a shot. They prefer to arrest them instead of just deterring them, knowing that they'll try eventually, and maybe in a spot without patrols or cameras.

For his second attempt, Julio César paid $1,200 to a friend in the United States who arranged for a coyote to show him a crossing point outside of the city. That time he made it, and worked for a year in the States until he was deported after a raid at a construction site in San Antonio, Texas.

This time he can't afford the coyote, and needs to rely on himself and his memory. "I want to inspect the place where I crossed back in 2005. See what the currents look like, and if there are agents watching, and then in January I'm going to cross alone and work up enough money to bring over Jessica and the kids safely."

This is the difference between Julio César and Roberto. Roberto dove in at a deep bend of the river because it was close to the shelter. He chose a spot where agents are on the lookout, and almost died in the attempt. Julio César, however, is waiting until January, studying the river, finding the shallows. This is the difference between knowing and not knowing.

Before saying goodbye, we arrange to accompany Julio on his scouting expedition the day after tomorrow.

Seven of El Abuelo's dealers stand just outside the shelter. They radio municipal police, and high-five and fist-bump when they arrive.

El Abuelo oversees all the *polleros* who use the route closest to the Atlantic, the one that runs through Tabasco and Veracruz before reaching Reynosa and Nuevo Laredo. It's a route plagued by kidnappings, where coyotes who don't pay put their migrants in danger of being held ransom for $300 to $500 a head. Los Zetas call that business the kidnapper express. But El Abuelo and his henchmen never have to deal with this problem. From Nuevo Laredo, the home base of many Zetas, El Abuelo forges deals that let his people cross largely without trouble. If you're in one of El Abuelo's circles, you can rest assured that Los

Zetas won't be a hindrance when you get to the city on the Rio Grande.

At four in the afternoon, migrants start to huddle on the sidewalk in front of the shelter.

Armando, a twenty-five-year-old Salvadoran, is there. He's one of those puzzling men who are addicted to the ways of the road. He's been wandering Mexico's streets since he was twelve years old. He travels north until hitting the border, works in whatever he can find, and goes back to El Salvador whenever he feels the need. He sums up his ambitions with one word: fun. He says he gets bored being in the same place for too long, that when he was a kid he went north to try to cross, and that little by little he got sold on this nomadic life. He became addicted to a road of assaults, rapes, mutilations, and kidnappings. It seems hard to understand migrants like Armando, yet there are many with similar stories. They are perfectly conscious of the risks they run, but there's an attractive perversity there that quickly turns them into adrenaline addicts. The Zetas do a good job of recruiting these types, many of them Central American, to work as spies on the trains.

Armando tells me that just a month ago he saw a body as he looked out over the river. "It was floating over there, by Viveros Park," he recalls. "That sort of thing happens because most guys go diving in at random, without studying the river first. And so one of two things happens: they get caught by Migration or they drown. I know where to cross, where it's shallow, but I don't want to go to the States."

I think I can see it, the difference between knowing and not knowing.

There are two patrol boats, three long-range, night-vision surveillance cameras, and some twenty reflectors and motion sensors covering the seven miles of the Rio Grande that separate Nuevo Laredo from Laredo, which is why wading in at one spot instead of another can make the difference between swimming into the arms of an agent or getting the chance to try your luck. But to try your luck you have to go to a less patrolled area, far from the city. That's Julio César's plan.

My conversation with Armando is interrupted by the leader of the gang made up of drug dealers and El Abuelo's troops. A guy about twenty-five years old, with a dragon tattoo on his neck, asks Edu: "Hey, what's that camera for?" Edu hastens to explain that he's taking pictures of migrants. We make it clear that whatever he's doing on his street corner is of no interest to us. "A twenty-eight," he says into his radio. And then he leaves.

Armando and I start talking again. Three more migrants sit down next to us. Then the guy with the dragon tattoo and another two from his group approach us. "Hey, that really is a kick-ass camera. Why don't you let me see it?" one of them says to Edu, who immediately starts shaking his head no. Then a red car shows up and drives close to us.

"Don't ask them, just get them in here!" orders the fat man at the wheel. Four men from the back of the car get out and walk toward us. We stand up and get ready to run, but Dragon Tattoo lets out a laugh and says, "Easy, easy, we're not going to kidnap you." They only wanted to let us know that we were on their turf. Just to scare us into understanding what could happen.

After that, they leave us alone and start to mingle with the thirty or so migrants sitting on the pavement. They trumpet their offer: "With El Abuelo! With El Abuelo! 1,800 dollars to Houston! We give you food, water, and shoes, and we cross you by boat. Come on, whoever wants to travel safely!"

Color comes back to the cheeks of the man sitting next to me. "I thought they were going to kidnap us," he whispers.

Kidnappings are an ever-growing threat on this route, and a lot of what goes on in the south is actually managed from two cities bordering the States—Nuevo Laredo and Reynosa. In these areas—which are entered by thousands of migrants every month—criminals rule, often with the complicity of the authorities, and shamelessly shout out offers on the streets as if they were selling tomatoes.

Eighty-three percent of the reports coming from the migrant shelter and recorded by the Center of Human Rights accuse Nuevo Laredo's city officers of being corrupt. In the past three months alone, from June to August 2009, 477 migrants have filed accounts of beatings, arbitrary detentions, kidnappings, and robbery. Over 80 percent of these migrants were from Honduras, Guatemala, and El Salvador.

"This used to be a peaceful place," explains José Luis Manso, the shelter director. "Before the shelter was built. But then this area became a big market for narcos and human smuggling. The situation is awful now. The police are in on it with the *polleros* and drug traffickers. This is where El Abuelo operates. His greatest income is from crossing Central Americans. He does a good job, illicit, sure, but at least whoever pays him can be pretty sure they'll get across okay. We've sent four municipal officers to ask the mayor for greater surveillance around the shelter."

The officers never got an answer. But Manso says that up until now, no promise has been fulfilled.

The shelter is stuck in this high-risk area. To describe the situation, Manso recounts a murder that happened only four days ago. "It was behind the shelter. Police violently knocked on the door in the middle of the night. They wanted information because they'd been told there'd been a fight between gangs, one Mexican and the other Central American, who mostly specialize in robbery. But then this strange thing happened. Only members from one gang were detained, which makes me think that the Central Americans who died or were hurt were actually migrants who resisted kidnapping."

Manso says that most Central Americans try to cross the river on their own: "They don't have the money, so they swim across or buy a car tire to help them keep afloat, and so they risk their lives."

I pick one of the shelter's migrants at random, a middle-aged Guatemalan. I ask him if he'll pay for a coyote. "Can't afford it," he answers. I ask him if he knows the river. "No." I ask him if he can tell me how he's going to cross. "By my faith in God," he says.

Before leaving the shelter, we make plans to meet with Julio César tomorrow, early in the morning in Hidalgo Park, to start our tour. The gang is still just outside the shelter walls, waiting for their prey.

They laugh shamelessly when they see us. But they leave us alone. We get on the bus.

It's just before sunrise. We're in Viveros Park, right where they found the two swollen corpses last week. Today there are two men fishing. The river is deep and the cold currents pull hard against the steep banks.

The Rio Grande doesn't belong to either of the countries it divides. A treaty signed at the beginning of the twentieth century permits each country to use its waters. Here, closer to its mouth than to its source, the river is already swollen by its three largest tributaries: the Picos River from the north, and the Conchos and Sabinas Rivers from the south. Here it's as wide as a football field, and even an expert swimmer would struggle against the swiftness of its currents.

A man fishing for catfish warns us: "When it gets dark you better leave. These hills fill up with drug mules at night. Plus there's bandits looking for people trying to cross." We take heed and decide to come back in full daylight.

Just as he promised, at eight o'clock on the dot, Julio César is sitting on a bench in Hidalgo Park. "Let's go," he tells us. "We need to jump on a bus." The area we're going to inspect, known as El Carrizo, is on the outskirts of the city.

The bus, far behind schedule, costs ten pesos. After waiting forty minutes at the stop, an employee announces the departure. We ride for a half an hour on the highway that runs from Monterrey to Nuevo Laredo, and still the sprawling suburbs of the city run on—dirt roads, half-built tract homes—until finally, at an unmarked spot along the highway, the bus stops and the three of us jump down. On the other side of the highway there are two dirt roads. Julio César points to the one on the right, which is narrower and a lot rockier. "That's the one," he says. "The other road is where the army patrols go."

We don't have to ask why there are army patrols. Along this stretch of border the formula is always the same: the wall, the back roads, and the military patrols add up to drug-trafficking routes.

We walk for thirty minutes on the abandoned trail. The sun burns down, though the winter temperatures rarely rise above eighty degrees. On each side of the path we see nothing but brambles and burs that keep catching onto our clothes.

Julio César starts reminiscing as we make our way: "Yeah, this little ranch here I remember. This is where they gave me water when I crossed back in 2005." We start to see how he got to know this place. The difference between knowing and not knowing is patience and hard work.

On his first attempt in 2005, when he swam into the hands of the Border Patrol, he realized he'd need to find a site with less activity, where a coyote wouldn't be able to trick him, and where being captured wasn't the most likely outcome. That is why he decided to start working for El Veracruzano.

El Veracruzano is a well-known figure around Nuevo Laredo. He's thirty-some years old and lives in Viveros Park, next to the migrant shelter, in a small clapboard shack full of inner tubes. He charges 200 pesos to ferry people across the river. Not too long ago, Julio César became El Veracruzano's right-hand man. He would cross the river and attach a rope to a tree on the US side. Then he would pull in the inner tubes ridden by migrants. The service can be understood, basically, as drowning insurance, and he and El Veracruzano would split the 200 pesos down the middle. There is no such thing, however, as Border Patrol insurance.

Julio César never tried crossing himself this way, explaining that it's a far cry from getting safely all the way to San Antonio, which is where he and most of the undocumented migrants crossing at this point are headed.

Little by little, while working hard for El Veracruzano and getting on his good side, Julio César saved up money to pay for his own coyote. "We never crossed less than fifteen people a week," he says, which added up to about $150 a week. Increasingly confident, El Veracruzano started toying with the idea of crossing outside of the city, where the Border Patrol was less ubiquitous, and there were small islands in the shallower parts of the river. That knowledge was something El Veracruzano kept close to his chest. He could have potentially lost a lot of business if migrants started finding out about better crossing zones. But he did finally tell Julio César of El Carrizo, who knew right away that that was where he was going to cross with his coyote.

Another half an hour passes, and we've left the dust path for the scrubland of a private ranch. We approach the front door of a small ranch house where a man, the first person we've encountered on our walk, is listening to a boom box at full volume. We wave to get his attention, and ask if we're on the right path to the river.

"Yeah," he answers. "Straight ahead. But be careful. Last week some bandits murdered a migrant and his coyote right around here."

This is a crossing point for those in the know, the path for coyotes and migrants with patience, but it's also far out of the city and a perfect location for assaults. In 2005, walking this same path, Julio César and his coyote were attacked by two masked men who acted as if they were back in La Arrocera: they stripped them both naked, looking for money even in the folds of their underwear.

Further down the path we enter onto another ranch. We're all very thirsty. But instead of finding a rest and some water, we see eight soldiers, all of them holding AR-15 assault rifles, watching us suspiciously from the ranch house. They approach and order us to identify ourselves. They ask for papers and search our bags. They know Julio César is undocumented, but in Mexico a soldier doesn't have the right to detain a migrant. They also know we're journalists.

"Excuse us," one of them says meekly. "We're out looking for drugs. A lot pass through here." As they let us go, the same soldier warns us: "Don't go down by the river. That's where people are getting mugged."

In another half an hour, walking up and down hills and through the brush, we start to hear the river. We stumble down a steep slope and finally arrive at the muddy bank of the Rio Grande. "Here it is," Julio César says, a smile on his face. He's arrived. His long, patient wait and careful research have paid off: he's finally found the spot where he crossed with his coyote back in 2005.

He sits down to consult a map he drew on a piece of paper. He traces a line with his long pinky nail, and outlines the plan: "The deal is that you have to cross at night. Once on the other side, you have to walk about seven hours to Laredo. From there you got to change clothes so you look decent, and then you'll have two options. One is to hit the back highways towards Cotula [a small Texan town], asking for water or food for your five- or six-night walk to San Antonio. The other is to jump on a cargo train that'll get you to San Antonio in an hour, except that there are checkpoints with dogs that'll be sniffing for you. If you want to ride the train you have to cover yourself with garlic and chilli to scare away the dogs. Because the cops don't actually get on the trains, they just follow the dogs. And then, once you're in San Antonio, you made it."

Except that he still hasn't finalized his crossing point. The current is strong enough that it would be difficult to swim, and he still has to figure out how deep the river is here.

We jump in. The water is cold. In the middle of the river there's a small island, so we can take a short break. In the deepest part the water reaches up to our necks, making it difficult to move forward. It's incredible that this is the famous Rio Grande, which has taken so many lives, and yet in crossing it we never lose our footing and, in the end, it only takes a few minutes.

We rest, hanging onto the river plants on the US side. It's not deep at all, but the current is still pulling hard at us. After another minute we cross back to the Mexican side.

"I'm going to go for it here," Julio César says confidently. We scramble up the steep bank, all of us still thirsty.

Norteña music blasts from the ranch house overlooking the river. It's a corrido that describes a Border Patrol agent falling into the hands of a narco-trafficker he caught dealing. We approach the house, yelling to announce our presence, not wanting to surprise anyone. We're greeted by a farmer who is trying to fix a reaping machine. He turns down the volume and I ask him if he sees a lot of migrants die while crossing the river.

"Die, no," the man responds. "Already dead, yes."

Julio César returns the bottle of water the farmer has given us.

The farmer explains: "They don't die here. The river isn't very deep at this point, except in the rainy season."

Julio César was thinking of crossing in January. The first rains come to Nuevo Laredo usually in April. He should have plenty of time.

"But you've seen dead bodies?" I ask.

"Now and again."

"How often?"

"I've seen two in the last two months," he says. "They get washed up on the little island. But they're all people who tried to cross in the city. The river pushes them down here. Last week a police boat recovered the last body on the island. It was already all swollen, lying there on the beach."

Julio César motions that it's time to start walking back, before it gets dark. He's got what he came for. Now he just needs to wait for the right moment. He knows that if he rushes things he'll put himself in danger. This is the difference in Nuevo Laredo between knowing and not knowing.

On the Typeface

The Beast is set in Monotype Fournier, a typeface based on the designs of the eighteenth-century printer and typefounder Pierre Simon Fournier. He in turn was influenced by the constructed type designs of the Romain du Roi, commissioned by Louis XIV in 1692, which eschewed the calligraphic influence of prior typefaces in favor of scientific precision and adherence to a grid.

With its vertical axis, pronounced contrast and unbracketed serifs, the Fournier face is an archetype of the "transitional" style in the evolution of Latin printing types—situated between the "old style" fonts such as Bembo and Garamond and the "modern" faces of Bodoni and Didot. Other distinguishing features include the proportionally low height of the capitals and the lowercase "f," with its tapered and declining crossbar.

The italics, which were designed independently, have an exaggerated slope with sharp terminals that retain the squared serifs in the descenders.

The Fournier design was commissioned as part of the Monotype Corporation's type revival program under the supervision of Stanley Morison in the 1920s. Two designs were cut based on the "St. Augustin Ordinaire" design shown in Fournier's *Manuel Typographique*. In Morison's absence, the wrong design was approved, resulting in the typeface now known as Fournier.